# NEW WORKS IN ACCOUNTING HISTORY

T0330904

*edited by*

**RICHARD P. BRIEF**
Leonard N. Stern School of Business
New York University

Routledge
Taylor & Francis Group

LONDON AND NEW YORK

# A CONCEPTUAL FRAMEWORK FOR FINANCIAL ACCOUNTING AND REPORTING

## VISION, TOOL, OR THREAT?

RICHARD MACVE, MA, MSC, FCA

Professor of Accounting
London School of Economics and
Political Science

Routledge
Taylor & Francis Group

LONDON AND NEW YORK

First published 1997
by Routledge

Published 2016 by Routledge
2 Park Square, Milton Park, Abingdon, Oxfordshire OX14 4RN
711 Third Avenue, New York, NY, 10017, USA

First issued in paperback 2016

*Routledge is an imprint of the Taylor & Francis Group,
an informa business*

**Library of Congress Cataloging-in-Publication Data**

Macve, Richard, 1940–
   A conceptual framework for financial accounting and reporting :
vision, tool, or threat? / Richard Macve.
      p.   cm. — (New works in accounting history)
   Includes bibliographical references.
   1. Accounting—Standards. 2. Accounting—Great Britain—Standards. 3. Accounting—United States—Standards. I. Title. II. Series.
HF5626.M33  1997
657—dc21

                                                        97-35910

ISBN 13: 978-1-138-99157-6 (pbk)
ISBN 13: 978-0-815-33035-6 (hbk)

# Dedication

With warm and grateful memories of 'Aber', the 'College by the Sea',
1979-1996.


*'Nid Byd, Byd Heb Wybodaeth'*

The motto of the University College of Wales, Aberystwyth:[1]
*'A life without knowledge is no life'*

---

[1] now the University of Wales, Aberystwyth.

# Contents

Page

## (III) THE FASB'S CONCEPTUAL FRAMEWORK—
## VISION, TOOL OR THREAT?

Page

# Introduction[1]

## THE STUDIES

Putting together this collection of my writings on the 'conceptual framework' has enabled me both to bring back into print the study (Macve, 1981) which I undertook for the UK's Accounting Standards Committee ('ASC'), and to consider how far the views I expressed there have stood the test of time as standard setters around the world have followed in the FASB's footsteps. The papers reprinted here were produced at intervals during the seventeen years that I occupied the Julian Hodge Chair of Accounting at the University of Wales, Aberystwyth[2] (including one year when I was a visiting faculty member at Rice University).

In the light of my 1981 study the ASC decided not to seek to develop a conceptual framework of the kind undertaken by the FASB in the USA (Ernst & Young, 1994, 4.4). However, by the end of that decade the pressures to demonstrate the coherence of the British standards programme, as articulated in the Dearing Report (CCAB, 1988)[3], led the new Accounting Standards Board to begin the development of its draft *Statement of Principles* (ASB, 1995).

There is now a plethora of such 'official' frameworks. The studies (often by prominent academics) that preceded them—for example the Stamp Report for Canada, reviewed in Macve (1981), the Barton Report for Australia, reviewed in Macve (1983a), and Solomons' *Guidelines* for the U.K., reviewed in Macve (1989a; 1989b)—individually took distinctive lines, but the 'official' frameworks subsequently issued, including that of the International Accounting Standards Committee (IASC, 1989) and the ASB's draft *Statement of Principles* (ASB, 1995), seem to me to be similar in all essential respects, and to have largely mirrored that of the FASB.[4] So the basic arguments of my 1981 study remain applicable to these more recent frameworks as well as to the FASB's original.

The studies that reappear here are the following:

(1) *Quaere Verum vel Recte Numerare* (Macve, 1980) was my inaugural lecture at the (then) University College of Wales, Aberystwyth, given shortly after I had been asked by Tom Watts to undertake my study for ASC. It encompasses most of what I had learned, after qualifying as a Chartered Accountant with Peat, Marwick, Mitchell & Co. (now KPMG) in London and joining the LSE as a lecturer from 1974 to 1978. The enormous intellectual debts I owe to Professors Will Baxter, Harold Edey, Ted French, Peter Watson, and Basil Yamey are obvious. The lecture explored the nature of the basic problem of how to determine the rules of accrual accounting when that problem is reduced to its essential core of how to allocate the results of multiperiod business activity over individual reporting periods, given the variety of purposes ('objectives') for which such reported results are used. If there is no clear answer to the problem even in the simplest situations, *a fortiori* standard setters will face much greater challenges in devising acceptable, coherent rules in more complex situations, e.g. when faced with economic uncertainties and market volatility due to changing interest rates, inflation, changing foreign currency rates, etc. and as new financial instruments and structures, and new varieties of business contracts, are devised. The lecture's essential message was that, while standard setters often argue that good disclosure is not a substitute for 'correct' accounting, and often appear to believe that moving towards greater use of current values will resolve many major difficulties of achieving good accounting, nevertheless one must equally understand that 'correct' accounting can never be a substitute for good disclosure and for explanation of the accounting principles adopted and assumptions made.[5]

(2) *A Conceptual Framework for Financial Accounting and Reporting: the possibilities for an agreed structure* was the report (Macve, 1981) prepared at the request of the Accounting Standards Committee, which was sponsored by the (then) Technical and Research Committee of the Institute of Chartered Accountants in England & Wales ('ICAEW').[6] In preparing the report I received a

great deal of wise counsel, especially from Professor Harold Edey and from Tom Watts. It included reviews not only of the FASB's project but also of UK studies such as *The Corporate Report* and the report of the Sandilands committee, and of Professor Edward Stamp's Canadian study. Its initial summary chapter contains its major arguments and implications, in particular that the FASB's original and largely instrumental conception of the development of the framework as a coherent basis for deriving consistent accounting standards, purportedly for the benefit of investors, based on abstract definitions of accounting elements and informational qualities, was a misunderstanding of the way in which conceptual thinking about accounting problems could help in considering individual accounting issues.

(3) This theme was further developed in the presentation that I was invited, by Professor Sandy Burton of Columbia University (formerly Chief Accountant of the SEC), to give at the 1983 Arthur Young Professors' Roundtable.[7] The Roundtable's theme that year was *The FASB—The First Ten Years*, and participants included the FASB chairman, Donald Kirk. My paper (Macve, 1983a), entitled 'The FASB's Conceptual Framework—Vision, Tool or Threat?', was written while I was visiting Rice University and attempted to give an evenhanded assessment of the benefits and costs of the FASB's long and expensive project. It considered the role of the project from two main perspectives—both as an 'intellectual enquiry' and as a 'legitimizing process' to demonstrate the expertise of the FASB and justify its claims to retain the authority to set standards.

At that time SFAC5 on 'recognition and measurement' had not yet been issued. Many people at the time were expecting that statement finally to apply the deductive framework of objectives, qualitative characteristics and definitions of elements and to set out the way in which the Board would proceed to determine individual and controversial accounting issues. As is well known, in the event SFAC5 (FASB, 1984) set out criteria which did little more than reassert the conclusions previously reached about definitions and qualitative characteristics underlying accounting choices, and state that deciding whether these lead to recognition is a matter of 'reasonable certainty' in each case. The recognition statements of other 'official' frameworks (e.g. IASC, 1989; ASB, 1995) have gone no further. It was the

Board's 'failure' in this respect that led Professor David Solomons (1986) to comment:

> Under a rigorous grading system I would give Concepts Statement No. 5 an F and require the Board to take the course over again—that is, to scrap the statement and start afresh.

Moreover, FAS33 (FASB, 1979), which represented the key element of the 'measurement' part of the project, had not taken a view on capital maintenance or on the respective merits of current values and current purchasing power measures but required experimental supplementary disclosures which enabled users to construct their own alternative views of entities' financial position and performance, in the context of changing prices. So no conclusions had been reached on this important practical aspect of the project either. (David Solomons was later to attempt to give clear guidance on both recognition and measurement issues in his own *Guidelines* (Solomons, 1989a).)

My paper benefited enormously from discussions with Professors Philip Bell and Stephen Zeff while I was at Rice University. It looked both at the underlying conceptual difficulties (already explored in Macve 1980 and 1981) and at the political realities facing the FASB and other standard setters and argued (p.197 in this volume):

> There are many other such questions one might raise. I believe it is extremely important that they are raised and examined now if the project is to make progress. In other words, I consider the stage to have been reached where what is most needed is development of understanding as to why such plausible arguments as those set forth in the present concepts statements do not either explain present practice, or give clear guidance on how to change it.
>
> The Board has preserved its flexibility so far. It may need to be especially careful not to lose it now and not to override some proper conceptual concerns.

Again (p.197 in this volume):

> I am not arguing for deliberate obfuscation of the issues—rather against the danger of representing the issues to be conceptually clear-cut when generally they are not. It is this very lack of clarity that makes it even harder

in accounting to distinguish the "political" and the "technical" than it is in many other fields. Indeed, I find one of the most fascinating aspects of accounting theory to be how little can be rigorously explained of the "technical" usefulness of a process that is such an important feature of modern economic life (and for which its practitioners are very well remunerated), and how difficult it is to show even what would be a "technical" improvement, apart from the political difficulties that plague all recommendations, scientific or unscientific, in any area of public policy. The danger lies in pretending that such ambiguities about accounting do not exist.

And finally (p.198 in this volume):

If I am right, the main danger is that of glossing over conceptual problems. This becomes more critical as the FASB's project now begins to deal directly with recognition and measurement questions. I would have preferred that these conceptual problems had been tackled head-on at the beginning—but I am convinced they will have to be faced in the end. "Truth is the daughter, not of Authority, but of Time" (Bacon, quoted by Baxter [1981][8]).

If the problems are acknowledged and faced, then I believe the conceptual framework project could considerably enhance respect for the difficult profession of accounting. It may help to reduce the danger of misguided political interference from those who believe that answers to accounting problems should be easy to find, and who attribute all the profession's failures to incompetence or self-serving.

So standard setters are wise not to make their frameworks explicit about the details of accounting issues—but equally this suggests that the kind of conceptual framework that standard setters should be referring to is not the kind they have generally been promulgating (e.g. Power, 1993; Archer, 1992, 1993; Dennis, 1997).

Unfortunately the normal sequence of publication of Roundtable proceedings in book form was interrupted, so that year's papers never appeared. Several times over the last fourteen years Steve Zeff has urged me to submit the paper for publication, but other pressures have always intervened to prevent me reworking and updating it for a journal, so that its inclusion in this volume now is its first publication. I have left it unchanged from the original (which included a review of Professor Alan Barton's Australian study), except that I have not reproduced here its Appendix I, which was simply the summary of my 1981 study, as that is of course already included here in reading (2). The paper contains an extensive bibliography of relevant literature available in 1983. Some major subsequent publications are cited in the references to this foreword.[9]

(4) 'The Conceptual Framework and Oil and Gas Accounting'. This piece is a compilation of three short articles which appeared in the weekly *Accountancy Age* in 1983 (Macve, 1983b, 1983c, 1983d). They were written while I was at Rice University in the style of a 'Letter from America', with Steve Zeff's encouragement and with considerable constructive criticism from Bala Dharan who was himself researching the impact of oil and gas disclosures under 'Reserve Recognition Accounting' at the time (Dharan, 1984). They were written in a populist style, based on the machinations then unfolding in the plot of the popular TV soap-opera *Dallas* (where, under a codicil to their father Jock Ewing's will, the Ewing brothers had to compete for the right to inherit Ewing Oil by each taking over half the family business and seeing who could more successfully run their half for a year). But I hope they bring out forcefully the conceptual and practical complexities underlying the FASB's objective of attempting to provide useful information for investors' decisions through conventional financial statements, whether based on historical cost or on current values (such as in 'Reserve Recognition Accounting'). Thus, for example (p.228 in this volume):

> The standard setters' solutions to the oil and gas accounting problem do not seem likely to tell us what we want to know—which brother has made his half of the company the better off. It would be possible to take a more cynical view and say it does not matter much who has *really* been more successful. We should take the accounting rules as given (like the rules of football) and the one who wins according to the rules is the winner. After all, whoever runs the company in future will continue to be judged by the figures he produces according to the accounting rules in force, so it makes sense to judge who shall run the company the same way. [But] other

> things being equal, different accounting methods only
> distribute the same total profit to different periods of the
> life of a business, so that a method which shows one
> brother more successful this period may show him less
> successful in a future period.

And (p.230 in this volume):

> So Jock's problem has no satisfactory solution. There
> is no theory which will tell us what accounting standards
> are the right ones for measuring this year's profit, even for
> this well-defined purpose. It looks unlikely that either
> brother will win by showing conclusively that he made
> more profit than the other. No wonder that *Dallas* and the
> FASB's search for the conceptual framework often appear
> to have a lot in common. They both go on and on. There's a
> lot of money involved and politics and power often seem
> likely to have more to do with the final outcome than
> reason and equity.

In preparing these articles for re-publication here I have removed
the connecting material that was inserted to link the three installments
in which they originally appeared, and added some bibliographic and
explanatory notes, but otherwise they are unchanged.

(5) 'Solomons' Guidelines: Where Do They Lead?', together with
(6) 'Questioning the Wisdom of Solomons', appeared in *Accountancy*
(Macve, 1989a, 1989b) as commentaries on the Solomons (1989a)
*Guidelines*.[10] As noted above, the FASB's and other frameworks had
'failed' (inevitably, in my view) to resolve the basic recognition and
measurement issues underlying the choice of particular accounting
principles. David Solomons, in a study for the Research Board of the
ICAEW, addressed to the Accounting Standards Committee, set about
rectifying both of these 'defects'.

Solomons' *Guidelines* set out clearly and forcefully his strongly
held views on how accounting should be improved—basically by
adopting the 'balance sheet approach' of measuring net assets at
current value and measuring a year's income or profit as the 'real'
increase in these values over that year. However, they did not (and to
my mind could not) resolve the underlying and fundamental
conceptual difficulties both with regard to the drawing of the
boundaries around what assets and liabilities are to be recognized and

measured in financial statements, and at how much, and with regard to the decision on how much of any change in their values is to be regarded as the income of an accounting period.

I remember enjoying a lively argument with David over these issues one sunny morning in the gardens of the London Business School, by Regents Park, and I hope he enjoyed it too. I learned a great deal, but we had to agree to continue to differ. His reply to my written criticisms appeared in *Accountancy* later in the same year (Solomons, 1989b). I am delighted that his *Guidelines* have now been reprinted by Garland.

## SUBSEQUENT DEVELOPMENTS

At the time the earlier papers in this collection were written, experiments with supplementary 'inflation accounting / current value accounting' statements were being inaugurated in both the UK and the USA. In the outcome, these experiments were finally abandoned in both countries. The move towards current values in some form did not, at least at that juncture, prove to be the way in which the perceived limitations (conceptual and practical) of much traditional 'historical cost' accounting were to be overcome. However, the standard setters in both countries (together with their counterparts in Australia and Canada, with whom, in company with the IASC, they form the 'G4+1' group) continue to express views that indicate that they regard moves towards current value based accounting as holding the key to the resolution of many accounting difficulties both of balance sheet presentation and of income measurement.[11] This appears to many (e.g. Ernst & Young, 1996) to be the ultimate logic of the conceptual framework that has been adopted by the G4+1 group—a logic that has become more forceful as the standard setters wrestle with the rapid growth in complex financial instruments and how to account for them.

In recent years I have revisited (with a number of colleagues) the ideas expressed in the papers reprinted here in a variety of contexts, exploring whether the framework established by FASB,[12] and largely followed by other standard setters, can give guidance on dealing with a range of emerging accounting problems. These have included developments in environmental accounting and reporting (Macve & Carey, 1992); issues in non-life insurance accounting (Harte & Macve,

1991; Macve with Gwilliam, 1993) as well as proposals for changing the principles of accounting for UK life insurance business (Horton & Macve, 1995); issues relating to accounting for listed investments (Macve & Jackson, 1991 and Horton & Macve, 1996), for long-term loans (Macve, 1984) and for goodwill (Arnold, *et al.*, 1992); and, most recently, debate over whether a Marxist approach could offer a clearer conceptual basis for accounting principles than that of FASB (Macve, forthcoming).

In each case the conclusion has remained broadly the same: the concepts of objectives, informational qualities, definitions of elements, recognition criteria and measurement criteria may help to structure discussion, to identify the questions to be asked, and to suggest useful lines of empirical investigation, but they do little in themselves to help determine where the accounting boundaries should be drawn, or how far gains and losses should be regarded as 'income', 'earnings' or 'profit', in individual cases.

Meanwhile, I have also been pursuing, with various colleagues, other lines of research aimed at the questions raised in part (C) of Macve (1983a) and at understanding the historical developments whereby accounting, despite the fundamental conceptual ambiguities underlying the numbers it reports, has become such a powerful process of control and pervasive disciplinary discourse in the modern management of business and other enterprises. Going behind the 'technical' and 'political' dimensions (as identified, e.g., in Macve 1981 and 1983a), I have been exploring the institutional and intellectual frameworks—the 'power-knowledge' regimes—within which the practices and discourses of modern accounting and accountability have become established (see e.g. Fleischman, Hoskin & Macve, 1995; Hoskin & Macve, 1994 and 1996).

In the UK a practitioner critique of the conceptual approach being followed by ASB and other standard setters has also recently been articulated. Ernst & Young's (1996) paper argues that the ASB may be correct in its 'balance sheet' and increasingly value-based approach as far as financial investment activities are concerned but that this is inappropriate for the traditional accounting problems of trading and manufacturing businesses. These can only be addressed by the traditional approach of allocation ('matching' with 'prudence') of costs and revenues.

Tweedie (1996) pp.54-7 rejects this criticism, arguing that the balance sheet definitions are best seen as an essential constraint on the excesses of 'matching' in order to outlaw balance-sheet 'what-you-may-call-its'. However he then alludes to a current issue in relation to the ASB's July 1996 discussion paper on *Derivatives and Other Financial Instruments*, namely how to account for 'hedges', not of current income or balance sheet items but of future transactions. ASB is not inclined to allow these to be deferred against the future income/expense: but Tweedie proposes that the 'real' situation be explained in the Operating and Financial Review (a recommended management commentary like the US (SEC mandated) 'Management Discussion and Analysis') and he even suggests including in the OFR *pro forma* reworked figures. One might be prompted to ask why the *Statement of Principles* (ASB, 1995) cannot get the 'true' performance into the accounts and why the accounts will only become (secondary?) 'matters of record' (Tweedie, 1996, p.57).

While I believe Ernst & Young are right to articulate a challenge to the ASB's draft framework, it remains unclear how Ernst & Young think the 'matching' approach that they favour can be any more likely to offer a consistent basis for accounting reform in future than it has in the past. Moreover, it is doubtful if they are even right to accept the ASB's 'valuation' approach for the purpose of measuring the income from investments and other financial instruments (Horton & Macve, 1996). The issues here come out forcefully in the current debate over reporting 'comprehensive income'.

Driven more, perhaps, by the difficulties of dealing with derivatives and other financial instruments than by the Conceptual Framework itself, both FASB and ASB are promoting statements of 'comprehensive income'. (The items comprising comprehensive income must, by definition, be included in articulated financial statements: the new proposals are concerned with how they should be presented and how allocated between the profit and loss account ('P&L') / income statement and the 'Statement of Total Recognised Gains and Losses' ('STRGL') in the UK or 'other comprehensive income' in the USA.)

The major difference between the two countries' approaches is that ASB (as in its FRS3 (ASB, 1992) and *Statement of Principles* Chapter 6 (ASB, 1995)) does not 'recycle' gains and losses from STRGL to P&L (e.g. as they are realized), while FASB would still 'reclassify' items from 'other comprehensive income' to 'net income'. The ASB's approach tends to make the STRGL an even more significant 'performance' statement, but the conceptual discussion in both countries has left unaddressed the basic issue of whether there are still some changes in the recorded values of net assets (other than contributions by or distributions to owners) which should be excluded from both performance statements (in the UK the P&L and the STRGL) and treated as equity adjustments (as they have been up until now in the USA).[13] Particular difficulties arise in relation to how much of any gains or losses on financial instruments arising from changes in interest rates should be reported in either performance statement. (These difficulties are discussed further in Horton & Macve, 1995 and 1996.)

The conceptual difficulties in respect both of interest-rate gains and losses and of hedging are of particular topical relevance in the light of IASC's recent discussion paper on accounting for financial instruments (IASC, 1997) and the pressure on IASC to deliver a set of 'core' standards within the next year under the agreement with IOSCO (Carsberg, 1996) At the heart of these difficulties are the boundaries of accounting recognition and the appropriate concept of capital maintenance. But why should a conceptually clear answer be more likely to be forthcoming in relation to the issues surrounding financial instruments than in relation to any others? (cf. IASC, 1997, Chapters 1 and 6).

## CONCLUSION

The major argument underlying all my papers reproduced in this volume is that an 'official' conceptual framework for financial and accounting and reporting is intrinsically incapable of resolving specific practical accounting issues. While this was undoubtedly the objective originally pursued by the FASB (as discussed further in Macve, 1981 and 1983a), it may now be argued that, as this was an unrealistic expectation, it is unfair to criticize the conceptual framework project on this basis. The role of conceptual thinking is more subtly interrelated with practice and with guiding changes in practice (e.g. Power, 1993; Lyas, 1993). Nevertheless, it seems that standard setters do continue to believe in the intrinsic correctness of their frameworks (albeit acknowledging the need for continuous updating to reflect new developments in practice, as well as the political necessity of making compromises on individual standards and of pursuing future changes through evolution rather than revolution (e.g. ASB, 1995)). In particular they appear to be currently locked into a 'balance sheet' syndrome of believing that correctly recognizing and measuring assets and liabilities will resolve issues of 'income measurement'.

Given the inherent conceptual limitations of 'income' and 'value' measurement, it remains unrealistic to expect official attempts to develop 'conceptual frameworks' for financial accounting and reporting to be able to provide a coherent basis for the resolution of accounting problems. It may be possible to improve the accounting for some parts of the financial statements, but this will often have to be a 'second best' solution, i.e. taking account of imperfections elsewhere. While the development of a common, and now increasingly familiar, terminology may clarify discussion (and assist accountancy education), the real debates will therefore continue to be over substantive accounting issues. The FASB has not succeeded, by establishing a framework of principles, in limiting the number of detailed standards required (currently about 125 and still rising (Delaney *et al.*, 1997)!). Moreover, standard setters' major problems are more often political. A framework, however technically correct, cannot solve the political problems of different interests and needs at the level of individual standards (e.g. Zeff, 1993). However, its very existence may assist the political justification of an 'independent' private-sector standard setter's role, while its ambiguity leaves scope for the negotiation and compromise that are essential in getting agreement to individual standards.

Accounting research continues to shed light on how accounting concepts and practice interrelate. For example, a recent development has been the attempt to link empirical research into the impact and usefulness of accounting disclosures—which, by focusing on 'information content' (e.g. Beaver, 1989) has previously had relatively little to say about the role of the formal articulation of, and aggregation of information within, financial statements—with theoretical understanding of the interrelationships between, on the one hand balance sheet book-values and accounting earnings measured on a 'clean-surplus' basis and, on the other, the fundamentals of security valuation (e.g. Ohlson, 1995; Brief & Peasnell, 1996). It is in such attempts to identify important research questions that conceptual thinking has its most valuable role to play. As I said in my study for the ASC (Macve, 1981):

> "the main value of thinking about the conceptual framework of accounting lies in developing understanding of what questions need answering and how they may be approached. In other words, a conceptual framework must be seen as a framework for investigation and research into solutions; not as a package of solutions."

# REFERENCES

Archer, S. (1992), 'On the Methodology of a Conceptual Framework for Financial Accounting. Part 1: An Historical and Jurisprudential Analysis', *Accounting, Business & Financial History*, 2/2 (September), pp.199-227.

———(1993), 'On the Methodology of a Conceptual Framework for Financial Accounting. Part 2: From Jurisprudence to Soft Systems Analysis', *Accounting, Business & Financial History*, 3/1 (March), pp.81-108.

Arnold, J., Boyle, P., Carey, A., Cooper, M., and Wild, K. (1991), *The Future Shape of Financial Reports*, London: ICAEW/ICAS.

Arnold, J., Egginton, D., Kirkham, L., Macve, R., and Peasnell, K. (1992), *Goodwill and Other Intangibles*, London: Research Board of ICAEW.

ASB (Accounting Standards Board) (1992), FRS3: *Reporting Financial Performance* (October; amended June 1993), London: ASB.

——— (1995), Exposure Draft: *Statement of Principles* (November), London: ASB.

Beaver, W. (1989), *Financial Reporting: An Accounting Revolution*, Prentice Hall, 2nd edn..

Brief, R. and Peasnell, K.V. (1996), *Clean Surplus: A Link Between Accounting and Finance*, New York and London: Garland

Carsberg, Sir Bryan (1996), 'The Role and Future Plans of the International Accounting Standards Committee', in I. Lapsley (ed.) *Essays in Accounting Thought: A Tribute to W.T. Baxter,* Edinburgh: ICAS, pp.68-84

CCAB (Consultative Committee of Accountancy Bodies) (1988), *The Making of Accounting Standards,* report of the review committee, Chairman, Sir Ron Dearing, London: Institute of Chartered Accountants in England & Wales.

Delaney, P.R., Adler, J.R., Epstein, B.J., and Foran, M.F. (1997), *GAAP 97: Interpretation and Application,* New York: Wiley.

Dennis, I.(1997), *What is a Conceptual Framework for Accounting?,* LSE ACCOUNTING working paper.

Dharan, B.G. (1984), 'Expectation Models and Potential Information Content of Oil and Gas Reserve Value Disclosures', *The Accounting Review,* April, pp.199-217.

Ernst & Young (1996), *The ASB's Framework: Time to Decide,* London: Ernst & Young

—— (1997), *UK GAAP,* 4th edition, 1994, London: Ernst & Young.

FASB (Financial Accounting Standards Board) (1984), SFAC5: *Recognition and Measurement in Financial Statements of Business Enterprises,* Stamford, Conn.: FASB.

—— (1979), Statement of Financial Accounting Standards No.33 ('FAS33'): *Financial Reporting and Changing Prices* (September), Stamford, Conn.: FASB.

Fleischman, R., Hoskin, K. and Macve, R. (1995), 'The Boulton & Watt Case: The Crux of Alternative Approaches to Accounting History?', *Accounting and Business Research,* 25/99 (Summer), pp.162-176.

Gore, J.P.O. (1992), *The FASB Conceptual Framework Project 1973-1985: An Analysis*, Manchester University Press.

Harte, G. and Macve, R. (1991), 'The Vehicle and General Insurance Company' in P. Taylor and S. Turley (eds.), *Case Studies in Financial Reporting*, Oxford: Philip Allan: pp.346-360.

Horton, J. and Macve, R. (1995), *Accounting Principles for Life Insurance: A True and Fair View?*, London: Research Board of ICAEW.

―― (1996), 'The "Amortized Cost" Basis for Fixed-Interest Investments: A Note on Economic, Actuarial and Accounting Concepts of Value and Income ', in I. Lapsley (ed.) *Essays in Accounting Thought: A Tribute to W.T. Baxter*, Edinburgh: ICAS, pp.127-155.

Hoskin, K.W. and Macve, R.H. (1994), 'Writing, Examining, Disciplining: The Genesis of Accounting's Modern Power' in A. Hopwood and P. Miller (eds.), *Accounting as Social and Institutional Practice*, Cambridge University Press, pp.67-97.

―― (1996), 'The Lawrence Manufacturing Co.: A Note on Early Cost Accounting in US Textile Mills', *Accounting, Business & Financial History*, 6:3 (December), pp.337-61.

IASC (International Accounting Standards Committee) (1989), *Framework for the Preparation and Presentation of Financial Statements*, London: IASC.

―― (1997), Discussion Paper: *Accounting for Financial Assets and Financial Liabilities* (March), London: IASC

Lyas, C. (1993), 'Accounting and Language', in Mumford, M.J. and Peasnell, K.V. (eds.), *Philosophical Perspectives on Accounting: Essays in Honour of Edward Stamp*, London & New York: Routledge, pp.156-76.

Macve, R.H. (1980), *Quaere Verum Vel Recte Numerare,* Inaugural Lecture, May 16th 1979, The University College of Wales, Aberystwyth (reprinted in this volume at pp.3-26).

—— (1981), *A Conceptual Framework for Financial Accounting and Reporting: the possibilities for an agreed structure.* A report prepared at the request of the Accounting Standards Committee, London: ICAEW (reprinted in this volume at pp.27-166).

—— (1983a), 'The FASB'S Conceptual Framework—Vision, Tool or Threat?', presented at the Arthur Young Professors' Roundtable: *The FASB—The First Ten Years,* May 7, 1983 (reprinted in this volume at pp.167-217).

—— (1983b), 'Jock's codicil creates problems at South Fork', *Accountancy Age* (June 30, p.19) (reprinted in this volume at pp.219-232).

—— (1983c), 'Dallas contest needs a few rules' (*Accountancy Age,* July 7, p.26) (reprinted in this volume at pp.219-232).

—— (1983d), 'No accounting for the plot of Dallas' (*Accountancy Age,* July 21, p.20) (reprinted in this volume at pp.219-232).

—— (1984), 'Accounting for Long-term Loans', in Carsberg, B.V. and Dev, S.F.D. (eds.), *External Financial Reporting* (London: Prentice-Hall), pp.90-108.

—— (1989a), 'Solomons' Guidelines: Where Do They Lead?', *Accountancy,* March, pp.20-21 (reprinted in this volume at pp.233-39).

—— (1989b), 'Questioning the Wisdom of Solomons', *Accountancy,* April, pp.26-27 (reprinted in this volume at pp.241-8).

—— (forthcoming), '*Capital* and Financial Accounting: A Commentary on Bryer's "A Marxist Critique of the FASB's Conceptual Framework" ', *Critical Perspectives on Accounting.*

Macve, R. and Carey, A. (1992), *Business, Accountancy and the Environment: A Policy and Research Agenda*, London: ICAEW.

Macve, R. with Gwilliam, D. (1993), *A Survey of Lloyd's Syndicate Accounts: Issues in Financial Reporting at Lloyd's*, London: ICAEW/Prentice Hall

Macve, R. and Jackson, J. (1991), *Marking to Market: Accounting for Marketable Securities in the Financial Services Industry*, London: ICAEW.

McMonnies, P. (ed.) (1988), *Making Corporate Reports Valuable*, ICAS and Kogan Page.

Mumford, M.J. (1989), 'The Search for a British Conceptual Framework: A Review Essay', *British Accounting Review* (December), pp.381-9.

Ohlson, J. (1995), 'Earnings, Book Value and Dividends in Security Valuation', *Contemporary Accounting Research* (Spring), pp.661-87.

Power, M.K. (1993), 'On the idea of a conceptual framework for financial reporting', in Mumford, M.J. and Peasnell, K.V. (eds.), *Philosophical Perspectives on Accounting: Essays in Honour of Edward Stamp*, London & New York: Routledge, pp. 44-61.

Solomons, D. (1986), 'The FASB's Conceptual Framework: An Evaluation', *Journal of Accountancy*, June, pp.114-116, 118, 120-22, 124 (reprinted in Zeff & Dharan, 1994, pp.120-30).

Solomons, D. (1989a), *Guidelines for Financial Reporting Standards*, London: ICAEW (reprinted New York and London: Garland, 1997).

Solomons, D. (1989b), 'The Solomons Guidelines: A Reply to the Critics', *Accountancy*, August, pp.21-23.

Tweedie, Sir David (1996), 'The Conceptual Framework and the Accounting Standards Board', in Lapsley, I. (ed.), *Essays in Accounting Thought: A Tribute to W.T. Baxter*, ICAS, pp.41-67.

Zeff, S.A. (1993), 'The Politics of Accounting Standards', *Economia Aziendale*, XII, 2, August, pp.125-42.

――, and Dharan, B.G. (1994), *Readings and Notes on Financial Accounting: Issues and Controversies*, 4th edn., New York: McGraw-Hill.

# NOTES

[1] I am grateful to Christopher Napier and Desmond Wright for their helpful comments on an earlier draft of this introduction.

[2] formerly the University College of Wales, Aberystwyth.

[3] In the Report's 'Summary of Principal Recommendations', the first three were:

> R1 Further work in a conceptual framework is desirable; it should be undertaken on a modest scale, with the level of expenditure being enhanced when the proposed Financial Reporting Council judges there to be a reliable basis for substantial progress (Section 7.2).

> R2 Accounting standards should be accompanied by a statement of the principles underlying them and of the reasons why alternatives were rejected (Section 7.3)

> R3 The concern should be with increasing the quality and timeliness of accounting standards and reducing the permitted options, and not with increasing their number (Section 8).

[4] In the U.K. there have also been reports issued under the aegis of professional accountancy bodies which have come out more strongly in favour of current value based approaches to reforming accounting than have the standard setting bodies' own frameworks. See for example McMonnies (1988) (reviewed in Mumford, 1989 and regarded by the current chairman of ASB as 'seminal' [Tweedie, 1996, p.49]) and Arnold *et al.* (1991).

[5] For this reprinting I have added some explanatory notes to the original text.

[6] now the Research Board of ICAEW

[7] As I recall, it was Professor David Solomons who had originally suggested to Sandy Burton that I be invited.

[8] This reference is given in full in the bibliography to Macve, 1983a.

[9] The papers reprinted in this volume refer to the original numberings of FASB Concepts Statements. In respect of business enterprises, these were subsequently revised to:

> SFAC No. 1: *Objectives of Financial Reporting by Business Enterprises*
> SFAC No. 2: *Qualitative Characteristics of Accounting Information*

SFAC No. 6: *Elements of Financial Statements* [replacing SFAC No. 3]
SFAC No. 5: *Recognition and Measurement in Financial Statements of Business Enterprises*

[10] For this reprinting I have added some bibliographic and explanatory notes.

[11] For example, Ch 5 of the ASB's draft *Statement of Principles* (ASB, 1995) favours 'value to the business' as the measurement basis and concludes that 'practice should develop by evolving in the direction of greater use of current values to the extent that this is consistent with the constraints of reliability and cost'.

[12] More extensive tracing of the development of the detail of FASB's statements has been undertaken by Gore (e.g., 1992).

[13] Ch 6 of the ASB's draft *Statement of Principles* (ASB, 1995) also now proposes that the Statement of Total Recognised Gains and Losses should include all gains and losses on 'infrastructure' items rather than basing the distinction between 'profit' and other gains on 'realisation'. Tweedie (1996, p.51) observes that the Board had wanted to do this at the time of FRS3 *Reporting Financial Performance* (ASB, 1992) but considered then that it was too radical a change to risk jeopardising the success of FRS3.

# Acknowledgments

I am grateful for permission from the copyright holders to reproduce the following publications:

*Quaere Verum vel Recte Numerare* Inaugural lecture as Julian Hodge Professor of Accounting at the University College of Wales, Aberystwyth,[1], given on 16 May 1979 (© Aberystwyth: University College of Wales, 1980). (Reading (I) in this volume.)

*A Conceptual Framework for Financial Accounting and Reporting: the possibilities for an agreed structure.* A report prepared at the request of the Accounting Standards Committee (© London: Institute of Chartered Accountants in England and Wales, 1981: ISBN 0-85291-3117). (Reading (II) in this volume.)

'The Conceptual Framework and Oil and Gas Accounting' [originally published as 'Jock's codicil creates problems at South Fork', *Accountancy Age* (June 30, 1983, p.19); 'Dallas contest needs a few rules' (*ibid.*, July 7, p.26); 'No accounting for the plot of Dallas' (*ibid.*, July 21, p.20)] (© VNU Business Publications Ltd., 1983). (Reading (IV) in this volume.)

'Solomons' Guidelines: Where Do They Lead?', *Accountancy*, March 1989, pp.20-21 (© Accountancy 1989). (Reading (V) in this volume.)

'Questioning the Wisdom of Solomons', *Accountancy*, April 1989, pp.26-27 (© Accountancy 1989). (Reading (VI) in this volume.)

In addition to all those whose from whose guidance I benefited when I originally wrote the papers reprinted here—who are acknowledged in the individual papers and in the introduction to this volume—I am particularly grateful to Professor Richard Brief and to

Desmond Wright, Head of Research at ICAEW, for their encouragement and support in enabling me to compile this collection.

Jean Matthews, Christine Hughes and Pam Williams deserve special thanks for their help in wordprocessing the original typescripts of the papers for presentation in this volume.

Richard Macve
LSE
London, July 10th, 1997

---

[1] now the University of Wales, Aberystwyth

# A Conceptual Framework for Financial Accounting and Reporting

(I)

# QUAERE VERUM VEL RECTE NUMERARE

Inaugural lecture by
Richard Macve, MA, MSc, FCA,
as Julian Hodge Professor of Accounting
at the University College of Wales, Aberystwyth,
given on 16 May 1979

# Quaere Verum vel Recte Numerare

The Latin of my title is barely grammatical; and a rough translation into barely grammatical English might be "Seek the truth or to count up correctly".

This sounds like a quotation, so I should acknowledge its source. Is it perhaps from some early textbook on accounting—for example the work of a mediaeval teacher at the University of Oxford, where estate accounting had become a regular part of the curriculum by the end of the 13th century?[1] I am afraid not. The appearance of antiquity is entirely bogus and the poor grammar is the result of my cobbling together two mottoes, firstly that of the Institute of Chartered Accountants of Scotland, "Quaere Verum", "Seek the truth", and secondly that of the Institute of Chartered Accountants in England and Wales, "Recte Numerare", "To count (or reckon) up correctly".

I have joined these together to make one theme, "Seek the truth or to count up correctly", because I wish to show in this lecture that although the accountant's task is primarily to produce numbers, this alone is not sufficient if he is to tell the truth. The numbers need to be supplemented, both on the accountant's side by an explanation of the bases and assumptions on which they have been calculated, and equally important on the side of those who use them by an understanding of the ways in which they have been prepared, and of the essential limitations which are imposed on them by the many difficulties the accountant faces in trying to express "the truth in numbers". Getting the numbers right—counting up correctly—may be a necessary but is certainly not a sufficient condition for seeking out the truth.

I shall develop the lecture as follows. Firstly I shall review briefly what accountants do, the tools they are able to employ, and the types of accounts they are able to produce, and give a brief outline of their historical development. I shall then describe some of the main uses to which accounts are put and the main users of them, and consider the skills and education that the accountant must have if he is to provide useful statements for their needs. I shall then illustrate the difficulties the accountant faces by dealing with one particular set of accounting reports—perhaps the best known to non-accountants—the annual published accounts of limited companies. I shall run through an example to illustrate what I see as the basic problems that arise in preparing these statements.

I will use this example to show why I believe that not only is it important for the accountant to explain his numbers, it is equally important for those who use his statements to have an understanding of what they can and cannot show, an understanding which I believe is not at present widespread. What is more, I shall argue that it will always be necessary to have these explanations and this understanding, given the nature of the world in which we live. In other words, I believe that understanding accounting is not merely a technical matter, a skill that needs to be mastered by those who are to produce accounts. It can be a valuable part of anyone's education. We do not all have to produce accounts, but directly or indirectly, we all have to use them.

What do accountants do? We clearly expect accountants to produce numbers. In English, the words "account" and "accounting" have wider meanings, as for example in "to give an account of the day's developments" or "there is no accounting for taste". But in Welsh, the notion seems more precise. "Cyfrifydd" is one who counts or reckons and the verb "cyfrif" corresponds almost exactly with the Latin "numerare".

What tools does the accountant employ? And what do the accounts that he produces show? I can give only a brief summary. First of all, the accountant finds it useful to be able to write. And the archaeological evidence of clay tablets found in Mesopotamia, dating from nearly 3,000 years before Christ, suggests that writing was invented in order to keep accounts.[2] Extensive and detailed records of inventories of physical assets and of transactions in them could be of assistance, not only to individuals, but also to traders, religious organizations and the state in keeping track of their resources.

A major step forward came with the introduction of coinage, which appeared in Western Asia Minor and in Greece in the late 7th and the 6th Centuries BC. The adoption of money as the normal medium of valuation and exchange made it possible to record possessions and transactions, not as so many things in physical quantities, but in terms of so many units of a particular currency.[3] The new importance and value of cash made the statement of cash receipts and payments a key accounting statement.

Much later came the introduction of Arabic numerals, which probably first reached Western Europe in the 10th Century AD. Arabic numerals have place value. In other words, when using Arabic numerals, it makes adding up easier if one lays out the figures in columns, one under another (which is no advantage with Roman numerals or other ancient numeral systems). It has therefore been argued that the gradual adoption of this new system (together with the introduction of paper to Europe during the same period) was a major factor that made possible the development of, what is perhaps the most famous invention of accounting, "double entry" book-keeping.[4] Our first printed description of the double entry system comes from the work of the mathematician Fra Luca Pacioli, who, in 1494 in Venice, published a work with the modest title of *Summa de Arithemetica, Geometria, Proportioni et Proportionalita*, "Everything about arithmetic, geometry and proportion". Pacioli included a section on commercial accounting and stated that the double entry system he was describing had been used in Venice for over 200 years, that is, from about the end of the 13th Century onwards. Some historians consider that there are examples of the method to be found in accounts from other northern Italian towns which date from even earlier than this.[5]

I shall not spend time describing the method to you. It is the outputs of the system not its mechanisms that are important to non-accountants. It is enough to say that the double entry method produces an integrated system for dealing with all the transactions and records of a business, and by its inbuilt checks and balances greatly increases the degree of control over the processing of a multitude of transactions into orderly accounts; and it added two new statements to the accountant's repertoire—the balance sheet and the profit and loss account.

So the accountant has at his disposal not only inventories of physical assets and of debts and liabilities; but also statements of cash receipts and payments, balance sheets and profit and loss accounts. And they are used not only to record past transactions and existing assets and liabilities, that is as "historical records", but also to set out plans about the future in a formal structure, that is they are presented as "budgets".

What do we want accounts for? And what training does the accountant need beyond basic literacy and numeracy, and drill in the mechanics of preparing accounts? The most important and ancient use of accounting is as an organized "memory" which enables individuals, and more importantly organizations of all kinds, to keep accurate and up-to-date records of their transactions, resources and obligations.[6] For commercial accounting the double entry system has been found to be an extremely efficient way of organizing this memory and in our own time the advent of computers has vastly increased the storage capacity of accounting systems and the processing of which they are capable. The modern accountant must understand computers.

We also use accounts as a basis for sharing out between interested parties the results of their economic activities, or for working out the contributions each is to make to the cost of some joint activity. Such shares may be matters of contract, for example the arrangements between partners, or between shareholders in a company, or between the government and a major defence contractor, or where employees are to be rewarded by some bonus or profit sharing scheme. They may be matters of statute law, like the division of assets on bankruptcy or liquidation; the administration of trusts and estates; or the assessment of the amount the state is to take the form of taxation, or these days, to grant by way of subsidy.

This aspect of accounting has therefore been heavily influenced by the law; the general commercial law, trust law, partnership law, company law and revenue, or tax, law. These provide a lot of work for accountants and accountants need to understand the relevant law.

Where accounts can affect the shares going to different groups in society, or to different countries, then the accountant begins to get involved in politics and even international politics. Consider for example the budget of the European Economic Community.

A third major use of accounting statements is in assisting with decisions and planning for the future, and in controlling and appraising the outcome of current activities. Whatever the objectives of individuals or organizations, it is important that they consider carefully the financial consequences of the alternative actions they contemplate, and the financial effects of the current actions of themselves and their subordinates or agents.

The problems they face are economic problems; choices about the allocation of resources, and the pursuit of efficiency, so as to obtain the best return or the lowest cost, and decisions about co-operative arrangements to be entered into with other parties and how costs and returns are to be shared. If the accountant's job is to provide information for such decisions and appraisals, he needs a grounding in economics and finance and in the mathematical and statistical techniques of modern management science.

And as decisions have to be made in large organizations, or at national and international level, there has been a growing awareness of a need to understand how the accounting information presented may be perceived by different individuals and groups; and how these perceptions, in turn, may affect the decisions they take or the attitudes they adopt to the decisions that are taken. So behavioural studies too are important.

For all these various uses of accounts, there are also a variety of users. Take large-scale businesses. In a modern economic organization there is a separation of the day-to-day control, in the hands of management, from the ownership, which in a limited company belongs to the shareholders, or in a nationalized industry, to the state. But others both inside and outside companies are interested in their economic performance, and need to know about it in order to make their own plans about spending, saving, investing and allocating capital; or to ensure that they receive their fair share; or to satisfy themselves that the resources of the company are properly safeguarded and utilized. So besides managements and shareholders, there are long-term lenders, bankers and the shorter-term creditors who have to appraise the state of companies when considering where to advance their money. The employees and their union representatives are concerned with the shares they are to receive in wages and other conditions. Competitors wish to know how their rivals are getting on.

The government seeks to act on behalf of the public interest in matters such as protecting consumers against unreasonably high prices or restrictive trade practices, for example through the Office of Fair Trading or the Monopolies Commission. The government also participates in the running of companies by itself taking investment stakes in various forms. The Board of Inland Revenue has to collect the legal amount due from companies, as defined by the prevailing tax law, and at a higher level the government has to decide its taxation policy in relation to companies, in the light of the likely consequences for the level of their activities and their investment, and how this may in turn affect the government's objectives for the management of the economy.

For all these various users (and one may think of others) the accounts of companies, whether individually, or aggregated at industry and national level, are an important source of information.

So the accountant prepares a number of different statements, for a number of different users. I now want to show you why for "sharing" and "decision-making" purposes the accounts cannot be taken simply at face value—why one needs not only explanations of the approaches and assumptions that the accountant has adopted, but an understanding of the difficulties he faces. To make this more concrete, I shall focus my attention on the accounts of commercial organizations, and in particular of limited companies, and I shall be talking about balance sheets and profit and loss accounts.

Companies are now the major form of private sector enterprise and I shall concentrate on their profit and loss accounts and balance sheets because these are the accounts that limited companies are legally required to publish—that is to send out to all shareholders and major lenders, as well as to make available for public inspection at the Companies Registration Offices in Cardiff, London and Edinburgh. Indeed, most users, other than the companies' own managements, rarely see any other form of accounts, and therefore the balance sheet and the profit and loss account have come to be commonly regarded as the prime accounting statements.

The main legal requirements are contained in the Companies Acts, which require an audited balance sheet and profit and loss account to be published each year by every limited company, together with an audit report which must state whether, in the opinion of the auditors, the balance sheet gives "a true and fair view" of the state of the company's affairs, and the profit and loss account gives "a true and fair view" of the profit or loss for the year.[7] So there is a weight of authority to foster the view that balance sheets and profit and loss accounts are the way to find out the truth about a company's financial affairs. In practice, nationalized industries follow similar reporting procedures, and unincorporated businesses too usually produce their annual results in the same form.

The legal requirements for these published accounts have in turn influenced the way accounts are presented internally for many management purposes. As the managers know that they will have to present their annual report to outsiders in the form of a balance sheet and profit and loss account, they ask for budgets of projected results for internal planning purposes, and for reports on progress during the year, to be prepared in the same form.

Perhaps it is time we did some accounting, to get some idea of the difficulties that accountants face in preparing accounts that "tell the truth".

Imagine an impoverished Aberystwyth student, whose grant has almost run out, and who decides to spend a summer weekend selling toffee-apples on the promenade outside this building. A very simple venture. On Saturday he buys 200 toffee-apples for £20. On Saturday he sells 100 apples at 20p each for £20 and on Sunday he sells the other 100 apples for £20. His total receipts are £40. His total payments were £20, so by the end of the weekend his receipts have exceeded his payments by £20 and he has doubled his money. A simpler set of facts would be hard to imagine.

An accountant might show these events in terms of an opening balance sheet, a closing balance sheet and a profit and loss account as follows:

| | Profit and Loss Account for Weekend | | Balance Sheets | |
| | | | at beginning | at end |
| | £ | | £ | £ |
| Sales | 40 | Capital paid in | 20 | 20 |
| Cost of Sales | 20 | Profit | — | 20 |
| Profit | 20 | | 20 | 40 |
| | | Cash | 20 | 40 |

The profit and loss account shows his sales of £40, less cost of sales £20, giving a profit of £20. The balance sheets, which list his resources and the claims upon them, show that he started the weekend with £20 cash, which was all his own capital, and that he ended it with £40 cash. So he has increased his capital by £20 profit.

It is clear that the student's profit over the weekend is £20. But suppose we ask the question, "How much profit did he make on Saturday and how much on Sunday?"—just as a company has to report how much profit it has made each year. If we review the events of the weekend, the sales for each day are clear, so that the profit we calculate for Saturday is going to depend on how we reckon the cost of 100 toffee-apples sold on Saturday. That will leave us with the cost of the closing stock on Saturday night, which will be the cost of the sales on Sunday. That will give us the profit for Saturday and the profit for Sunday.

Is this difficult? It seems natural to say that if in total the toffee apples cost £20, and he sold half of them on Saturday and the other half on Sunday, then the cost of the apples sold on Saturday was £10 and so was the cost of the apples sold on Sunday. That gives us £10 profit on Saturday and £10 profit on Sunday. His accounts would look like this:

|  | Profit and Loss Account | | | Balance Sheet |
|  | Saturday | Sunday | | Saturday night |
|  | £ | £ | | £ |
| Sales | 20 | 20 | Capital paid in | 20 |
| Cost of Sales | 10 | 10 | Profit | 10 |
| Profit | 10 | 10 | | 30 |
|  |  |  | Stock | 10 |
|  |  |  | Cash | 20 |
|  |  |  | | 30 |

Each day's profit and loss account shows sales of £20, and cost of sales £10, giving a profit of £10 each day. His opening and closing balance sheets will be the same as before, but now he can also prepare an intermediate balance sheet for Saturday night. This shows the cash he has recovered—£20—and also the closing stock which was reckoned to cost £10. So his total assets are £30. He started with capital of £20, his profit for Saturday is £10 and everything balances correctly.

But considering the same sequence of events one could equally well say that what happened on Saturday was that he spent £20 on buying toffee-apples, and by the end of Saturday he had got his £20 back. Then on Sunday he made £20 profit. By the end of Saturday he was back to where he started in terms of cash; and he also had 100 unsold apples which it turned out he was able to sell for £20 on Sunday, so ending the weekend £20 better off than when he started. In other words he could regard the cost of the apples sold on Saturday as £20, and by the end of Saturday he was left with 100 apples which had cost him nothing, as he had got his money back. Then his accounts would show a profit by the end of Saturday of nothing, and a profit on Sunday of £20. The accounts would look like this:

|              | Profit and Loss Account | | | Balance Sheet |
|              | Saturday | Sunday | | Saturday night |
|              | £ | £ | | £ |
| Sales        | 20 | 20 | Capital paid in | 20 |
| Cost of Sales | 20 | — | Profit | — |
| Profit       | — | 20 | | 20 |
|              | | | Stock | — |
|              | | | Cash | 20 |
|              | | | | 20 |

In the balance sheet on Saturday night he shows the cash recovered of £20 as before—but now he shows nothing for the stock that is left as he reckons this cost him nothing. His assets at this stage are stated in total at £20, and no profit as yet is shown. Then on Sunday he sells the remaining apples for £20 and so makes his £20 profit.

This seems a perfectly reasonable treatment of how the profit arises even though we know that on Sunday the rest of the apples were successfully sold. But of course in real life he would not know on Saturday night how much he was going to sell the apples for on Sunday. After all it might rain on Sunday, so that if he stands in the wet, the apples could be spoiled, and anyway there would not be many people around to buy them. Then if he was a prudent or cautious young man, he might well say when reckoning his profit on Saturday night, that as there is no guarantee that he will be able to sell the apples tomorrow all he can say at this stage is that he has got his money back and has so far broken even. This uncertainty about the future would strengthen the case for this method of allocating profit between the two days.

Alternatively, one could say that on Saturday he spent £20 on 200 apples; by the end of Saturday he had got his £20 back and he also still had 100 apples which he could sell for £20. So that he was £20 better off by the end of Saturday, and had therefore made his profit of £20 that day. Consequently, he made no profit on Sunday. The value of his remaining stocks on Saturday night was £20 and therefore the effective cost of what he had sold on Saturday was nothing.

His accounts would look like this:

|  | Profit and Loss Account | | | Balance Sheet |
|  | Saturday | Sunday | | Saturday night |
|  | £ | £ | | £ |
| Sales | 20 | 20 | Capital paid in | 20 |
| Cost of sales | — | 20 | Profit | 20 |
| Profit | 20 | — | | 40 |
| | | | Stock | 20 |
| | | | Cash | 20 |
| | | | | 40 |

So his balance sheet on Saturday night shows his total assets as £40 (the £20 cash he has recovered that day and the £20 that he can sell the remaining apples for), and his profit and loss account for Saturday shows how his capital has increased by £20.

The normal objection to that allocation in common practice (when the result of the next period is what we do not know) would be that it is not very prudent of him, on Saturday night, to value the stock at what he hopes to sell it for on Sunday, because he does not know whether or not in fact he will be able to sell it. He would be counting his chickens before they are hatched. But then, one can also doubt whether the first method (which showed his stock on Saturday night at £10) is prudent. If he does not know that he is going to be able to sell the apples, then it seems wrong to take any profit on Saturday, even the more modest profit of £10.

So far we have three versions of how his £20 profit arose over the two days—£10 on Saturday and £10 on Sunday; nothing on Saturday and £20 on Sunday; £20 on Saturday and nothing on Sunday. I think many accountants might say that the first method is the most reasonable one of splitting up the costs and arriving at the profit, because it seems to give the fairest measure of what it would cost him to buy 100 apples each day.

But is that likely? The wholesaler might well charge, say, for batches up to 150 toffee-apples, 12p each (so 100 apples cost £12); while for batches over 150 the price is 10p each (so 200 apples cost £20). That is a perfectly normal commercial arrangement; the more you buy the cheaper you get it. So our student could have bought 100 apples on Saturday, which would have cost him £12, sold those for £20 and made a profit of £8 that day. And then on Sunday he could again have bought 100 apples for £12, sold them for £20 and again made a profit of £8.

That of course would solve all our accounting problems about when he made his profit—he would have made £8 each day. But unfortunately it would mean that he made less profit over all—£16 instead of £20. He does better by buying one batch of 200 apples to sell over the two days because he gets them for £20 in total, saving £4. That is to say the additional cost of the second 100 apples is only £8 when he buys all in one batch. The cost of the first 100 is £12, while the additional cost of the second 100 is only £8.

Now it might be a better, more useful way of measuring his costs, which would tie in better with the decisions he has to make, to measure not the average costs of 10p per apple, but the additional or incremental costs of buying more apples. In which case it is of course completely arbitrary which day's 100 apples we say were the first lot and which the second lot. We could either say that the apples sold on Saturday cost £12 so that the ones sold on Sunday cost £8; which would give us a profit on Saturday of £8 and a profit on Sunday of £12. Or we could say that the ones sold on Saturday cost only £8 and those sold on Sunday cost £12; so that the profit on Saturday was £12 and the profit on Sunday was £8.

So now we have five different calculations:-

| Cost of Apples sold on Saturday £ | Stock on Saturday night = cost of sales on Sunday £ | Profit on Saturday £ | Profit on Sunday £ |
|---|---|---|---|
| (1) 10 | 10 | 10 | 10 |
| (2) 20 | - | - | 20 |
| (3) - | 20 | 20 | - |
| (4) 12 | 8 | 8 | 12 |
| (5) 8 | 12 | 12 | 8 |

Looking at these alternatives we can see that the amount of the profit shown for Saturday is a direct function of the amount at which the stock is stated in the balance sheet on Saturday night. At one extreme he could reckon all the profit to be earned immediately, by stating the stock at selling price; at the other extreme he could say that there is no profit until the final outcome has been realized by stating his stock at nothing. And one could take almost any intermediate result. What the accountant does in practice is to find some result in between the two extremes, which he does by adopting an allocation method that puts a figure on the assets in his balance sheet that is somewhere between zero and the amount which he expects to be realized from their sale or to be earned from their use. He cannot say that his result is 'right', because in real life there is always the problem that a business has, by the end of each accounting year, reinvested in a set of further assets whose value is often uncertain, and essentially a function of what is going to happen next in the future—and the future is uncertain.

So even for that simple situation (about the simplest situation I could think of), I have managed to find five different ways of saying how much profit was made on Saturday and how much profit was made on Sunday. In other words, profit figures are not facts, they are just opinions—opinions arrived at by adopting some acceptable rule for their calculation.

What is more, I have avoided any of the problems and complexities that are normally regarded as explaining why it is difficult to arrive at the correct profit figure for a period. For example, there are no problems of changing prices; no problems of deciding what to do if apples now cost say 15p each to buy, because prices have risen with inflation. I have no problem of continuous reinvestment in new assets in an ongoing business; in this case, we do know the final outcome of this business venture. I have no long-term assets, whose useful life is uncertain and whose depreciation needs to be considered; no research and development expenditure whose outcome is problematical, and the treatment of which needs to be decided. No problems of sales on credit and the consequent doubts about whether the customers' debts will be paid. No long-term sales contracts where receipts are to be spread over several periods, so that it is not clear how much sales income belongs to each period. No special or peculiar circumstances of this kind of business to explain the individual practices adopted in arriving at the profits.

In short, I have none of the problems of complex businesses, that one normally has to deal with in trying to work out each period's profits. But nevertheless, I am at a loss to say which of these five possible methods gives the "true profit" each day.

Well, if there is no single correct way of calculating profit in such a simple situation, then *a fortiori* there is no single correct way of doing it in the more complex situations that we actually meet in real life. Even in the simplest situation we have to adopt some acceptable set of procedural rules, and so in more complex situations we have to adopt more complex rules; and it is hardly surprising that there are a large number of different procedures that accountants may adopt in what, to all intents and purposes, seem to be similar situations.[8]

What implications does all this have for the use of the accountant's figures, and for the users for whom they are prepared?

I talked earlier of "memory", "sharing" and "decision-making" uses. There is little problem with the "memory" function as almost any arbitrary system of assigning numbers will do for this purpose—and I shall say no more about it.

The problems arise with the "sharing" and "decision-making" functions, and it is clear that if the users of accounts are to understand their significance for these purposes, then firstly the accountant needs to explain clearly how the numbers are arrived at—what "accounting policies" have been adopted, to use the technical jargon—and secondly that those who read the accounts need to understand how the information the accountant presents is relevant for the purposes for which they wish to use it. In particular, they must be clear about the limitations to what the accounting figures can show, given the uncertainty about what the future holds.

These two requirements—for explanation and understanding of the significance of the numbers—could only be avoided if it was already perfectly clear what approach the accountant had adopted (for example because it was generally known that all accountants use the same method, or a particular method had been specified for a particular purpose by agreement between the interested parties) and if the accountant was able to provide precisely the numbers that the users wanted for the purposes they had in mind.

So for the remainder of this lecture I intend to discuss some of the developments that have recently taken place, or are being investigated by practising accountants and academic researchers, to try and improve published accounts. I shall discuss three aspects of this problem:

- disclosure of accounting policies,
- elimination of the diversity of practice,
- improving relevance to users.

Firstly, disclosure. It is obvious that the accountant must make clear what bases he has adopted in presenting the figures. This is of course easier with the internal accounts of an organization, where the management are in a position to ask the accountant to explain the figures or to rework them on to different bases.

Nevertheless, it is a serious criticism of published accounts that for a long period no attempt was made to explain the methods that had been used to compute the results. Although the Companies Acts specify the details of what items are to be disclosed they do not say much about the ways in which the figures are to be calculated. On the whole, this has been left to company directors and their accountants.[9] There is, moreover, no legal requirement to explain the bases on which many of the figures have been arrived at. In Britain it is only since 1971, when the professional accounting bodies issued their Statement of Standard Accounting Practice No.2 (called *Disclosure of Accounting Policies*), that there has been a conscious effort to try and explain in the annual accounts the bases on which the figures have been arrived at.

The adoption of the attitude that one does need to explain how the figures are calculated has been a major reform of accounting practice and is a great improvement over the previous attitude—dating from a more authoritarian, paternalistic age—which implied that the figures must be right just because the auditors reported that they gave a "true and fair view" of a company's results and its state of affairs.

The second matter to consider is how to reduce the diversity of practice. In Britain, the major professional bodies of accountants attempt to do this through the work of the Accounting Standards Committee, which was set up, nearly ten years ago now, in January 1970. Fifteen accounting standards have so far been issued, as well as a number of consultative papers ("exposure drafts") for future standards. In the USA the Financial Accounting Standards Board is proceeding with a similar programme. There have also been attempts at international co-operation between accountants on accounting standards through the International Accounting Standards Committee. More important, the Council of Ministers of the European Community has approved the second and fourth directives dealing with companies and their accounts, which impose standard requirements throughout the community in respect of a number of matters of disclosure and also of approved accounting treatment.

One of the main aims of standards is to define approved methods of accounting, primarily with a view to improving the comparability of the accounts of different companies. They have not been entirely successful and it is not hard to understand why. We have already seen that there is no obviously correct way to determine how profits should be measured, or assets and liabilities stated in the balance sheet.

Deciding on a method has therefore often reduced to picking the method that most people seem to use, or indeed to picking any method just in order to get one answer. Objections follow from those who prefer other methods.

Where the lobbies are strong enough, in several instances standards have had to be changed, or rewritten to accommodate more than one method. Indeed some researchers regard the process of setting accounting standards as an interesting problem in political science.

It seems clear from out earlier illustration that settling these disputes cannot be done by appealing to some "correct" notion of profit. If it can be done at all it must be by approaching the problem rather from the direction of what the accounting information is wanted for and by whom, how far their individual interests can be met, and, where these diverge, how they can be reconciled. The profession has realized that a sound theoretical framework is needed in order to tackle this problem successfully. Recently the Accounting Standards Committee has asked us to carry out research here, in the accounting department at Aberystwyth, into the problem of finding an agreed conceptual framework for setting accounting standards; and we shall shortly be starting work on this enquiry.

But for the purpose of this lecture, I am not so much concerned with the problem of how, if at all, one determines the "right" method. Rather, I want to point out that even if some unique method can be chosen, the accountant will still need to explain the assumptions on which his figures are calculated if they are to inform his readers.

Take for example the problem of depreciation. Assets with long lives are bought and some way of spreading their costs over their useful life has to be found for calculating annual profits. To do this, it is necessary not only to know how much the assets originally cost—usually, but not always fairly straightforward—but also how long they will last and what residual sale value, if any, they will have at the end of their useful life. One can then choose some method of allocating the cost over the estimated useful life to leave the residual value by the end of the last period. The accountant has many such methods, for example, "straight-line" depreciation, "reducing balance", "sum of the digits", "service units"—there are many others.

How much uniformity can a standard achieve? In fact the present standard on depreciation only goes so far as to require that depreciation should allocate the cost, less estimated residual value, of assets "as fairly as possible to the periods expected to benefit from their use".[10] This of course leaves us with the very problem that we faced in dealing with the toffee-apple seller—indeed the problem now extends over a large number of periods. As we have seen, almost any answer would be "fair".

The standard could, I suppose, go further and say for example that everyone should use "straight-line" depreciation, a method which allocates an equal amount of cost to each period of the asset's life. But even so, two different accountants could still produce different annual depreciation figures for the same asset, because they could legitimately make different estimates of the likely useful life and residual value, given that both of these are uncertain matters until the life of the asset is eventually complete. These estimates depend on how one foresees the events of the future, the ways in which the company's management is likely to respond to these events, and the decisions they are likely to take about how the asset is to be used, or when it is to be disposed of.

So even if all companies used "straight-line" depreciation, one could still not interpret the depreciation figure in a company's accounts, or compare the depreciation between different companies, without knowing what assumptions had been made about useful life and residual value, and also without some understanding of the factors, economic or otherwise, that might influence the ways in which the company's management could decide to utilize its assets. And one could draw similar conclusions by considering almost any other accounting problem for which a variety of practices is employed.

I have talked about disclosure, and about standardization of practice—finally I want to deal with suggestions that have been made for making the published accounts give information that is more relevant to the needs of those who use them.

The real problem with balance sheets and profit and loss accounts, as far as the purposes of "sharing" and "decision making" are concerned, is that their orientation is too much to the past. They are essentially backward looking statements not forward looking. Although the accountant is careful to avoid overstating the figures for the assets in his balance sheet, compared with the future cash they are likely to bring in, and tries to include all liabilities that have been incurred, the preparation of accounts is, as we have seen, mainly a matter of choosing a rule by which to allocate past cash payments and past cash receipts to different periods. Indeed the normal description of conventional practice is "historical cost" accounting.

But if one is looking to the balance sheet and profit and loss account as a basis either for sharing out the rewards of past endeavours, or as a guide to decisions about where to allocate resources for the future, then one is really hoping that they will tell one something about how well off the company is, and what its prospects are for the future. In other words, one is asking how valuable the business is, and how the efforts of those working in it have helped to increase its value.

But the value of any item, whether an individual asset or a business as a whole, is fundamentally a matter of the benefits that are expected to flow from it in the future, not a matter of the costs that have been expended on it in the past. In economics, "bygones are forever bygones". True, it is only sensible to expend costs on assets if one thinks that they will, as a result, have a value greater than or equal to their cost. But that does not mean that expending the cost will make items valuable.

There has been a growing awareness—in academic circles for at least the past forty years—of the severe limitations of "historical cost" accounts in providing information that is relevant to those who receive them.[11] The awareness has become widespread in recent years, as a period of high inflation has emphasized how quickly balance sheet figures can get out of step with current values; and how dangerous it can be to calculate profit by setting the costs of assets bought in earlier periods, when prices were low, against the sales income of later periods in which they are used, when prices are high. This produces large "money" profit figures, when it can be argued that the "real" profits are small or maybe non-existent.[12]

I shall discuss briefly one of the cures that has been suggested, that of shifting the emphasis in published accounts from past costs to current values. There are other possible approaches, but I do not have time to consider them all, and my main purpose is to emphasize that any such reforms are likely to place an even greater importance on the need for the accountant to explain his assumptions and the ways in which he has arrived at his figures, and on the need for the user of accounts to have a good understanding of how the information presented may be relevant to his own processes of forming the expectations about the future on which he will base the decisions he has to take.

The proposed cure is to make the balance sheet a valuation statement, and the profit and loss account a statement of changes in values. This was the basic recommendation of the Sandilands Report on inflation accounting, that was published nearly four years ago now in 1975.[13] That there are many difficulties is clear from the fact that, in spite of a lot of research effort and discussion, no agreed way of implementing the recommendations has yet been found. Value is not a simple notion. One must ask "Value to whom?", "When?", and "On what conditions?"

Where good market prices are available, these questions can be answered—although one has to decide whether value means "buying price", "selling price" or some "value in use". It is a simple matter to find the value of a quoted share by looking up the price in the financial press. It is perhaps not too difficult to arrange for real property to be valued by a qualified surveyor. But where good market prices are not available, assessment of value is not so easy. It is for example extremely difficult to form an estimate of the value of a modern, complex, technologically sophisticated, industrial plant devoted almost entirely to the manufacture of some specific product. Its value is almost entirely dependent on the demand for the product it produces. Where such an asset has a long life, assessment of its value may require the prediction of the demand for its product, often a highly uncertain matter, for many years into the future.

Such assessments have to be made by managements when deciding whether to invest in such assets, or when to replace or scrap them, and management accountants are familiar with the need to prepare budgets to assist managers in making these decisions. But that is a far cry from stating these uncertain estimates as valuations in a published balance sheet.

Furthermore, there is the extremely difficult problem of inter-relationships between assets working together in a business. In my little example, there was only the toffee-apple seller's stock of toffee-apples for which one might assess a value. But many major businesses utilize highly interdependent complexes of assets—consider for example a chemical company. Here there may be little meaning to be attached to the value of any individual item in the complex. Adding up any such individual values may give a very poor valuation in total. One can only usefully appraise the entire asset complex as a whole.

Again, for many companies, their value lies not just in their saleable stock, or in their land and buildings, or even in valuable plant and equipment; but in "intangibles" such as the value of the organization that has been built up; of a team of people with varied experience and skills; of contacts with customers and suppliers; of a well-known product name; of access to particular sources of finance; perhaps of some monopoly power in the markets in which they sell.[14]

In other words, when one starts to ask for valuations of assets in balance sheets, the only satisfactory answer in many cases may be a valuation of the business as a whole, and an assessment of its entire future prospects. Moreover, the figures one gets will only be as good as the forecasting ability of the directors and accountants who produce them. So if asset valuations are to become the basis of annual accounts, it will be even more important that they are accompanied by a clear explanation of the assumptions that have been made in preparing the necessary estimates about the future, and of the methods by which values have been attributed to individual assets. Only then can the user, reading the accounts, form any assessment of the reliability of the figures, and be able to compare them with his own assessments, based on information from this and other sources, of what the future seems likely to hold for the company.

The move towards valuations, and a number of alternative approaches to ways of reforming published accounts, together seek to eliminate irrelevant information contained in present balance sheets and profit and loss accounts, and substitute more relevant information. They aim to find new ways of collecting, aggregating and presenting data that will be of greater use for the purposes for which accounts are wanted. But because "relevant information" in this context is a highly subjective notion, since one is dealing with the problems of appraising a highly uncertain future, these reforms will not eliminate the need for the accountant to explain, and for the user to understand, what lies behind the preparation of the figures in accounts—rather they will emphasize that need.

To summarize: in this lecture I have looked at what accountants do, and how they turn facts about a business's past, and estimates about its future, into numbers. I have looked at some of the difficulties they face in doing this, and commented on the disciplines they need to master if they are to do it well—disciplines which are taught and studied here at Aberystwyth.[15]

I hope I have said enough to indicate why accounting is more than just trying to get the numbers right, and why accounting is not just for accountants. Not only must accountants explain their figures, those who use the accounts must understand their subjectivity and appreciate the essential limitations to what the accountant can report—limitations that are not the accountant's fault, but which arise from our imperfect understanding of the uncertain world in which we live.

In short, numbers alone are not enough. There must be explanation and understanding if the accountant is to help those who read his accounts to find out the truth. So if the day ever dawns when the various professional bodies of accountants (who at present pursue an independent existence) should decide to unite under one banner, a good motto, if poor Latin, might be:

"QUAERE VERUM ATQUE RECTE NUMERARE"

"Seek the truth, and try to get the numbers right as well".

## REFERENCES

1. Oschinsky, D., 'Medieval Treatises on Estate Accounting', in Littleton, A.C. and Yamey, B.S. (eds.), *Studies in the History of Accounting* (London: Sweet & Maxwell, 1956).

2. Keister, O. R., 'The Mechanics of Mesopotamian Record-keeping', in Chatfield, M. (ed.), *Contemporary Studies in the Evolution of Accounting Thought* (Belmont, California: Dickenson, 1968).[*]

3. De Ste Croix, G.E.M., 'Greek and Roman Accounting', in Littleton and Yamey, *op.cit.*

4. De Ste Croix, G.E.M., *ibid.*[**]

5. De Roover, R., 'The Development of Accounting Prior to Luca Pacioli according to the Account-books of Medieval Merchants', in Littleton and Yamey, *op.cit.*

6. See Edey, H.C., *Introduction to Accounting*, Chapter 1, 4th edition (London: Hutchinson, 1978).

7. The Companies Acts 1948 to 1976 and, in particular, The Companies Act 1967, Section 14.***

8. For further discussion see Thomas, A.L., 'Allocation: the Fallacy and the Theorists', in Baxter, W.T. and Davidson, S. (eds.), *Studies in Accounting*, 3rd edition (London: The Institute of Chartered Accountants in England and Wales, 1977).

9. Yamey, B.S. 'Some Topics in the History of Financial Accounting in England 1500–1900', in Baxter and Davidson, *op.cit.*

10. Statement of Standard Accounting Practice Number 12 *Accounting for Depreciation* (London: The Institute of Chartered Accountants in England and Wales, 1977).

11. See Edwards, R.S., 'The Nature and Measurement of Income', in Baxter and Davidson, *op.cit.* and Bonbright, J.C., *Valuation of Property* (New York: McGraw-Hill, 1937; reprinted Charlottesville, Virginia: Michie, 1965).

12. For a full discussion of the problems of accounting in a period of inflation see Baxter, W.T., *Accounting Values and Inflation* (London: McGraw-Hill, 1975).****

13. *Inflation Accounting: Report of the Inflation Accounting Committee*, Cmnd 6225 (London: HMSO, 1975).*****

14. For further discussion see Edey, H.C., 'Deprival Value and Financial Accounting', in Edey, H.C. and Yamey, B.S. (eds.), *Debits, Credits, Finance and Profits* (London: Sweet & Maxwell, 1974).

15. For further discussion see Carsberg, B.V. and Hope, A.J.B. (eds.), *Current Issues in Accounting* (Deddington, Oxford: Philip Allan, 1977).

# NOTES TO THIS REPRINTING

---

[*] See now also Macve, R.H., review of Schmandt-Besserat, D., *Before Writing: From Counting to Cuneiform* Vol I (Austin: University of Texas Press, 1992), in *Accounting and Business Research,* 92 (Autumn 1993), pp.526-7.

[**] See now also Macve, R.H., 'Pacioli's Legacy' in Lee, T.A., Bishop, A.C., and Parker R.H. (eds.), *Accounting History from the Renaissance to the Present: A Remembrance of Luca Pacioli* (New York: Garland, 1996), pp.3-30.

[***] The requirements are now in the Companies Act 1985.

[****] Now reprinted (Oxford: Philip Allan, 1984)

[*****] For an analysis of the Sandilands proposals see Appendix IV to Macve, R.H., *A Conceptual Framework for Financial Accounting and Reporting: the possibilities for developing an agreed structure.* (London: ICAEW, 1981), reprinted in this volume at pp.137-142.

(II)

A report prepared at the request of the
Accounting Standards Committee

# A Conceptual Framework for Financial Accounting and Reporting

The possibilities for an agreed structure

RICHARD MACVE, MA, MSc, FCA
*(Julian Hodge Professor of Accounting at the
University College of Wales, Aberystwyth)*

# Contents

# Preface

The terms of reference given to Professor Macve were "to review critically current literature and opinion in the UK, US and elsewhere with a view to forming preliminary conclusions as to the possibilities of developing an agreed conceptual framework for setting accounting standards and the nature of such a framework; and to identify areas for further research". It was further agreed that in this work Professor Macve should put the emphasis on a conceptual framework for financial accounting and reporting.

The Accounting Standards Committee (ASC) is most grateful to Professor Macve for undertaking this task in a particularly difficult and important area, and also to the Technical and Research Committee of the Institute of Chartered Accountants in England and Wales for sponsoring it.

The ASC is sure that Professor Macve's report will aid and stimulate public discussion and thought on the steps that should now be taken by ASC in the development of an agreed framework that would be of practical benefit. The ASC encourages this discussion and invites comments. The ASC will warmly welcome comment on all aspects of the subject; it seems however that the following points emerging from Professor Macve's report may be worth special attention by commentators:

1     Professor Macve suggests that the value of the current attempts to explore the "conceptual framework" lies mainly in the discipline the process imposes in identifying the important areas where judgement is needed on questions of accounting policy, and of stimulating enquiry about users' needs and how to satisfy them. He suggests that it is unlikely that an "agreed conceptual framework" can be found that will give explicit guidance on what is appropriate in preparing financial statements. The important thing in his view is that the effort is made, and seen to be made, to ask the relevant questions with respect to users' needs, to methods that can satisfy these and their

visible and hidden costs, and to possible conflicts between needs. Do commentators accept that the best chance of success is likely to be found by giving emphasis to the direct approach to usefulness and users' needs?

2    Chapter 10 of the report contains Professor Macve's suggestions for further work. The first is to monitor the development of FASB work on the conceptual framework project and the development of thinking on this subject in other countries: it can be taken for granted that this will be done. On the other suggestions, comment is especially invited on whether each is regarded as appropriate and practical and the relative priority which should be given to them. There is no need for commentators to confine themselves to the suggestions listed in Chapter 10: constructive suggestions for other steps to be taken will be very welcome.

The ASC would appreciate receiving comments not later than 31 December 1981. Comments should be sent to:

> The Accounting Standards Committee
> PO Box 433
> Chartered Accountants' Hall
> Moorgate Place
> London EC2P 2BJ

All replies will be regarded as on public record unless confidentiality is requested by the commentator.

TR WATTS
Chairman
The Accounting Standards Committee
August 1981

# Acknowledgments

I would like to acknowledge my gratitude to the Technical and Research Committee of the Institute of Chartered Accountants in England and Wales ('ICAEW') for sponsoring this study and to the Financial Accounting Standards Board ('FASB') for allowing me to visit their headquarters, to have discussions with their staff and to observe their process for setting accounting standards. I am grateful too for permission to quote from several FASB publications, as well as from the other reports summarised in the Appendices.

A large number of people have helped me greatly in discussions, and by their comments on an earlier draft of this report, although, of course, they would not necessarily agree with the views expressed in it and are in no way responsible for its remaining faults. They include Will Baxter, Michael Bromwich, Bryan Carsberg, Graham Corbett, Harold Edey, Kenneth Gee, Henry Gold, Anthony Hopwood, Jack Kitchen, Richard Laughlin, Tony Lowe, Derek Macve, Anthony Puxty, Walter Reid, Michael Renshall, David Solomons, Reed Storey, Andrew Thomas, Tom Watts, Chris Westwick and Michael Young, together with my colleagues in the University of Wales, especially Christopher Cowton, Clive Emmanuel, Neil Garrod and David Gwilliam. I am grateful to them all, and particularly to Harold Edey for his advice and guidance.

Eileen Evans deserves special thanks for her determination in turning my illegible manuscript into clear typescript.

Richard Macve
Aberystwyth
31 May 1981

# 1. Summary

1. The role of a 'conceptual framework' is to provide a structure for thinking about what is 'better' accounting and financial reporting. It is a theoretical endeavour with the practical aim of clarifying the objectives of financial reporting, and how alternative practices are likely to help achieve those objectives. Whether as a company director, a chief accountant, an auditor or an accounting standard setter, one cannot make a rational choice of accounting procedures without some framework of principle. The purpose of the FASB project and other similar studies is to discover how much common agreement there is about objectives and the means to those objectives.

2. There is general agreement that a set of accounts should (and does) give information about the financial situation, progress and prospects of a business or other entity, and about how different individuals or groups share in, or contribute to, its financial results. But there are inherent limitations to what the accounts can show. There is no unambiguous or correct definition of 'income' and 'value' on which to base measures of profit and net assets. Considerable difficulties arise from:
a) 'absence of comprehensiveness' because, except in the simplest cases, it is not possible to reflect in its accounts all the attributes contributing to an entity's value and to changes in its value;
b) the need for 'allocations' over products, activities and time in identifying the individual components of income and value (which requires subjective judgments in choosing the most appropriate rules), and
c) uncertainty about the future, which imposes a need to make estimates even of those attributes which can be identified and accounted for, and which inevitably requires subjective judgments.

3.  There is general agreement that accounting must be useful (so that improvements must similarly be judged by their usefulness) but there is otherwise little agreement about objectives and the means to achieve them. Lack of agreement may be explained as due to uncertainty, variety of needs and conflicts of interest.

    a)  Uncertainty.
    Even when considering information for some specific purpose, or some particular use, there are considerable difficulties in establishing what actually is useful. It is difficult to discover precisely what accounting information is used and how; and it is difficult to show exactly how some proposed accounting information would be useful in making assessments about the future. Assumptions are hard to test. An experimental attitude to developments in accounting is needed, but given the complexity and uncertainty of the economic environment, people are often unlikely to agree on what information is most useful.

    b)  Variety of needs.
    Different users will have different needs for accounting information depending on the situation and decisions they face, their level of understanding, and the alternative sources of information available to them. One 'general purpose' set of accounts is obviously more economical to produce than many different 'tailor-made' sets, but recognising this is not sufficient to indicate what information this set should contain or how far it should cater for different requirements.
    Published accounts are used for a number of different purposes. A broad distinction can be made between 'economic' and 'legal' purposes. The desire for certainty in legal matters can conflict with that for business reality in economic matters, so that a general purpose set of financial statements may reflect an uneasy compromise between these different needs.

    c)  Conflicts of interest.
    The different individuals and groups involved with financial reporting, whether as users, preparers or auditors, often have conflicting economic interests, and any decisions about accounting practices (which will affect them all) have to be made after weighing up the consequences for these different parties and what

their respective rights are. These problems make accounting and the establishment of a conceptual framework a 'political' as well as a 'technical' matter.

4. FASB have argued that business accounts should serve the interest of users in the amount, timing and uncertainty of future cash flows of business enterprises. This is a way of stating the common interest of users in the financial future of an enterprise, including the way in which its results are shared out (or deficits contributed). FASB have also argued that the primary focus of the financial statements of businesses should be on reporting earnings (or income), but the relationship between this activity and the objective of providing useful indications about business prospects has not been conclusively established. The examination by FASB of the qualitative characteristics of useful information and its definitions of the elements of balance sheets and profit and loss accounts do not offer much practical assistance in showing how this objective is to be achieved, nor more generally in indicating how to decide questions about accounting methods, and about what information will be the most useful, practicable and acceptable to include in financial reports.

5. Other recent studies in the U.K. and Canada have adopted a similar approach to FASB—discussing users, their needs and the qualitative characteristics of useful information. However, they have not attempted authoritative definitions of accounting terms, and they have given more recognition to the need to balance the rights of the different parties involved when assessing useful, practical and acceptable developments. Each of them has suggested a number of interesting possibilities for accounting developments, but none has examined explicitly what people do in fact find useful in accounts, nor demonstrated rigorously how the particular accounting recommendations suggested would satisfy user needs.

   None of these attempts has been able to provide the material for establishing an 'agreed conceptual framework' in the terms referred to in 1. above.

6. The chief implication of the uncertainty about what is useful information, and of the need to reconcile the interests of different

parties, is that what is 'good (or better) accounting' is fundamentally a subjective matter.

Regulation of accounting practice (e.g. by accounting standards) cannot remove the need for subjective judgment by individual users, managements, accountants and auditors in assessing economic uncertainties. There is inevitably some latitude in presentation of financial results. Clear explanations of the bases and assumptions on which financial statements have been prepared are therefore particularly important. There are also political issues as to the extent to which regulation is needed to reconcile different interests, and where the authority for deciding matters of accounting disclosure and policy should reside.

Accounting theory cannot give complete, precise answers to accounting problems. The history of the development of accounting suggests that it serves many purposes reasonably well rather than any one purpose very well. It therefore seems unlikely that searching for an agreed conceptual framework of theory in abstraction from individual problems of disclosure and method will be successful. What is important is that in identifying and considering particular problems there should be questioning of purpose, of likely consequences, and of how user needs and different interests will be served. In this way, there can be rational debate of the issues and the areas where judgment is needed can be more clearly identified. A 'conceptual framework' for accounting should be regarded rather as a common basis for identifying issues, for asking questions and for carrying out research than as a package of solutions.

7.   Areas of further work which seem particularly relevant include:
      a) monitoring of the further development of FASB's project as it moves from more abstract considerations to specific possibilities for reporting profit and loss account and balance sheet items; monitoring the progress of the U.S. inflation accounting experiment; and reviewing ideas and developments in other countries (particularly in continental Europe).
      b) Analysis and empirical study of the relationships between different methods of profit calculation and the realities of financial performance under various conditions.

c) Empirical study of how, and to what extent, financial accounts are actually used for various purposes, and what their shortcomings are seen to be.

d) Study of the contribution that the methods of management accounting can make to financial reporting, and of the relationship between them.

e) Exploration of, and experiment with, provision of information outside the traditional accounting statements (balance sheet and profit and loss account) which may assist in forming a better overall view of the financial affairs of reporting entities.

f) Study of the process by which changes in accounting practice are introduced; the role of regulation; and how and why accounting practices have changed in the past.

g) Exploration of ways of communicating effectively, to those who use them, the limitations of what accounts can show.

# 2. Introduction

In its consultative document on 'Setting Accounting Standards',[1] the last two questions raised by the Accounting Standards Committee ('ASC') were:

> 7.1. Is it accepted that there is at present no single 'model' or 'agreed conceptual framework' which can be used as the touchstone for accounting standards?
>
> 7.2. Should the ASC encourage research into the possibility of finding an acceptable 'model'?

Those who submitted written responses to ASC[2] were almost unanimous in answering 'yes' to the first question, and although divided on the second, the majority again said 'yes'. Those who answered 'no' apparently did so because they considered it would be impossible to develop an agreed framework what would be of any practical benefit, and among those who answered 'yes' many appeared to take the view that there is little hope of success, or at least that any success lies a long way off. On the other hand, a large number of respondents (and in particular many of the larger firms of Chartered Accountants) said that they consider such research to be a priority and that there is an urgent need to develop a theoretical underpinning to meet the charges of inconsistency and *ad hoc* rationalisation that are commonly made against present standards and exposure drafts. Several of these respondents rejected the arguments given in 'Setting Accounting Standards' to explain why an agreed framework is not possible at present, and several argued that substantial areas of agreement could be identified already. The view was often expressed that the research should start by taking account of the work of the Financial Accounting Standards Board (FASB) in the U.S.A. and of 'The Corporate Report'[3] in this country, and that it is important to aim for international agreement.

This study attempts to make that start. The terms of reference set for it were 'to review critically current literature and opinion in the U.K., U.S. and elsewhere with a view to forming preliminary conclusions as to the possibilities of developing an agreed conceptual framework for setting accounting standards and the nature of such a framework; and to identify areas for further research'.

This is a wide remit, so to make it manageable I have tackled it in the following way.

First, I have put the emphasis on 'financial accounting and reporting' rather than on 'accounting standards' in order to keep separate questions about the criteria for determining the contents of the published accounts (with which I deal) from questions about the need for, and extent of, authoritative standards, and about the appropriate constitution and methods of procedure for a standard setting body. These latter questions have recently been tackled in the ASC's own report on 'Setting Accounting Standards'.[4] Nevertheless, questions about financial accounting and reporting and about accounting standards are obviously interrelated and I have included some comments on the implications for standard setting in my conclusions in Chapter 9.

Second, I have followed the suggestions cited above from the respondents to the consultative document on 'Setting Accounting Standards' and I have based my study, in large part, on the FASB's conceptual framework project[5] and on 'The Corporate Report'. The FASB's project is of course still in progress, but is, I think, now sufficiently far advanced for an assessment to be made of its likely benefits. I have also added the Sandilands Report[6] in the U.K., and the research study recently prepared by Professor Edward Stamp for the Canadian Institute of Chartered Accountants[7] (hereafter the 'Stamp Report') as these two reports also tackle fundamental questions about the nature, purpose and future development of financial accounting.

These various reports themselves comprise a weighty bulk of literature—and they represent only a fraction of a mass of writing produced by practising and academic accountants, whether as individuals or as members of study groups and committees. I have therefore seen my main task in this study as that of trying to distil and evaluate their contributions.

I have therefore summarised the major elements of these reports in the Appendices (I—V), while in the main chapters of my own report I give my interpretation and evaluation of them.

In setting out the chapters of my own report I have followed the line of development which I personally find most helpful in thinking about the topics that I cover, which does not exactly tally with the structure of any of these other reports. So I have made references as I go along to those parts of the reports that are relevant to the matter in hand. I have therefore also provided an overview of each of the reports in Chapters 7 and 8.

The line of development in my own report will be recognised, by those familiar with 'SOATATA',[8] to follow a similar path through the various areas of accounting theory. However, the conclusions are rather different, being closer to those in Peasnell's review of SOATATA.[9] In addition, while SOATATA deals mainly with the U.S. literature, this report refers mainly to British opinion on the problems that it surveys.

I have given some references to further reading (indicated by numerical superscripts in the text). These have been chosen on the whole for their relative clarity of exposition and their ready availability (many of them are in ASC or ICAEW publications). Those who wish to explore the literature more thoroughly should find in these sources sufficient guidance to further references.

# REFERENCES—CHAPTER 2

1. Setting Accounting Standards: a consultative document, ASC, 1978.

2. Submissions on the Accounting Standards Committee's Consultative Document: Setting Accounting Standards, in two volumes, ASC, 1979.

3. The Corporate Report, a discussion paper, ASSC, 1975.

4. Setting Accounting Standards: Report and Recommendations by the Accounting Standards Committee, 1981.

5. Extracts are quoted by permission.

6. Inflation Accounting: Report of the Inflation Accounting Committee (chairman F.E.P. Sandilands, Esq., CBE (later Sir Francis Sandilands)), Cmnd 6225, London: HMSO, 1975. Extracts are quoted by permission.

7. Corporate Reporting: Its Future Evolution, Toronto, Canada: Canadian Institute of Chartered Accountants, 1980. Extracts are quoted by permission.

8. Statement on Accounting Theory and Theory Acceptance, Committee on Concepts and Standards for External Financial Reports, American Accounting Association, 1977 ('SOATATA').

9. K.V. Peasnell, 'Statement of Accounting Theory and Theory Acceptance', *Accounting and Business Research*, No.31, Summer 1978.

# 3. What is a 'Conceptual Framework' and Why is it Needed?

It is often not entirely clear what people mean when they talk about a 'conceptual framework' for accounting. It has been defined by FASB as 'a constitution, a coherent system of interrelated objectives and fundamentals that can lead to consistent standards and that prescribes the nature, function and limits of financial accounting and financial statements'.[1] In general terms then, it is a basic structure for organising one's thinking about what one is trying to do and how to go about it. So in asking whether there is, or can be, an agreed conceptual framework for accounting, one is asking basic questions of the kind: For whom and by whom are accounts to be prepared? For what purposes are they wanted? What kind of accounting reports are suitable for these purposes? How far do present accounts fit the bill, and how could accounting practices be improved to make them more suitable?'

The first two questions deal with what are often called the 'objectives' of accounting; the remainder with the form and content of accounts and the methods of preparing them. An 'agreed conceptual framework' may be seen as an agreed set of answers to these questions, which would provide a consistent approach for making decisions about choices of accounting practice and for setting accounting standards. In short, the search is for the criteria for deciding what is 'better accounting'. It is a theoretical endeavour with an extremely practical end in view.

The importance of thinking about these questions is clear. Anyone recommending a particular accounting practice must necessarily base his views on an implicit conceptual framework—and it is therefore important, if there is to be rational discussion and evaluation of the proposal, to try and make that framework explicit. Whether as a company director or accountant choosing an accounting policy; or as an auditor deciding whether a proposed treatment gives a 'true and fair view'; or as a member of ASC discussing a proposed standard; one can give only an arbitrary or capricious decision, or one based solely on precedent, unless one has some idea about what is trying to be achieved and how the decision will help. So, if, for example, one supports a recommendation for an accounting standard requiring uniform disclosure of leasing commitments, one must be assumed to have some view of the likely consequences of such a requirement, and whose interests will be served by it.

One may be uncertain both about one's aims and about the likely consequences of one's action; and as a member of a committee one may find one's colleagues having very different views, so that often some compromise is needed. Nevertheless, giving a rational judgment implies that one must be prepared to state the grounds for one's own opinion, or for supporting the committee's view.

The attempt to develop an agreed conceptual framework is an attempt to establish a common framework of theory that will both identify the important basic questions to be asked, and, it is hoped, produce substantial areas of agreement about how the answers are to be found, so that it will become clearer how individual accounting problems should be resolved than is the case at present.

ASC has suggested[2] that such a framework or 'model' would need to comprise 'a selected and defined set of accounting procedures compatible with a single set of definitions of 'profit', the 'balance sheet', 'capital maintenance', etc.' and that 'this is a luxury which evades us at the moment'. Thus, the problem is viewed in the context of the current requirements of the U.K. Companies Acts that the annual accounts (balance sheet and profit and loss account) should give 'a true and fair view of the state of affairs of the company . . . and . . . of the profit or loss . . . for the financial year'.[3]

Similarly, FASB's conceptual framework project is largely concerned with how assets, liabilities and equity, and the components of income, are to be calculated and reported. I will therefore begin my review of the possibilities for developing an agreed conceptual framework by discussing the problems that arise in determining 'profit' and 'net assets'.

# REFERENCES—CHAPTER 3

1. in 'Scope and Implications of the Conceptual Framework Project', December 2$^{nd}$, 1976, at page 2.

2. in 'Setting Accounting Standards', 1978, chapter 7.

3. The Companies Act, 1948, section 149.

# 4. 'Profit', 'Balance Sheet', 'Capital Maintenance' etc.

The reason for the focus of financial accounting practice on the calculation of 'profit' (or 'income') and net assets is clear. All those who have an interest in, or are affected by, the activities of a business (or other organisation) are interested in its 'performance' and 'financial situation' (how well it is doing and is likely to do in the future) and in judging whether they are getting a fair and reasonable share of the wealth it is creating (or alternatively in ensuring that its success or failure is not unduly at their expense). Whether they are investors, employees, customers, government agencies or whoever, they want to know about the 'wealth' of the entity and changes in this wealth.

It would therefore be extremely helpful if the accounts could reflect in a single periodic figure of 'profit' (or 'loss' as the case may be) the improvement (or worsening) over the period in the financial state of the entity (and how this result is shared among the various interested parties) so providing an indication of how successful its management has been and of what might be expected in future.

However, most people familiar with accounting would accept that it is unrealistic to suppose that the financial accounts can provide a complete and accurate picture either of the current worth of an entity, or of changes in its value over time—that they can completely measure even its financial success or failure in a quantitatively precise way (let alone other aspects of its activities). Correspondingly, it is idle to look for a 'correct' definition of 'profit', 'capital' etc.

The reasons why this is unachievable can perhaps be briefly rehearsed, at the risk of oversimplifying a complex topic that has generated an extensive literature.[1] Analyses of the concepts of 'income' and 'wealth' have shown that only under the most idealised economic conditions could these concepts be defined unambiguously—

and under those conditions there would be no need to measure them. In the real world, changing and uncertain, where imperfect markets are the rule, unique and settled prices for each economic resource are not available, so that measurement of wealth and changes in wealth necessarily require approximation methods which are to some extent arbitrary and require professional judgment in their application.

Three main sources of difficulty (often interrelated) may be identified: absence of comprehensiveness; need for allocations; and uncertainty. They affect the preparation of accounts in even the simplest situations (the further complexities caused by situations such as inflation and changing foreign exchange rates are well known and will not be discussed here). I will outline these three difficulties in terms of business accounts, but similar considerations apply to the accounts of all types of entity.

## ABSENCE OF COMPREHENSIVENESS

Much as one may wish that the balance sheet could be seen as a statement of wealth and the profit and loss account or income statement as explaining how changes in that wealth have occurred, it is obvious that the accounts cannot include all relevant magnitudes, and that the total of the balance sheet cannot be the 'value of the business'. Important aspects which contribute to its financial success cannot be routinely measured, for example the value of the organizational pattern that has been built up, the training and skill of its employees, its business contacts, market power and so forth. There is one exception, on those occasions when a business is purchased and 'goodwill' is recorded. But as time passes the amount on the goodwill account ceases to have relevance and there is no way of assessing the current goodwill of a business without attempting to make a valuation—necessarily subjective—of the business as a whole.

Similarly, other aspects which are regarded as assets separate from goodwill are usually excluded, e.g. the benefits of research and much development activity.

If successive balance sheets do not record a business's total wealth, then it is unlikely that the profit and loss account will record all the changes in that wealth.[2]

## NEED FOR ALLOCATIONS

By this is meant the need to split some total into two or more elements (conversely viewed as the 'aggregation problem').

A feature of business accounts (perhaps one of their most useful features in controlling business operations) is that they 'add up'. Individual assets and liabilities add up to 'net assets'; individual revenues and expenses add up to profit and losses; assets and liabilities of individual departments, divisions and subsidiary companies can be consolidated; and individual periods' profits add up to the business's life time results. Unfortunately, in many aspects of economic life, the whole is usually more (or less) than the sum of its parts and conversely, given the value of the whole, there is often no one valid basis for separately identifying the share of that value attributable to each of the parts, and for allocating it to each.[3]

Similarly, because of interrelationships over time, there is often no correct way of splitting up the overall results of a business over its life into the amount attributable to each period. The concepts set out in SSAP2[4] of 'accrual' and 'matching' purport to do this, but the very difficulties attending their practical application (e.g. in such matters as depreciation and deferred tax) are indicative of the underlying problem, and of the need to resort to arbitrary rules or subjective judgments.

These 'allocation' problems become more serious as the complexity of business increases, and take different forms in different types of businesses, but they arise even in the simplest cases.

## UNCERTAINTY

Profit and loss accounts may appear to be about the 'past' and balance sheets may appear to be about the 'present'. But as is well known their preparation requires many estimates about the future. To follow the concepts set out in SSAP2 one has first to ask 'Is the business a going concern?' Such a question can only be answered by making subjective judgments about future events.

Having decided that it is, one still needs to consider such questions as the recoverability of the debts, the saleability of the stocks, potential benefits of expenditure on development and advertising, the likely useful lives of fixed assets, provisions for liabilities incurred but not yet paid and so on, in deciding what may be 'carried forward' in the balance sheet and what must be 'written off'; all, to a greater or lesser extent, requiring estimates about the future.

In making these estimates, accountants exercise 'prudence', and as is well known this may often lead to conflicts with the attempt to allocate costs and benefits of operations as realistically as possible to different periods ('accrual' or 'matching'). Under present conventions, prudence prevails. Similarly, conventions of 'realization' and so forth attempt to deal with the risks and uncertainty involved in assessing business performance by limiting what may be reported as profit until its estimation is 'reasonably certain'—but what is 'reasonably certain' must also often be a matter of subjective judgment.

What is more, estimates are likely to change. So any measure of a period's results will include, to a lesser or greater extent, the consequences of the changes to previous estimates about the remaining future that have been made during the period.[5]

Consideration of these difficulties of trying to represent the economic realities of an entity's financial position and progress in a set of accounts, makes it clear that any such attempt can normally only produce a 'second best' answer and that there can be no 'correct' definitions of how 'profit', 'net assets' etc. are to be calculated.

Any rules that are made in order to try and standardize the approach to these problems must therefore both be justified by the purposes for which the accounts are being prepared; and also, if their application is not to produce arbitrary effects, allow scope for the exercise of professional judgment.

These conceptual difficulties are explored extensively in the Stamp Report (see Appendix V) but have only been relatively briefly discussed in the FASB's project. However, the problems have clearly manifested themselves in relation to the attempt, in SFAC3, to define the 'elements of financial statements of business enterprises' (see Chapter 7).

## CONCLUSION

One way of looking at the problems raised in this chapter is to say that if accountants merely reported present cash balances and past cash flows, they would have few problems. But going beyond this to try and measure 'net assets' and 'profit' they run into difficulties requiring the exercise of professional judgment. Given that they cannot hope to provide a perfectly satisfactory representation of an entity's financial state of affairs, performance and prospects, the question is 'how much additional information beyond the cash data is it useful for them to provide, and in what form?'[6]

In the next chapter, I will therefore look at how far one can get, in trying to establish principles for financial accounting and reporting, by asking 'What is useful accounting information?'.

## REFERENCES—CHAPTER 4

1. For a classic exploration of the problems, see Sir Ronald Edwards, 'The Nature and Measurement of Income', in W.T. Baxter and S. Davidson (eds.), Studies in Accounting, 3rd edition, London: ICAEW, 1977.

For a recent survey of the literature see G. Whittington, 'The British contribution to income theory', in M. Bromwich and A.G. Hopwood (eds.), Essays in British Accounting Research, London: Pitman, 1981.

2. H.C. Edey, 'The Nature of Profit', *Accounting and Business Research,* No.1, Winter 1970 (reprinted in R.H. Parker (ed.), Readings in Accounting and Business Research, 1970-77, London: ICAEW, 1978).

3. A.L. Thomas, 'Allocation: the Fallacy and the Theorists', in Baxter and Davidson, *op.cit.*

4. Statement of Standard Accounting Practice No.2.: Disclosure of Accounting Policies, ASC, 1971.

5. For example, see H.C. Edey, 'Accounting Principles and Business Reality', *Accountancy*, Vol.74, November and December 1963 (reprinted in B.V. Carsberg and H.C. Edey (eds.), Modern Financial Management, Harmondsworth, Middlesex: Penguin, 1969).

6. T.A. Lee, 'Enterprise Income: Survival or Decline and Fall?', *Accounting and Business Research*, No.15, Summer 1974 (reprinted in Parker, *op.cit*).

# 5. Useful Accounting Information

## DECISION USEFULNESS

Everyone agrees that accounts must be useful: accounting is not an end in itself, it must serve some purpose. From this viewpoint, the elements of defining a conceptual framework for accounting have been argued to be as follows:[1]

A. Identify the potential users of accounts (either as individuals, or more commonly grouped by some common interest) who are to be served.
B. For each user or group, identify the decisions they have to take, and the factors relevant to their decisions.
C. For each decision, identify the accounting information that can be provided and how it will be useful to them in assessing those factors.
D. In each case, compare the benefits of providing the accounting information with the costs of doing so, since in choosing between alternative types of information to provide (e.g. between different accounting disclosures, or different accounting methods) one will wish to choose the alternative which has the greatest value, i.e. the greatest benefit in excess of cost.

The structure of this approach is clear enough, and it is a general approach, applicable equally to 'financial accounting' (i.e. the basis of published accounts) and to 'management accounting' (i.e. internal accounts).

It may be objected that people do not only, or mainly, read accounts to assist them make their financial decisions; but rather to check on the honesty and stewardship of management; to confirm compliance with company law; to check the reasonableness of the dividend being declared and so forth. This is an empty objection, as is readily seen if it is accepted that no one would read the accounts for these purposes unless there was some possibility of 'doing something about it'; in other words, the possibility of making a decision.

In principle, the approach set out in A—D above requires a comprehensive examination of all users, all uses and all possible accounting practices and ways of utilising them, and a system of review to adapt to changes in these in course of time.

This line of thinking suggests that there are likely to be many difficulties in finding a 'universal' answer to what is wanted. They can be summarised by saying that analysis of 'decision usefulness' shows that, in general, the value of information depends on the particular decision taker (including his level of understanding and the other knowledge he has), the particular decision he has to take, and the particular circumstances in which he has to take it. Potentially, all information is useful for decisions, and it is generally a subjective matter (i.e. peculiar to each individual) whether the benefits of using any particular information are expected to exceed the costs of collecting, processing and understanding it.[2]

In FASB's conceptual framework project, SFAC2 on 'Qualitative Characteristics of Accounting Information' discusses many of these difficulties, which may be categorised as 'variety of needs' and 'conflicts of interest', and which I will discuss in some more detail in the next chapter. However, in the last chapter I referred to the common interest amongst users of accounts in assessing the financial situation, progress and prospects of business and other entities, and how the rewards and costs of their activities are shared. The various studies that I am reviewing in this report take this common interest as a starting point in developing their ideas about the characteristics of a useful 'general purpose' set of financial accounts.

## PREDICTING FUTURE CASH FLOWS

This common interest is usually expressed in the accounting literature (as it is by FASB in SFAC1 on 'Objectives of Financial Statements of Business Enterprises') as an interest in predicting the amount, timing and uncertainty of future cash flows. The merit of this formulation is that it puts in clear and simple terms the essence of what ought rationally to concern people about the financial affairs of the entities they are interested in, whether they are 'outsiders' or involved directly in their management. Thus, shareholders are ultimately concerned with the dividends a business is likely to be able to pay; employees with the salaries, wages and pensions they can hope for, and the working conditions their employer can afford to provide; suppliers with their customers' ability to pay them, and so on—all questions about the cash that the relevant entity will be able to generate, control and distribute. Given the fairly universal practice in advanced economies of using cash as the medium for exchanging economic resources, one can describe the consequences of most economic activity in terms of the resulting cash inflows and outflows.

In the same way, one can view financial management in terms of ensuring that the entity's long-term and short-term cash budgets show a satisfactory relationship between cash inflows and outflows. One can express ideas like 'Choose the most profitable course of action' in terms of 'Choose the action which offers the most desirable pattern of future cash flows'. Similarly one can describe the financial conditions for survival, the nature of financial success, and the financial relationships of entities to those involved in and interested in their activities in terms of their present and future cash flows.[3]

In the end, it is the ability of the entity to provide cash at the time needed and in the amount needed that interests all users. This is not to say that the financial aspects of its activities are the sole item of concern. However, they are an integral part of the successful management of any organization, whatever its objectives are considered to be, and they can be best described in terms of their likely cash consequences.

People therefore want information that will assist them in forming their assessments of likely future cash flows. As SFAC2 clearly argues, this does not mean that the information must itself be a forecast. Relevant information is data, whether about the past, the present, or about other people's forecasts of the future, that a decision maker can use to improve his own predictions about the future. This 'feedback' information can have predictive value—a report of what has actually happened may be useful, e.g. in comparison with previous attempts at prediction, in improving the way in which future predictions are made. Indeed, anything which helps one understand better 'how the world works' has predictive value, and the term is little more than a tautology for, or definition of, the 'usefulness' of a piece of information. In the present context then, it would be useful if accounts could provide information that would in some way assist the prediction of future cash flows of business, and other, organizations—and do so better than information available from other sources.

## UNCERTAINTY

How does one determine what information actually is best for predicting future cash flows (and is better provided by the accounts rather than from other sources)? One would like an empirical demonstration of its superior 'predictive ability'. Unfortunately there is at present very little rigorous knowledge about the predictive ability of various kinds of accounting information.

While the principles of the kind of test that is needed are clear,[4] the difficulties in carrying it out are very great, and the empirical work that has been done so far offers little help in the choice of accounting methods. Such work requires extension of the skills of econometricians to the level of individual businesses, and given the difficulties of all economic forecasting and the uncertainties and complexities of the business environment, the results are often difficult to interpret.[5]

A more 'philosophical' difficulty about the attempt to identify the predictive power of financial information arises from the fact that the predictions are essentially about human behaviour—which introduces the possibility of reaction to the predictions. People make predictions in order to assist their decisions—and their subsequent actions can then help to confirm or negate the predictions as they decide whether to accept or try and alter the future they see.[6]

Again predictions may affect other people's behaviour, and thus become self-fulfilling or self-defeating. SFAC2 makes this point in relation to interpreting the factors that may enable one to predict bankruptcy. If predictions about future failures are believed by those who supply business with credit, then they may be 'proved' by becoming self-fulfilling as the credit is withdrawn. Many accountants are only too aware of this problem when considering the effect of issuing an audit qualification referring to doubts about 'going concern'. The qualification itself may destroy the confidence that could have kept the business going. So while there is no doubt that making the attempt to test the usefulness of information for predicting future cash flows is important, and encourages an experimental, scientific approach to questions of improving accounting disclosure and measurement (as FAS33 calls for an 'experiment' with inflation accounting—see Appendix I), nevertheless the difficulties that lie in the way of establishing any conclusive results imply that opinions are likely to diverge on what is the most useful information to require in accounts.

Similarly, if one attempts to discover what information people actually use, and how they use it, in making financial decisions—or tries to find out what they would like to have—one is likely to get conflicting and confusing results as different people attach different significance to different types of information.

## INCOME

One question of obvious interest is 'How useful are the 'income' figures that accounts presently provide, and would different methods of calculating and presenting them make them more useful?'

FASB, in SFAC1, argues that, in order to provide users of accounts with information that will be useful in making assessments of the amounts, timing and uncertainty of future cash flows, the 'primary focus' of financial reporting is on measures of 'earnings' (restated in SFAC3 on 'elements' as 'comprehensive income') and its components, together with statements of economic resources and claims, and information about cash flow or other funds flows.

A possible rationale for this view is set out in the discussion memorandum on 'Reporting Earnings' where it is suggested that, in order to predict future cash flows, users may predict future income or earnings and then convert these to predictions of future cash flows. In order to predict future income they may use past income, and in order to understand the relationship between income and cash flow they may use comparisons of past income and past cash flow. The memorandum then explores suggestions for how income statements might be analysed and presented to make them more useful for the purpose of predicting future income.

Those ideas are developed further in the recent discussion memorandum on 'Funds Flow, Liquidity and Financial Flexibility', which suggests ways in which funds flow statements may be presented to help understanding of the relationship between income and cash flows; and how balance sheet items may be classified for assisting prediction of liquidity problems (see Appendix I).

However, as yet, the suggested relationships have little empirical support.[7] Indeed, as the 'earnings memorandum' itself disarmingly points out, what evidence there is so far on the usefulness of past reported income in predicting future reported income is not encouraging—but equally this may reflect the inadequacies of present measures and presentation and the situation may therefore improve if new methods are experimented with, or if more attention is paid to the individual components of income than to the 'bottom line.'

## STOCK MARKET EVIDENCE

Tests of the ways in which investors presently use reported accounting profits, and more generally of how the stock market processes information, have been undertaken, mostly in relation to the U.S. stock market (the 'efficient markets' research). The conclusions (which seem to apply also to other major stock markets) suggest that while there is a general association, on average, between the behaviour of share prices and the announcement of accounting profits, there are few associations fine enough to enable one to discriminate between the effect of different disclosures, presentations and measurement bases.[8]

However, there is fairly consistent evidence that the market is unlikely to be 'fooled' by differences in the presentation or measurement methods used by different companies that do not in themselves reflect significant differences in economic situation. Thus, arbitrary choices of method of the kind discussed in the last chapter (e.g. of depreciation method or method of deferred tax calculation) are unlikely to affect share prices, and in this sense it does not matter which method of calculating profit is used.[9] The more important question in this context is: what information is it useful and cost-effective to disclose, or to confirm by means of the published accounts, and what should be left to be collected by the market from other sources? Similarly, how much of the information that companies publish should be subject to audit scrutiny?

It is clear that the stock market makes prompt use of many sources of information,[10] so that the particular contribution made by the audited accounting information is not easy to disentangle. The procedural or 'methodological' difficulties of the tests made (in which investigators try and assess how differently a company's share price has behaved from how one would have expected it to behave, given the behaviour of other share prices; and how much of the difference is attributable to the variation in accounting information) are considerable, and the scope and significance of the conclusions need to be stated with particular care—so that they are correspondingly difficult to summarize.

Again, tests of the stock market's overall reaction have little to say about the effects of different reporting methods on individual investors—and of course nothing directly to say about users outside the stock market. Moreover, the tests must inevitably be based on the information that is currently provided. Evaluation of new alternatives for presenting information about companies' results must await testing until they are available and people are familiar with using them.

It is not therefore possible to come to precise conclusions from the empirical work available[11] about the 'usefulness' of accounting income or profit figures, or about how they can be made more useful for the purpose of 'predicting likely future cash flows'. The FASB discussion memorandum on 'Reporting Earnings' suggests a number of interesting ideas, and it seems equally important to consider other ways of improving the information content of company reports, e.g. improvements in management explanations accompanying the figures; the provision of direct forecasts; or various non-financial statistics, and so forth.

## CONCLUSION

It is important to consider the usefulness of accounting information in considering how to improve financial accounting and reporting. But the difficulties of testing its usefulness—in particular of establishing exactly how it will be relevant for appraising the uncertain financial future of business concerns and other organizations—suggest that different people will necessarily form their own subjective judgments on this matter and therefore are likely to disagree about what information the accounts should provide. There is no clear answer to the questions raised in the conclusion of the last chapter.

The problem is compounded when one considers the different needs of, and conflicts of interest between, different parties, which are discussed further in the next chapter.

## REFERENCES—CHAPTER 5

1. See for example, B.Carsberg, A. Hope and R.W. Scapens: 'The Objectives of Published Accounting Reports', *Accounting and Business Research*, No.15, Summer 1974 (reprinted in R.H. Parker (ed.), Readings in Accounting and Business Research, *op.cit.*); P. Bird, 'Objectives and Methods of Financial Reporting: A Generalised Search Procedure', *Accounting and Business Research*, No. 19, Summer 1975.

2. See for example, J.R. Mace, 'Value of information', in J. Arnold, B. Carsberg and R. Scapens (eds.), Topics in Management Accounting, Deddington, Oxford: Philip Allan, 1980.

3. H.C. Edey, 'The Logic of Financial Accounting', Deloitte, Haskins + Sells Lecture, Cardiff: University College, 1980.

4. B. Carsberg, J. Arnold and A. Hope, 'Predictive Value: A Criterion for Choice of Accounting Method', in Baxter and Davidson, Studies in Accounting, *op.cit.*

5. See for example, G. Foster, Financial Statement Analysis, Englewood Cliffs, N.J.: Prentice-Hall, 1978, especially chapters 4 and 14; C.R. Emmanuel and R.H. Pick, 'The Predictive Ability of U.K. Segment Reports', *Journal of Business Finance and Accounting*, 7,2, Summer, 1980.

6. See for example, A. Ryan, The Philosophy of the Social Sciences, London: Macmillan, 1970, chapter 9.

7. See for example, S. Dev, 'Financial Accounts—what they do and don't reveal', 1979 City-Association Accounting Lecture, *The Certified Accountant*, August, 1979.

8. See for example, G.Foster, *op.cit.*, especially chapters 10 and 11; G.J. Benston, 'Investors' Use of Financial Accounting Statement Numbers: A Review of Evidence from Stock Market Research', 1979 Arthur Young Lecture, Glasgow: The University Press, 1981.

9. W.H. Beaver, 'What should be the FASB's objectives?', *Journal of Accountancy*, August 1973 (reprinted in D. Fraser, M. O'Connor and P. Schelluch (eds.), Issues in External Reporting, revised edition, Kensington, NSW: New South Wales University Press, 1979).

10. See for example, A. Hopwood, Accounting and Human Behaviour, London: Haymarket (Accountancy Age Books), 1974; Englewood Cliffs, N.J.: Prentice-Hall, 1976, Chapter 8.

11. For a recent survey, see K.V. Peasnell, 'Empirical research in financial accounting', in Bromwich and Hopwood, Essays in British Accounting Research, *op.cit.*

# 6. Variety of Needs and Conflicts of Interest

The last chapter suggested that there is likely to be disagreement on what is 'useful' accounting information because of the difficulties of rigorous and conclusive demonstration of the relative 'predictive value' of different types of information in the uncertain and complex environment of economic activity.

This chapter considers two other factors likely to lead to disagreement—the variety of user needs and conflicts of interest between different parties (problems which are discussed fairly extensively by FASB in SFAC2 and in Professor Stamp's report).

## VARIETY OF USER NEEDS

Although all users may be argued to have a common interest in the 'future cash flows' of an enterprise, the actions that different users can take may be very different, so that they are likely to be interested in somewhat different aspects of its financial situation, and in different levels of detail about its activities.

For example, different classes of investors and lenders may want more or less detailed reports according to the extent of their financial commitment to an enterprise, and the extent to which they can exercise control over its activities. Employees may want information relating to their particular location or activity within an organization. Customers (or government agencies acting on their behalf) may want details about costs and prices of individual products. Host governments of multinationals may want information about transfer pricing policies, comparative cost structures etc. Some of these users have the power to call for the special information they need, but as SFAC2 points out, constructing a suitable set of 'general purpose' accounts for the rest has somehow to cope with the fact that different individuals have different needs for information, given the particular situation they face in taking a decision, and the information they have from other sources.

Again, different users have different levels of understanding of financial matters, so that there are questions about whether different reports are needed for more sophisticated and less sophisticated users.

## VARIETY OF PURPOSE

Users want accounting information for different purposes. FASB has concentrated on the importance of information to assist in predicting the amounts, timing and risk of future enterprise cash flows, which, as I have argued, is what people need to try and assess when making decisions, whether at enterprise level about investment, credit or wage negotiations, or at government level about intervention and control of industry, taxation policy, etc.—often called 'economic' decisions.

Other decisions (relating primarily to sharing out 'surpluses') are more constrained by legal requirements or contractual arrangements, for example in determining the maximum size of the dividend that may be paid to the shareholders; the amount of tax to be paid; the amount of bonuses and payments to be made under profit-sharing schemes. Here clear rules are needed in order that the various parties can check that the relevant law or agreement has been observed and that their rights have been respected. Ideally, such 'shareouts' would be based on agreement about 'how well off' or 'how much better off' the business is, requiring the same kind of estimates as are needed in making 'economic' decisions, but in an uncertain world, where all of the interested parties can have their own views on this (as has been discussed in the last two chapters), this approach would often be likely to result in dispute. To minimize dispute, and the need for litigation and arbitration by the courts, the rules are based as far as is possible on objective measures, with an emphasis on 'consistency' so that any underpayments in one period are likely to be balanced by overpayments in a later period.

Thus, the U.K. taxing statutes provide their own allocation rules for matters such as depreciation, stock consumption and write-offs of intangibles, and disallow provisions based on the more subjective estimates of future losses and liabilities. Similarly, the rules for legal dividend calculations, or for use in contracts such as profit sharing agreements and commission schemes, try as far possible to keep towards the objective end of the spectrum. This not only reduces the opportunity for manipulation by managements and makes the auditor's task easier, but also, by providing clearer rules, tries to protect both of them from the risk of liability for negligent statements, or from unwittingly transgressing the law.

Such 'legalistic' calculations are unlikely to be as relevant for the purpose of forming the most realistic estimate possible of 'how well the business is doing' (its economic performance), where attempts to assess the likely future consequences of current decisions and events are needed, lying at the more subjective end of the spectrum.

It has consequently been argued[1] that these different kinds of purposes for which accounts are wanted are so different that one general purpose set will not do and that two kinds of approach to profit measurement are needed. One for purposes where cautious prudent methods are wanted, to provide an acceptable basis for 'legal' payments, and one for purposes where the aim is to provide calculations more useful for assessing performance and the 'economic reality' of the operation. Thus it has long been the case in the U.K. (unlike several continental European countries) that the accounting methods laid down by the tax laws are distinct from those that are adopted in the financial accounts. But the legal rules relating to distributable profits remain a constraining factor on financial accounts in the U.K.,[2] whereas in the U.S.A. FASB appears to have been able to ignore these 'legal' aspects in developing its 'conceptual framework'.

However, even if one separates these two aspects (the 'legal' and the 'economic' orientated), the difficulty of course remains of specifying more precisely what is wanted for each of them, beyond the general observation that the one needs to be more 'prudent' and 'objective' than the other.[3]

## THE IDENTIFICATION OF COSTS AND BENEFITS

While the assessment of the benefits of information is mainly a matter of trying to judge its potential usefulness (as discussed in the last chapter), nevertheless there will only be a net advantage to users from having the information if the benefits exceed the costs—including costs of collecting, processing and reporting it, and, in the case of information in the financial accounts, having it audited. When information requirements are changed, there will also be the costs of adapting to the new procedures.

Many of these costs will be hard to measure, particularly in the case of new disclosure requirements or new measurement methods. Moreover, the costs and benefits may fall to different groups (e.g. benefits to various external readers of the accounts; costs to the firms that have to produce them) so that conflicts of interest will often have to be resolved. SFAC2 gives attention to these questions and argues that, in most cases, any assessments will be extremely difficult to make, almost impossible to quantify precisely and therefore largely a matter of judgment.

## WIDER CONFLICTS OF INTEREST

There may also be conflicts of economic interest between different potential users or between users and preparers[4] (or between either of these and auditors, e.g. in respect of liability for misleading information). In the environment of published accounts one is not just choosing which users to provide with information: for information given to any party will be equally available to all.

For example, while it may be thought desirable for investors or employees to have a substantial and precise knowledge about management's future strategies and plans if they are to form a realistic assessment of a company's financial position, the consequent availability of such information to a company's competitors may be thought so to endanger the company's prospects, or to have such adverse consequences on the incentives for the company's management to search for and exploit favourable opportunities, that not only may the management resist proposals to increase such disclosure, the investors or employees themselves may often prefer that the information should remain confidential until the plans are realized or the delicate negotiations concluded.

On the whole this seems to be the current attitude, on both sides of the Atlantic, in relation to the disclosure of detailed management forecasts on a regular basis. Where foreign competition is seen as a serious threat there are further exemptions available from the normal current level of disclosure (e.g. in the U.K. for shipping under the provisions of the Companies Acts, 'in the national interest', at the discretion of the Department of Trade), as there are also where 'public confidence' is vital (e.g. for banks and insurance companies).[5]

So there is likely to be disagreement between different users, and between users and preparers, over what are the proper circumstances for, and level of, disclosure of organizations' financial affairs. Views about the likely 'economic consequences' of different policies will be cited (e.g. see the terms of reference of the Sandilands committee). Moreover the arguments are likely to run deeper than any economic cost/benefit analysis, and to reflect more fundamental attitudes about 'accountability' and the balance of freedom of information and respect for confidentiality, which in turn reflect different and changing social and political attitudes. Attitudes now are very different from those at the time of the 'Royal Mail' case.[6]

## VESTED INTERESTS

Similarly, there may be disputes over proposals to standardize or change rules for measuring profit, assets, etc. (and consequently 'return on capital employed', 'price-earnings ratio' and so on), because of vested interests in the results of present methods.

People have such vested interests, for example because their management remuneration is related to reported profits, or their ability to borrow is related to their published debt/equity ratio, or because they believe that the opportunities for raising capital, the risk of government intervention in their industry, or the results of bargaining with other interests will be affected by the size of the profit figures they report. An accounting policy or standard which favours one method over another may therefore adversely affect a number of vested interests, who will wish to 'lobby' for their own method and produce arguments to justify their present practice.[7] If there is no clear basis for preferring one method to another (which is often likely to be the case for the reasons discussed in the last two chapters), there will be pressure for compromises, or exemptions for special interest groups. SFAC2 acknowledges the difficulties of achieving 'neutrality' in setting accounting standards.

## CONCLUSION

Recognition of the variety of user needs and of conflicts between different interests and different rights leads to the view that reaching agreement on the form and content of financial statements is as much a 'political' process, a search for compromise between different parties, as it is a search for the methods which are 'technically' best.[8]

It may be political both in the wider sense of being to do with people's rights and interests in society, and sometimes also in the more ordinary sense of being a matter where support will be canvassed for one view or another; lobbies formed; and occasionally governments asked (or themselves see a need) to intervene.

Given that the theories of politics and social choice themselves have no 'agreed conceptual framework', then by implication accounting, in this respect, has to cope without one as well.

This chapter and the previous one have reviewed a number of difficulties that arise in trying to develop a conceptual framework for financial accounting by asking 'How can accounts be made most useful?' In particular the difficulties caused by the uncertainties and complexities of predicting economic affairs; the likely variety of information requirements; and the potential conflicts of interest between different parties have been discussed.

In the next two chapters I will briefly review the various reports, that are summarized in Appendices I—V, and comment on how they tackle these difficulties.

## REFERENCES—CHAPTER 6

1. The Corporate Report, 7.14; P.G. Corbett, 'How Many Profits?', delivered at ICAEW Annual Conference, Cambridge, July 1975 and reprinted in *Accountants' Weekly*, 20 July 1979; H.C. Edey, 'Why all-purpose accounts will not do', *Accountancy*, Vol. 89, October 1978.

2. The Companies Act 1980, Part III (which implements the requirements of the EEC 2nd Directive on company law); The Companies Bill, 1981 (which implements the requirements of the EEC 4th Directive on company law); for the previous situation, see E.A. French, 'The Evolution of the Dividend Law of England', in Baxter and Davidson, Studies in Accounting, *op.cit.*

3. For the difficulties in relation to dividends, see E.A. French, *op.cit.*, and in relation to taxation, see The Structure and Reform of Direct Taxation, Report of a Committee chaired by Professor J.E. Meade, The Institute for Fiscal Studies, London: George, Allen and Unwin, 1978.

4. E. Stamp, 'The Watts Report: An Uncertain Trumpet', *The Accountant's Magazine*, January 1979 (reprinted in Vol.II of the submissions on Setting Accounting Standards).

5. Companies Act 1967, Schedule 2, Part III.

6. Sir Patrick Hastings, 'The Case of the Royal Mail', in Baxter and Davidson, *op.cit.*

7. R.L. Watts, and J.L. Zimmerman, 'The Demand for and Supply of Accounting Theories: The Market for Excuses', *The Accounting Review*, Vol. LIV, No.2, April 1979.

8. A. Hope, 'Accounting Policy: Theory or Pragmatism or Both?', 1979 (printed in Vol.II of the submissions on Setting Accounting Standards); contrast: D. Solomons, 'The Politicization of Accounting', *The Journal of Accountancy*, November 1978.

# 7. The Conceptual Framework Project of FASB

I review the background reasons for FASB's commitment to the 'Conceptual Framework' project and give an outline of the major steps so far taken in its development in Appendix I. Here I shall merely aim to identify, in an extremely summarized form, the main thrust of the project.

While a number of areas are being explored by the Board, initial conclusions were reached in SFAC1 'Objectives of Financial Reporting by Business Enterprises' which is concerned with 'general purpose external financial reporting'. These may be summarized as follows:

1. The users on whose decisions attention is focused are investors and creditors, but other users have similar needs.

2. The main factor of importance for the decisions they have to take is the assessment of the amount, timing and uncertainty of the future cash flows of the business enterprises in which they are interested.

3. The primary focus of financial reporting is on the provision of measures of enterprise income together with information about enterprises' economic resources, obligations and owners' equity. Information about past cash flows is also useful, and so are explanations by management about the accounts.

From the starting point of SFAC1, the remainder of the project is largely concerned with exploring how the traditional financial accounting statements (balance sheets, profit and loss accounts and statements of source and application of funds) should be constructed and presented to make them more useful in assisting investors and creditors and others to assess the amount, timing and risk of future cash flows. SFAC3 'Elements of Financial Statements of Business Enterprises' contains definitions of some of the characteristics of assets, liabilities, revenues, expenses etc. that are necessary if they are to appear in the accounts, and other areas of the project, still under way, tackle recognition, measurement and presentation questions (see Appendix I and Figure 1).

As well as tackling these specifically 'accounting' problems the Board has also issued a conceptual statement, SFAC2 'Qualitative Characteristics of Accounting Information', which discusses the general characteristics which make information valuable, and which may also be helpful in assessing the value of accounting information. The most important characteristic is said to be that of 'usefulness for decision making', which in turn implies a need for 'relevance' and for 'reliability'. An important aspect of 'relevance' is that information must have 'predictive value' or 'feedback value' or both, and there are a number of subsidiary attributes which help to ensure the relevance and reliability of information. However, the statement also points out that a major difficulty in applying these characteristics is that the qualities may conflict.

SFAC2 also stresses the need for the benefits of information to exceed the costs if it is actually to be worth providing, but acknowledges many difficulties in identifying these costs and benefits and in weighing up their effect on different interested parties (their 'economic consequences').[1] By and large SFAC2 represents a more 'philosophical' discussion of the basic notion of 'usefulness' rather than being concerned with developing any specific guidance on what particular steps should be taken that would make accounting more useful.

The fourth statement to date (SFAC4 'Objectives of Financial Reporting by Nonbusiness Organizations') deals with 'general purpose external financial reporting' and runs parallel to SFAC1. Its main conclusions may be summarized as:

1.  The users on whose decisions attention is focused are present and potential resource providers; but other users have similar needs.

2. They need to assess the services that a nonbusiness organization provides and its ability to continue to provide those services; and how the management discharges its stewardship responsibilities.

3. The most useful information is information about organizations' economic resources and obligations and how they change; together with information about service efforts and accomplishments. Information about past cash flows is also useful, and so are explanations by management about the accounts.

In the light of these conclusions, the Board considers that it is not necessary to develop an independent conceptual framework for any particular category of entities, but rather to give appropriate consideration to different reporting objectives and concepts, that may apply only to certain types of entities, within an integrated conceptual framework.

The main development of the project therefore follows the line of asking 'What is useful accounting information?' and, particularly in SFAC2, considering many of the difficulties that arise in judging what is likely to be most useful and acceptable to the interested parties. However, some particular features of FASB's approach are worth noting.

## 'INVESTORS AND CREDITORS' AND 'CASH FLOWS'

SFAC1 and its background papers give an extensive description of the operation of a 'market economy' and of the role of capital and credit, in order to derive the objective of providing information useful for investment, credit and other similar decisions, and to identify the users' interest in the amount, timing and uncertainty of future cash flows. However, SFAC1 rightly says (para.30) that the objectives are directed towards the common interest of various potential users in the ability of an enterprise to generate favorable cash flows. This, as I have previously argued, is a good description of a general focus of interest of all users in any economy where cash is the normal medium of exchange, whatever the objectives of the enterprise being considered.

However, SFAC4 does not refer in the same way to a general interest in 'future cash flows', because, I suppose, the activities of nonbusiness organizations, although valuable, are often charitable, and do not bring in any cash. Similarly, they may obtain resources (e.g. through voluntary assistance, and donations of supplies, equipment etc.) that do not involve cash outflows. Therefore, exchanges for cash may comprise a relatively small part of their total transactions. Nevertheless, assessing their 'ability to continue to provide services' must, at least in part, require assessment of their financial situation and prospects; of what cash outflows will be required and where the money will come from; and of how the money may be contributed by various sources and allocated to various purposes. To my mind, in the case of these organizations too, it is these potential 'cash flows' that best sum up the financial aspects with which the accounts are most obviously concerned.

## THE FOCUS ON 'INCOME'

In the light of present accounting practice it is understandable that the main focus of the project should be on the calculation of 'income' or 'profit' and of 'net assets'. However, I have already commented (in Chapters 4 and 5) on the difficulties associated with trying to establish agreed rules for how these should be calculated and presented, whether the approach taken is to ask 'How best to represent economic reality?', or 'How to provide the most useful accounting information?'.

## 'QUALITATIVE CHARACTERISTICS OF ACCOUNTING INFORMATION'

All the reports deal with these (see Figure 4), and FASB (in SFAC2) and Professor Stamp give them particular importance. The question therefore arises: Does sorting out what one means by the term 'useful information' (by identifying what the characteristics of useful information are in general) significantly advance the ability to resolve disputes over whether some particular proposal will provide useful information? Does it, that is, help in establishing the 'conceptual framework' that FASB is looking for? Obviously, it will help debate if terms are used clearly and consistently; but there are three main reasons for thinking that this help will be limited. Firstly, such characteristics have been identified in many studies and have not obviously led to any greater agreement about particular problems. Secondly, defining usefulness in terms of say 'relevance' and 'reliability' only shifts the area of disagreement over any particular problem back from 'Is this information useful?' to 'Is this information reliable?' or 'Is it relevant?' (i.e. it may merely lead to word-shuffling). Thirdly, the criteria may often conflict and one needs some other criterion by which to resolve these conflicts. As SFAC2 acknowledges in para 31:

> The challenge is to define in more detail what makes accounting information useful for decision making. If there is a serious difference of opinion it is not over the general nature of characteristics such as relevance and reliability, which clearly occupy an important place in the hierarchy of qualities that make information useful. There may indeed be some disagreement about their relative importance. But more serious disagreement arises over the choice between two accounting methods (for example, methods of allocating costs or recognizing revenues) if the choice involves a judgment about which method will produce more relevant or more reliable results or a judgment about whether the superior relevance of the results of one method outweighs the superior reliability of the results of the other.

As there seems to be no way of resolving such conflicts except by settling individual accounting problems, general discussions of these various characteristics, and of their relative importance, are unlikely to be of much assistance.

## 'DEFINITIONS OF ELEMENTS'

SFAC3 sets out definitions of ten basic elements of balance sheets and profit and loss accounts (see Appendix I & Fig.5). However, it again seems unlikely that they will be of much assistance in resolving individual accounting problems. The statement itself points out that it expects most assets and liabilities in present practice to continue to qualify as assets or liabilities under the definitions; and emphasises that the definitions neither require nor presage upheavals in present practice, although they may in due time lead to some evolutionary changes in practice or at least in the way certain items are viewed. In the light of these remarks, it is difficult to understand why the Board believes that 'they should be especially helpful . . . in analyzing and resolving new financial accounting issues as they arise' (SFAC3 p.xiii).

The main reason why they are unlikely to help is that they merely push all the problems back to other stages. Thus the definitions give characteristics *necessary* for something to qualify as an element, for example, as an asset—but they are not *sufficient* to decide whether it is an asset. This also requires consideration of 'recognition criteria' (i.e. the rules for deciding *when* to include something or the effect of something in financial statements) as well as settling of the 'measurement' and 'presentation' questions (i.e. determining *how* it should be included). Moreover, the definitions given are so general that they are unlikely to exclude anything that one might reasonably want to include.

As several commentators have observed,[2] the most interesting example in the appendix to SFAC3 is that of deferred taxes. The discussion there indicates that the definitions are in fact compatible with two methods (i.e. the 'liability' and the 'net of tax' methods) out of the three most widely suggested methods of accounting for the tax effects of timing differences, and with a possible rationale for the third (the 'deferral') method, and moreover do not either require tax allocation or rule it out (paras.163-165). It is thus hard to see how they are to help resolve accounting arguments—and this is largely because they are as yet incomplete until the recognition and measurement criteria are established too. Indeed, SFAC3 itself says (in introducing the examples that illustrate the concepts) that in many cases 'although the points are conceptually significant, they may be practically trivial—that is the results may appear to make little difference in practice' (para.153). It does not say why a 'trivial' matter is also 'significant'.

In my opinion, it is hard to see any practical benefit arising from this area of FASB's conceptual framework project. Indeed, it is not clear why one cannot go straight from the objective of providing useful information to discussing difficult accounting problems in terms of the 'usefulness' of different answers, rather than by the circuitous route of qualitative criteria, definitions, recognition and measurement criteria. At least it seems to me to be no more likely that an agreed answer will be reached by this longer and more involved route than by tackling the problems head on.[3]

## CONCLUSION

Given the difficulties experienced in arriving at 'useful' definitions of the elements of profit and loss accounts and balance sheets, it seems to me likely that the continuing attempts to develop 'recognition criteria' and 'measurement rules', that can both command general acceptance and have any impact on individual accounting disputes in relation to profit and net asset calculation, will be similarly unsuccessful. From this point of view, the most valuable parts of the project are the inflation accounting 'experiment', and the ideas raised in the discussion memoranda on 'Reporting Earnings' and 'Reporting Funds Flow, Liquidity and Financial Flexibility', which discuss specific issues and suggest useful improvements that may be made to present reporting practices. Of the 'concepts statements', SFAC2 clearly sets out many of the conceptual problems in assessing what is 'useful information'.

## REFERENCES—CHAPTER 7

1. S.A. Zeff, 'The Rise of "Economic Consequences" ', *Journal of Accountancy*, December 1978.

2. e.g. N. Dopuch and S. Sunder, 'FASB's Statements on Objectives and Elements of Financial Accounting: A Review', *The Accounting Review*, January 1980; the Stamp Report, Chapter 9, para. 50

3. For a general discussion of the problems of providing authoritative definitions, see J. Kitchen, 'Costing Terminology' in W.T. Baxter and S. Davidson (eds.), Studies in Accounting Theory, 2nd edition, London: Sweet and Maxwell, 1962 (reprinted from *Accounting Research*, February 1954).

# 8. The Other Reports

The basic structure of the other reports (summarised in Appendices III-V) is similar to that of FASB's conceptual framework project. They identify users, uses and potentially useful information; indicate costs, benefits and potential conflicts; and point out some of the difficulties of getting agreement on matters of accounting policy and accounting standards. The differences seem to be largely matters of emphasis.

## THE CORPORATE REPORT

The Corporate Report (see Appendix III) concludes that the 'fundamental objective of corporate reports is to communicate economic measurements of and information about the resources and the performance of the reporting entity useful to those having reasonable rights to such information', and outlines the general qualitative characteristics such information should have. This seems to capture the essence of the FASB's broad objectives for both business and nonbusiness organisations, as well as emphasising the important condition that 'usefulness to users' is not enough, but practicability and acceptability to other users and preparers (and by implication auditors?) is necessary too. For the extent of disclosure is a question of mutual rights and obligations, and thus of the 'accountability' of the reporting entity to those with whom it has dealings or who are otherwise affected by or affect its activities (including 'society as a whole').

But from this objective the report moves in a rather different direction from FASB, concentrating more on the need to consider the rights of different users; to widen the range of entities obliged to give a public account of their activities; and to alter the emphasis as to which users corporate reports should address. There are suggestions for

*81*

altering the focus of the traditional accounting statements (e.g. to
'value added' instead of 'profit'; more details of transactions with
government etc.) and adding indicators of responsibility and
performance of other kinds (e.g. employment reports). In relation to
the calculation of profit and loss and balance sheet items, the report
does suggest a need to split 'performance' oriented from 'prudence'
oriented calculations (similar to the 'economic' and 'legal' oriented
uses I discussed in Chapter 6 above), to use current purchasing power
measures, and to explore the possibilities of using a range of value
measures, but no specific proposals in relation to existing accounting
procedures are developed.


# SANDILANDS

The Sandilands Report (see Appendix IV) follows a similar approach
but its main concern, of course, is with the problem of changing prices.
By and large, it takes the 'usefulness' of ordinary historical cost
accounts for granted when prices are stable, but argues that their
usefulness has been so severely eroded in an inflationary environment
that there is a need to substitute current cost valuations and to report a
revised figure of 'operating profit' if user needs for information that
will help them to assess the position, performance and prospects of
businesses are to be met in a way that will be acceptable to company
managements. The report is then largely devoted to developing what is
argued to be an evolutionary and practicable approach to current cost
accounting.

The 'measurement' problems addressed in the Sandilands Report
have been considered by FASB in the development of FAS33 on
'changing prices'—but as I point out in Appendix I FASB have
adopted an 'experimental' approach of requiring supplementary
information on more than one basis (requiring both current cost and
current purchasing power measures and taking no decision on 'capital
maintenance concepts') with a commitment to review the results in
some years' time. The Sandilands Report argues for the usefulness of
its measure of current cost profit on the grounds that it will be useful if
accounts show as a measure of profit the amount that could go on
being distributed in all future years 'if revenues earned and costs

incurred in future years were the same as in the year of account' (para.166—see Appendix IV).

This argument is confused. Either it is an empty tautology which is true of all measures of profit (as 'profit' may be defined as 'revenues' less 'costs'); or it is wrong if it means that this year's current cost profit (i.e. excluding 'holding gains') will be repeated in future years if conditions/prices do not change any further. For in general, this year's current cost profit will reflect the effect of the changing conditions and prices throughout the year, not the profit that would have been obtained if everything had occurred under year-end conditions (and defining 'year-end conditions' would itself not be straightforward in respect of many aspects of the economic environment). Alternatively, if the (changing) conditions prevailing during the current year were somehow to be repeated in future years, then it would be the current cost profit plus the holding gains accruing that would be repeated; though of course the *analysis* of the total gains into these two elements could well be argued to be useful for making predictions about the future (as suggested in FAS33).

The Sandilands report also notes some of the limitations of accounting (including the problems of uncertainty in accounting measurement; the need for allocations; and the difficulties of prediction in the business environment). However, its concern is not to explore how these issues are to be resolved, and it merely observes that the ASC is developing its standards programme to attempt to eliminate some of the diversity of current practice.

## STAMP

More recently there has been Professor Stamp's report (outlined in Appendix V) prepared for the Research Department of the Canadian Institute of Chartered Accountants. This undertakes a much more extensive review of the problems (several of them said to be 'irresolvable') of income and value measurement, of the conflicts between user needs, of the difficulties of setting accounting standards, and of the doubts raised by 'efficient markets' evidence about the need for 'unique measurement standards'—and indeed whether investors do use the information in published accounts. Neither FASB's statements nor the British reports raise so many of the relevant problems.

Nevertheless the view is taken that as standards are needed, and must be enforced, then the accounting profession must deal with the problems of defining income and value (lest governments do it instead in an arbitrary fashion) and (apparently) that 'measurement' standards are equally, if not more, important than disclosure standards.

The approach is similar to that of the other studies. Given a primary objective of ensuring that the legitimate needs of users are properly met the report considers the same sorts of users, user needs and rights to information, and similar desirable (but often conflicting) qualitative characteristics of useful information. In addition, it is urged that accounting standard setting should be an evolutionary process, and that there are important parallels with the development of law as a means for resolving conflicts and defining boundaries of acceptable behaviour.

The report takes issue with what it sees as FASB's approach in four main areas: the range of users to be considered; the importance of 'accountability'; the use of 'predictive ability' as a criterion; and the approach to be adopted in developing a conceptual framework (particularly doubting the value of authoritative 'definitions' of assets, liabilities etc.). As I have already commented on these matters in earlier chapters, I will not discuss them further here.

The report goes considerably further than the other studies (including those of FASB) in listing major conceptual problems that arise in developing any framework. However, while mentioning several interesting ideas for further exploration, the report does not offer significantly more help in developing a set of principles that will resolve particular accounting disputes, and does not itself offer unequivocal conclusions about useful changes in accounting practice.

## CONCLUSION

So far as the development of a 'conceptual framework' is concerned, it is difficult to see that the conclusions offered by these various reports (including FASB's project and the many other similar studies that have preceded them) go much beyond listing the conceptual problems and stating the common sense view that accounting must be useful; that it is about the financial affairs of individuals and organisations, whether business or 'nonbusiness', and that one must respect the interests and rights of the different individuals and groups who have an interest in their financial affairs, so that accounting policies and standards must be practicable and acceptable.

Nevertheless, although the notions of usefulness, the qualitative characteristics of useful information and the preliminary identifications of users and user needs offered by such studies are insufficient even to begin to resolve many accounting problems, they do raise important matters that must be dealt with. In the next chapter I shall argue for the view that this is the most than can, at least at present, usefully be expected of them; and that the main value of thinking about the conceptual framework of accounting lies in developing understanding of what questions need answering and how they may be approached. In other words, a conceptual framework must be seen as a framework for investigation and research into solutions; not as a package of solutions.[1]

# REFERENCES—CHAPTER 8

1. B.V. Carsberg, Presentation at FASB Symposium: Conceptual Framework for Financial Accounting and Reporting, June 24, 1980 (transcript published by FASB, pp.109 and following).

# 9. Implications For Financial Accounting and Reporting

In this chapter I consider some implications of the problems that have been reviewed in this report.

The chief implication of course is that people may properly disagree about what is 'good accounting'—it is fundamentally a subjective matter. The lack of objective criteria is due both to the uncertainty of the environment in which accounting takes place, and to the need to reconcile the interests of the different parties involved in the accounting process.

The first of these—uncertainty—can lead to disagreement on what is a good 'technical' solution to an accounting problem. In reporting profit and net assets there is a need for subjective judgments about the future in order to make the necessary estimates and allocations, and to decide what further information needs to be given to supplement the necessarily incomplete picture of an enterprise's financial situation, so that overall a 'true and fair' view is given. More generally, in deciding what information it is useful to provide there is often a need for judgment in deciding what is likely to be relevant, and in assessing the costs and benefits of providing it.

The second factor—the interests of different parties—means that 'technical' solutions alone are not sufficient to resolve accounting problems—the social and political consequences must be considered too. Personal value judgments are needed as to whose interests are to be recognised. When one takes these two kinds of difficulties together, one is faced by a situation of potentially great confusion; and one for which there seems unlikely to be any 'universal' solution.

Whether there will be agreement on what information should be provided for general use as a matter of routine by a set of financial (or management) accounts seems likely to depend largely on how much similarity of situation and purpose there is among the various users of and uses for the accounts; on how much agreement there is on the usefulness and value of different types of information in those circumstances; and on what economies of cost or other advantages are anticipated from agreement on a common package. Personal, organisational, social, institutional and cultural factors are all likely to influence the choices made. In some cases agreement will be more readily forthcoming than in others.

# ACCOUNTING STANDARDS

What are the implications for the role of accounting standards and other forms of regulation of accounting practice? How far can, and should, the rules go? Again, one can consider the 'technical' and the 'political' problems.

The 'technical' problems (relating mainly to the uncertainty of the economic environment) impose inevitable limitations on what standards can achieve in trying to ensure that 'the same economic facts are treated in the same way'. In the context of profit and net asset measurement, standards can lay down procedures but cannot determine how people will estimate the future and therefore what are seen as 'the same economic facts' by different company managements.

Consequently, it is inevitable that, to the extent that such estimates are required, managements have some latitude in the calculation of the performance measure by which they are judged, and that one cannot precisely determine the borderline between justifiable and unjustifiable optimism in the presentation of results (or, similarly, between reasonable prudence and excessive conservatism). In many businesses (e.g. long term contractors; high technology concerns; insurance companies) such areas of estimation may be the most significant factors in the determination of their overall results. The auditors can exercise their own judgment, but often will not be in as good a position as the experienced management to form a realistic opinion.[1]

In such situations the emphasis must be on disclosure of relevant information, and on explanation of the procedures adopted and important assumptions made, if readers of the accounts are to be able best to assess their relevance for their own needs. Again, because the accounts cannot give a complete picture of the financial state of the reporting entity, one needs to allow for the limitations of any particular accounting procedure in helping to give a 'true and fair' view overall, and consider what additional disclosures and supporting explanations are needed. Furthermore, a procedure relating to a particular area (such as stock valuation, depreciation, deferred taxation etc.) needs to be considered in relation to those for other areas, as it is the combination of procedures that determines the overall picture.

Turning to the 'political' factors, the basic questions that arise are 'Is regulation needed, and if so, who should have the authority to decide questions of accounting policy?' One approach to these questions is from the viewpoint of 'information economics' and 'welfare economics'.

Recognition that 'accounting information' is something whose possession is valuable and which requires costs to produce, and that different people have different needs for it, has led to economic analysis of the nature of the demand for it, and the conditions for its supply—and to recommendations on how the 'optimal level' should be achieved.[2] Some analysts stress the 'private value' of the information (so that disclosure to others is itself something to be bargained over) and recommend that the determination of how much should be supplied, and how it should be produced, should be left to a bargaining or 'market' process between those directly concerned (and therefore argued to be in the best position to appreciate the costs and benefits) in order to advance the most efficient solution. This will lead to a variety of disclosures and practices according to individual circumstances.

Other analysts would stress the 'externalities' of the activities of businesses (and other organisations)—that is the effects they have (costs they impose or benefits they bring) on those who cannot directly bargain with them, but who consequently have an interest in information about them. Again, analysis of the demand for and supply of the 'commodity' information suggests that, as it tends to be 'jointly supplied' (is but one part of a contractual relationship rather than being negotiated and 'priced' separately), or because, once produced, it easily becomes costlessly available for use by many people (is essentially what economists call a 'public good'), therefore it cannot be left to 'market forces' to determine the 'optimal' amount and type of information to be provided—there is a strong case for intervention in determining what should be provided.

Such analyses attempt to assess how 'efficiency' (in balancing costs and benefits) is likely best to be achieved—but others would stress the potential importance of accounting information in redistributing power and economic advantage and the consequent political significance of the way in which accounting policies and disclosures are chosen, and of which entities are made to give a public account and whose rights are given priority. So, as the 'private' or the 'public' values of information are emphasised, and the 'technical' and the 'political', there is an inclination to recommend less or more standard setting and accounting regulation.

At one extreme, a wholly 'free market' supporter would see no benefit to users from government regulation of company accounting (or by bodies like FASB and ASC)—or at least argue that while such interventions may theoretically appear to remedy failures of the 'market solution', in practice they lead only to bureaucratisation and greater inefficiency.[3] At the other extreme, some favour accounting (and auditing) regulation coming directly and entirely under government supervision.

Having indicated the importance of such institutional matters in relation to regulation of accounting policy, I do not propose to discuss them further as they reflect more general concerns about the appropriate institutional and political arrangements for intervening in the economy that arise also in respect of many non-accounting matters.


## ACCOUNTING THEORY

How can accounting theory help in matters of accounting policy? The general conclusion must be that the development of 'accounting theory' to date is not such as to offer definite guidance. There has certainly been an expansion of awareness of what information it is possible and practicable to report in an accounting framework and of what the possible uses of such information might be. There has been less advance in understanding how actually to choose from among the variety of reporting possibilities, and what the long run consequences of alternative choices may be.

It is not easy to assess the merits of alternative accounting options and methods as compared with current practice, and judgments have to be made (as in the case of current cost accounting). Given that a potential improvement is thought possible, there is then the question of whether it is worth the extra costs, or the costs of change. In making judgment one is hampered by having very limited knowledge about a wide range of relevant questions—for example: What factors have led to the adoption of the present accounting practices? Are these now seen to be inappropriate, or is it rather that conditions have changed so that they are no longer relevant? Do present practices in fact have beneficial consequences and effects (possibly quite different from those originally intended) that have not been taken full account of by those who recommend change?

What use do various individuals and groups in fact make of the accounting information? Does this differ significantly depending on whether one is dealing with accounting within organisations, or with accounting by organisations to those outside? Do people want changes and, if so, what changes? How does one find this out? How does one allow for the possibility that their expressed needs may be limited by their experience of current practices and lack of awareness or understanding of the potential usefulness of alternative procedures?

Will changes that seem suitable for one purpose be suitable for other purposes? What will the consequences be for other institutional arrangements within organisations and within society? Whose rights will be adversely affected? And so on. It is not easy to find clear, general answers to these kinds of questions. It is perhaps even more difficult to be sure that one is even asking the right questions—let alone all the right questions.[4]

If it is not precisely clear how accounting is used and what it is useful for, it may seem strange that accounting has come to be regarded with such importance and that accountants' services are so much in demand. However, a plausible view of the strength of accounting is that its value lies, not in serving any one purpose particularly well, but in economically serving a number of purposes reasonably well.

One may view the history of accounting as one of continuous adaptations and modifications to meet additional demands (rather than as one of clear design as the ideal tool to achieve some particular end)—to keep track of resources and to check the honesty of subordinates and agents; to provide a basis for sharing out rewards and costs; as an instrument of management planning and control; as an indication of economic performance; and so on. Indeed in many circumstances the value of accounting may lie more in the discipline that the process imposes of systematically keeping track of events and resources, and in trying to from a comprehensive and consistent view of the overall position of an enterprise as a useful basis for further enquiry, than in any precise usefulness of the figures it can produce.[5]

From this viewpoint, it is no surprise to find tensions between alternative views of which purposes future developments should aim to serve, and arguments about what disciplines (e.g. economics, law, management science, psychology, organisation theory) should provide an underpinning for these developments. Indeed these tensions continually raise the question of whether accounting can go on being an 'adequate all rounder' or whether the time has come for it to divide into a number of specialist branches, some perhaps barely recognisable as 'traditional' accounting.

If accounting has so far developed in a rather pragmatic way for many different reasons, then it is also no surprise that it is difficult to offer any general theory or complete conceptual framework that will explain it fully—just as it is difficult to write any general history that fully explains how it has developed so far.[6]

Diversity of views about origins and purposes is a common feature of many social institutions: medicine, education, marriage, law, politics, religion and so on. There is disagreement about their past and present functions in society, and about what objectives should guide their future development. It seems that similar ambiguities are associated with accounting. Once one starts to ask 'How is accounting useful and how can it be made more useful'? one is launched into what seems to be an endless series of further questions; and immediate clear answers are few and far between. But it is the acknowledgment that such questions are important and need answering, and that tradition and experience alone are not enough to provide the answers (especially as new conditions change the demands that are made, and technological developments change the possibilities) that give accounting its professional status, as well as the justification for its study as an academic discipline.

It therefore seems idle to hope for an 'agreed conceptual framework' or general accounting theory of a type that will give explicit guidance on what is appropriate in preparing financial statements, or on what will improve accounting practice. The important thing is that the effort is made, and seen to be made, to ask the relevant questions with respect to users' needs; the methods that can satisfy these and their visible and hidden costs; and possible conflicts between needs. This will not always ensure agreement: conversely people may 'agree to agree' even though they reject the reasons given for the proposed change in practice. But in the absence of such justifications, action can only be arbitrary, or based merely on precedent.

This is a view of a conceptual framework for accounting theory primarily as an aid to suggesting what are the important questions to try and answer, rather than as providing a formula or set of formulas such that solutions to particular accounting problems can be readily derived. This view implies that all accounting research is potentially research into 'the conceptual framework of accounting'—for it is as bits of evidence, knowledge and new ideas are accumulated that there will come gradual, and sometimes sudden, changes in the overall view that people have about what 'accounting' is about; which in turn will suggest new questions to ask.[7]

## CONCLUSION

The value of the current attempts to explore the 'conceptual framework' lies, in my opinion, mainly in the discipline the process imposes of identifying the important areas where judgment is needed on questions of accounting policy, and of stimulating enquiry with regard to users' needs and how to satisfy them.

In the final chapter, I shall offer some (necessarily personal) suggestions for work that may be of assistance to ASC in following up this report.

# REFERENCES—CHAPTER 9

1. A.M.C. Morison, 'The Role of the Reporting Accountant Today', *The Accountant's Magazine*, 74, January and February 1970 (reprinted in Baxter and Davidson, Studies in Accounting, *op.cit.*).

2. For example, see M. Bromwich, 'In Support of the Accounting Standards Committee: An Academic View' (printed in Vol. II of the submissions on 'Setting Accounting Standards', *op.cit.*), and 'The Setting of Accounting Standards: the contribution of research' in Bromwich and Hopwood, Essays in British Accounting Research, *op.cit.*

3. e.g. G.J. Benston, 'The Establishment and Enforcement of Accounting Standards: Methods, Benefits and Costs', *Accounting and Business Research*, No.41, Winter 1980.,

4. S. Burchell, C. Clubb, A. Hopwood, J. Hughes and J. Nahapiet, 'The Roles of Accounting in Organizations and Society', *Accounting, Organizations and Society*, Vol.5, No.1, 1980.

5. W.T. Baxter, 'The Future of Company Financial Reporting', in T.A. Lee (ed.), Developments in Financial Reporting, Deddington, Oxford: Philip Allan, 1981.

6. B.S. Yamey, 'Some Reflections on the Writing of a General History of Accounting', *Accounting and Business Research*, No. 42, Spring 1981.

7. See, for example, A. Ryan, The Philosophy of the Social Sciences, *op.cit.*, especially chapters 4 and 10.

# 10. Suggestions for Further Work

The most obvious need is for work to develop knowledge of the ways in which the profit statements, balance sheets, funds flow statements and other information in financial reports can, and do, assist people to form their estimates about the financial position, performance and prospects of businesses and other entities. This suggests a number of areas of research.

a) *Monitor FASB's work, and developments in other countries.*
First, there is a need to monitor the development of FASB's work on the 'conceptual framework project'. The questions addressed in the Board's discussion memoranda on 'Reporting Earnings and 'Funds Flow, Liquidity and Financial Flexibility' are concerned with possible improvements in disclosure and presentation of information, and it would be useful to review the public comments and the exposure draft when they are published. The Board is soon to issue a Research Report on the topic of 'user needs' and is currently considering what research would be helpful in monitoring its 'inflation accounting' experiment. A paper on this will also be published soon, which could suggest useful comparative studies that might be undertaken in the U.K.

There is also a need to monitor the development of thinking in other countries. My study has been confined to some developments in the U.S.A., U.K. and Canada, but European ideas are obviously also of particular interest.

b) *Economic significance of accounting measures.*
Second, there is a more general need to develop knowledge of the way different profit and asset measures behave under different economic circumstances, and how they (and corresponding measures of 'rate of return') may be related to the 'real' financial performance of enterprises. This can be tackled by mathematical, econometric and statistical analysis; and by simulation of different possible conditions.[1]

It is vitally important that accountants should develop their understanding of the ways in which the numbers they produce may best be interpreted when analysing the financial situation of businesses and other organisations.

c) *What do people find accounts useful for? What are their complaints?*

Third, it is obviously important to increase knowledge of the ways in which accounts are actually used by people, and to try to assess the significance of the empirical work that has been, and is being, carried out. As I said in Chapter 5 above, it is not easy to derive obvious conclusions from much of the work done so far, but this kind of work is important if one is to take seriously the question 'What are accounts useful for'?

Clues may also come from considering the kinds of information called for on special occasions, such as during a takeover or when issuing a prospectus; or by specialist users who have the power to obtain the information they want, such as banks with major participating interests and supervisory authorities.[2] How far could these (e.g. profit forecasts)[3] usefully become part of the routine general purpose financial accounts?

While much of the work done to date has concentrated on investors and creditors, and on companies listed on stock exchanges, the needs of those dealing with private businesses, with nationalised industries and with nonbusiness organisations in the private and public sectors require consideration too; as do the needs of different classes of user.[4]

Such investigations may be likened to the 'market research' that the manufacturer of a product may carry out to try and identify what the customers want. Another way of tackling this is to analyse customers' complaints about faulty products—which for published accounts suggests that analysis of cases where DoT investigations have been held into a company's affairs, or of other *causes célèbres*, may shed useful light on where present accounting practices have failed to meet the public's reasonable expectations, and what kinds of improvement may best remedy these deficiencies. My own impressions from some work I have recently been doing on this[5] are that the kinds of problems concerned with measuring profits that have been tackled in many accounting standards seem unlikely to have been as significant a factor as the more basic questions of adequate disclosure (particularly of the nature of the estimates and assumptions made in arriving at the figures) and of the adequacy of the management accounting system for orderly running of the business and as a suitable basis for the preparation of annual accounts. However, further work is needed before such impressions can be confirmed or rejected.

d) *Relationships between financial and management accounting.*
There is a good case for arguing that the management accounting procedures that are found most useful for running businesses are also likely to be the most useful for giving outsiders an impression of how well a company is being run—or, if this is not so, then the particular features in the external reporting environment that impose an alternative approach need to be carefully examined and understood. Thus, the problems facing the top management of a large diversified business with overseas subsidiaries, in developing a suitable accounting system for reporting at Board level, seem in many ways the same as those facing ASC in setting suitable standards for general use in published accounts. Again, it seems likely that innovation and experimentation with new methods will more often take place in management accounting than in the more constrained legalistic environment of published accounts.

There are also pressures the other way. New external requirements impose new internal procedures, and one can examine how beneficial for management purposes this effect is. Similarly, in trying to understand the merits and consequences of alternative accounting policies, or how important it is to have a standard for a particular area, one needs to understand the reasons why different company managements have chosen the policies they presently use—and why they themselves make changes in them from time to time.

There is also a need to explore ways of developing the contribution to financial reporting to be made by management explanations of choices of accounting policies, of the bases for estimates, and of the significance of the reported results. Thus, for example, the present standard on deferred taxation[6] requires the provision of only as much deferred tax as a company's management considers is needed having regard to likely future capital expenditure etc., but there is no requirement to explain the *assumptions* on which the provision has been calculated, which are needed in order to interpret the figure sensibly.

A casual survey of major British companies' presentation of supplementary current cost figures suggests there is at present usually little or no attempt by the Chairman or Directors to explain how they see the significance of the two different profit figures they now present—e.g. in relation to the size of the dividend they have decided to propose.[7]

e) *Supplementary information.*
Fifth, there is the need to consider more widely what information is to be provided outside the framework of the balance sheet and profit and loss account, and what other significant items may need disclosure. Some recent U.K. standards may be seen as examples of this line of thinking. Consideration of 'post balance sheet events.'[8] and of 'contingencies'[9] aims to overcome some of the limitations of the main accounts in indicating future eventualities.

Generally, the use of supplementary information may often provide a more convenient means of experimenting with new requirements and of avoiding problems of legal constraints (e.g. imposed by European law) on what may be included in the main accounts and how the items must be measured. Indeed, the emphasis on providing 'useful information' and the difficulties previously discussed of assessing what is useful (and to whom) suggest that a more 'experimental' approach to questions of accounting policy is often likely to be more fruitful than trying to settle arguments over what is right.

f) *The problems of making changes in accounting practice.*
Sixth, there is need to study the process of introducing changes in accounting practice, including the visible and hidden consequences of changes and the 'economic consequences'; the kinds of demands and pressures that are likely to arise; and how the problem of implementation may best be managed.[10] There have been some general studies (mainly in the U.S.A.) of the problems that have faced standard setting bodies in the past in this respect,[11] but there is also a need for clear studies of the particular circumstances that have surrounded the introduction of new requirements and the setting of individual standards, and of the lessons that may be learned from this experience—about 'what users want'; about the scope of regulation; and about implications for future changes.[12] Similarly, historical studies of major developments in accounting practice that have

occurred in the past are illuminating, particularly in comparing developments that have occurred as a result of regulation or legislation with developments that have occurred 'spontaneously'.[13]

g) *Public education.*
Finally, I would suggest there is still a need to consider how best to explain publicly the limitations of financial accounts, given the problems that have been discussed in previous chapters. Should each set of accounts (like a packet of cigarettes) carry a warning, or should this be left to 'covering' statements (e.g. of the SSAP2 type), or to a more general attempt to achieve public education and understanding of the difficulties accountants face in trying to turn facts about a business's past, and estimates about its future, into a meaningful financial report?[14]

# REFERENCES—CHAPTER 10

1.  See for example, G. Foster, Financial Statement Analysis, *op.cit.*, *passim*.

    G. Whittington, 'On the Use of the Accounting Rate of Return in Empirical Research', *Accounting and Business Research*, No.35, Summer 1978.

    J. Arnold and M. El-Azma, 'A Study of the Relative Usefulness of Six Accounting Measures of Income', Research Committee Occasional Paper No.13, London: ICAEW, 1978.

2.  See for example the Report of the Tribunal appointed to enquire into certain issues in relation to the circumstances leading up to the cessation of trading by the Vehicle and General Insurance Co. Ltd., London: HMSO, 1972, Ch.II Part I; and also: 'The Measurement of Liquidity' and 'The Measurement of Capital', London: Bank of England, 1980.

3.  S. Dev, 'Statements of Company Prospects', *Accounting and Business Research*, No.16, Autumn 1974.

4.  See, for example, the survey articles by J.R. Perrin, C. Tomkins and P. Bird in Bromwich and Hopwood, Essays in British Accounting Research, *op.cit.*

5.  with M.Sc. students at The London School of Economics and Political Science, G. Harte (now at the University of Stirling), T. McDonnell and C. Shepherd. P. Russell at the University of Manchester is also working on DoT reports.

6.  SSAP15, Accounting for deferred taxation, ASC, 1978.

7.  as A.D. Macve has pointed out to me.

8.  SSAP17, Accounting for post balance sheet events, ASC, 1980.

9.  SSAP18, Accounting for contingencies, ASC, 1980.

10. For an overview, see L. Kelly-Newton, Accounting Policy Formulation: The Role of Corporate Management, Reading, Mass.: Addison-Wesley, 1980.

11. S.A. Zeff, Forging Accounting Principles in Five Countries (1971 Arthur Andersen lectures at the University of Edinburgh), Champaign, Illinois: Stipes, 1972.

    C.T. Horngren, 'The Marketing of Accounting Standards', *Journal of Accountancy*, October, 1973.

    M. Moonitz, Obtaining Agreement on Standards in the Accounting Profession, Studies in Accounting Research No.8, American Accounting Association, 1974.

12. See for example C.A. Westwick, 'The Lessons to be Learned from the Development of Inflation Accounting in the U.K.', *Accounting and Business Research*, No.40, Autumn 1980.

13. For example see J. Kitchen, 'The Accounts of British Holding Company Groups: some thoughts on development in the early years', *Accounting and Business Research*, No.6, Spring 1972.

    R.L. Watts and J.L. Zimmerman, 'The Demand for and Supply of Accounting Theories', *op.cit.*

    J.R. Edwards and C. Baber, 'Dowlais Iron Company; Accounting Policies and Procedures for Profit Measurement and Reporting Purposes', *Accounting and Business Research*, No.34, Spring 1979.

    R.H. Parker, 'The study of accounting history' in Bromwich and Hopwood, *op.cit.*

14. R.H. Macve, 'Quaere Verum Vel Recte Numerare' (Inaugural Lecture, 1979), Aberystwyth: University College of Wales, 1980.

# Appendix I: The Conceptual Framework Project of FASB

## INTRODUCTION

The Board's work on this project has been in progress for nearly eight years now, and has always had high priority and taken a large share of its resources. Some impression of the size of the effort that has been devoted to it may be gained from the fact that the Annual Report of the Financial Accounting Foundation for 1980 shows total expenditure on the activities of the Board and its related bodies for the year approaching US $8million, while the Board's director of research and technical activities recently estimated (during the symposium held in June 1980) that this project was occupying approximately 40% of the staff's effort. The areas of the conceptual framework project comprise a large part of the Board's 'technical plan' (see Figure 2), and the Board's publications on the project already amount to over 3000 pages (of which statements of concepts and standards amount to some 400 pages). In addition, there are the transcripts of comments received and of public hearings and conferences held, which in turn reflect the enormous input of time and thought that is being made by those likely to be affected by the Board's decisions (see Appendix II).

The scale of this effort is unparalleled elsewhere in the world, and this alone makes FASB's work of particular interest. It is also felt by many that the effort it has made to collect the views of interested parties give the results an important degree of validity that studies by individual academics, or more limited studies by professional groups, have previously lacked.

The reasons for the current interest in, and the large commitment of resources being made to, this project by FASB may be traced to the pressures that have been brought to bear on it and its predecessors, and particularly expressions of public dissatisfaction with accounting and auditing and calls for greater government intervention. In undertaking the project, the Board no doubt wishes to counter criticisms made of its predecessors that they followed a 'fire fighting' approach without developing any underlying philosophy as a basis for consistent accounting principles, and thereby to establish that it has the necessary technical expertise in accounting matters to be the appropriate body to be entrusted with standard setting.[1]

As the Accounting Principles Board (APB) of the American Institute of Certified Public Accountants (AICPA) was born out of dissatisfaction with its predecessor, the Committee on Accounting Procedure (CAP), so FASB was born out of dissatisfaction with the APB. The AICPA set up two committees in April 1971. The report of the Wheat Committee's study on Establishing Financial Accounting Standards, issued in March 1972, dealt with the constitution and financing of the new FASB, which was then set up in 1973. The report of the study group on the Objectives of Financial Statements (the Trueblood report of October 1973) dealt with topics that have become the first stage of the FASB's conceptual framework project.

FASB in turn has taken various steps to increase general recognition of its authority as the proper body to establish the fundamental principles and to set standards. There is its 'due process' of full consultation with its 'constituents', the various users, preparers and auditors of accounts. Thus, before a statement is issued there is a lengthy procedure of investigation and consultation which starts normally with the appointment of a 'task force' to explore the issues, leading to the production of a discussion memorandum (or other initial paper) in which comment on them is invited (often preceded or accompanied by a 'research report' from an outside researcher). Then follows an exposure draft, and then finally a statement (with opportunities to comment and 'public hearings' along the way).

In addition, the Board's own meetings are held in public, and it produces regular reports on its agenda, on its meetings and on the statements made by, and the activities of, its members. The constitution of the Board itself has recently changed so that there is no longer any requirement for a majority of its seven members to be from public accounting practice.

Matters of enforcement are handled in the Board's relationships, both with the accounting profession (the AICPA's rules impose an obligation on its members normally to qualify their audit reports in cases of non-compliance with FASB standards), and with the Federal Securities and Exchange Commission (SEC).

Many commentators see FASB as the 'last chance' for keeping standard setting 'in the private sector' and consider that its survival in this role depends to a large extent on how successful it is judged to be in developing its conceptual framework project, and in tackling, in particular, the controversial topics of inflation accounting and foreign currency translation. This perception of its role, as the only alternative to greater government regulation, probably explains why the Board generally seems to enjoy strong financial and moral support from the leaders of the financial and business community in the U.S.A. and why it has itself stressed the role of good accounting in assisting the functioning of the capital market in a free enterprise economy and emphasized the importance of public confidence in accounting for confidence in business as a whole. As it said in 'Scope and Implications of the Conceptual Framework Project' in 1976, 'skepticism about financial reporting . . . creates adverse public opinion, which may be the antecedent of unjustified government regulation. Every company, every industry stands to suffer because of skepticism about financial reporting'.

Given that, on several occasions, existing accounting standards have trailed behind regulations issued by the SEC requiring new disclosures (e.g. the requirements for disclosure of replacement cost information and of the value of oil and gas reserves; and more recently for managements to discuss and analyze their companies' 'liquidity' and 'capital resources')[2] there is a strong incentive for FASB to establish principles that will enable the private sector to recapture the initiative in settling where the boundaries of useful accounting information should lie, and how they should be moved over time in response to changing needs and conditions.

The AICPA's concern also reflects the concerns of its members as auditors. As it is the auditors who are in the front line (whether in the U.S.A., the U.K. or elsewhere) when problems with accounting standards and other regulations arise, they too are vitally concerned with the nature of the authoritative backing for the standards that are adopted.

In the United States in recent years there have been investigations of auditing practices and of the structure of the profession by committees of Congress and of the Senate, starting in 1976 with the

Moss committee and the Metcalf committee, following public disquiet over a number of business scandals and bankruptcies.

Many people have argued that the flexibility of practices permitted by 'generally accepted accounting principles' has been a significant factor in reducing public confidence in the auditing profession;[3] that the search for better accounting principles is a vital part of the effort to restore the auditors' credibility; and that the cornerstone for the building of a sound edifice of acceptable accounting standards is the conceptual framework project. Comparisons can readily be extended to other countries, and to the international arena.

It is illuminating therefore to see the current interest in a conceptual framework, and particularly the significance that is attached to its development by FASB, in the context of the current pressures on the profession both as accountants and auditors (and by extension on the self-regulatory system for business as a whole). Nevertheless, in considering the more fundamental questions about the nature and purpose of financial reporting, I believe it is more important to take FASB's conceptual framework project (and other similar studies) at face value and to evaluate their contribution in terms of what has actually been said, and the arguments that have been presented.

This Appendix therefore outlines the main stages of the development of the project and the contents of the more important publications in it. A full list of publications is given in Appendix II.

## THE DEVELOPMENT OF THE PROJECT

The project really began, shortly after the setting up of the FASB in 1973, when the AICPA published the report of the Trueblood Committee on 'Objectives of Financial Statements' which specified a number of objectives and identified a number of desirable 'qualitative characteristics' of accounting information. The FASB considered this Report and in June 1974 issued a discussion memorandum entitled 'Conceptual Framework for Accounting and Reporting: Consideration of the Report of the Study Group on the Objectives of Financial Statements' which asked for comments on the issues raised. A public hearing was held in September 1974. In December 1976, the Board published a summary of its aims for the project in a paper called

'Scope and Implications of the Conceptual Framework Project', where the main areas to be tackled were identified. Subsequently, these have been extended and at present include (see Figure 1):

A. Objectives of financial reporting (i.e. considering for what purpose and for whom financial reports are prepared, and broadly what type of information they should contain).

B. Qualitative characteristics of financial information (including consideration of relevance, reliability etc. and the problems of conflicting qualities).

C. Elements of financial statements of enterprises (basically considering the nature of assets, liabilities and capital and the constituents of income).

D. Recognition criteria (the rules or conventions that should determine when an item is included as an asset or liability, or as a part of income in the financial statements).

E. Measurement (e.g. use of historical cost, replacement cost etc. to value assets and liabilities; and whether the unit of measure should be money or purchasing power).

F. 'Financial statements' and 'financial reporting' (what financial information should be in the 'financial statements' and notes thereto rather than provided by other forms of financial reporting; the identity, number and form of the financial statements; and whether all sizes of enterprise should be required to present the same information).

G. Reporting 'comprehensive income' and its components (what the form and content of the income statement should be, how information about income should be analyzed and presented, what choice of capital maintenance concepts should be made, whether some components should be presented as the 'earnings' of the enterprise and what additional information might be disclosed).

H. Funds flow, liquidity and financial flexibility (the form and content of 'flow of funds' statements; what information about cash flows and their relationship to income should be disclosed and how it should be analyzed and presented; how information about the liquidity and adaptability, or 'financial flexibility' of an enterprise can be provided).

These various areas of the conceptual framework project deal both with fairly abstract subjects, such as the formulation of basic objectives and qualitative characteristics, and with more concrete subjects where specific practical recommendations for action may be reached. Thus areas A, B and C have each been completed by the issue of a 'Statement of Financial Accounting Concepts' (SFAC). Such statements set out the basic objectives and concepts that the Board will use in developing accounting standards. They are intended primarily to serve as guides to the Board itself, but also to explain publicly the basis behind the Board's approach and thus increase general confidence in published accounts. These statements do not contain specific requirements for accounting practice, and thus do not have the effect of the Board's 'Statements of Financial Accounting Standards' (which are the equivalent of SSAPs in the UK.). Thus, they do not impose any obligation on auditors to consider qualifying their reports in cases of non-compliance.

As progress is made through the other parts of the project, from the general underlying concepts to more specific rules and procedures, the stage will be reached at which accounting standards, requiring compliance, can be issued. Thus, the statement issued in 1979 on 'changing prices' (which covers many aspects of the 'measurement' area—E) is an Accounting Standard, not a SFAC. Similarly, areas G and H (and possibly D and F) could lead directly to accounting standards (probably as well as concepts statements) if the conclusions produce recommendations specific enough for compliance to be monitored.

The progress so far in each of these areas of the conceptual framework is as follows (see also Figure 2 and Appendix II):

A.  SFAC1 was issued in November 1978 entitled 'Objectives of Financial Reporting by Business Enterprises'. SFAC4 on 'Objectives of Financial Reporting by Nonbusiness Organizations' was issued in December 1980. The Board has recently added to its agenda the topic of 'reporting the performance of nonbusiness organizations' in order to consider the types of information that meet the objectives in SFAC4.

B. SFAC2 'Qualitative Characteristics of Accounting Information' was issued in May 1980.

C. SFAC3 'Elements of Financial Statements of Business Enterprises' was issued in December 1980.

D. Two research reports have been published. 'Recognition of Contractual Rights and Obligations' by Professor Yuji Ijiri, published in December 1980, explores whether 'wholly executory' contracts should be reflected in the balance sheet as assets and liabilities (e.g. purchases ordered rather than purchased delivered) and suggests that a possible criterion of 'firmness of commitment' should be explored further in considering this question. 'Survey of Present Practices in Recognizing Revenues, Expenses, Gains and Losses' by Professor Henry R. Jaenicke surveys current practice and current financial accounting standards, and finds inconsistencies in the times at which these elements of income are recognized as between different industries and different circumstances, which development of the conceptual framework should eliminate. A Discussion Memorandum on the issues involved is planned by the Board for later in 1981.

E. The preface to the exposure draft 'Financial Reporting and Changing Prices', published in December 1978, commented that the proposed statement was 'based on the measurement phase of the Board's project on a conceptual framework for financial accounting and reporting' and that it drew on SFAC1. The statement of financial accounting standards (No.33) was published in September 1979. Four supplementary statements (Nos.39-41 & 46) dealing with specialized assets were issued in late 1980 and early 1981. Further significant conceptual work on measurement is not expected until experience is gained on the supplementary information required by these standards.

It may be noted that an exposure draft on foreign currency translation was issued in August 1980, which contains proposals to replace FAS8 (in particular proposing the use of current rates for all balance sheet items). It has not, however, been classified by FASB as part of the 'measurement phase' of the conceptual framework project. Public hearings were held in December 1980 and a revised draft is scheduled for later in 1981.

F.  An initial 'invitation to comment' on 'Financial Statements and Other Means of Financial Reporting' was issued in May 1980, raising issues about where information should be given in financial reports. The next steps are to be determined in the light of the comments received. Another part of this area focuses on reporting by small businesses and an initial discussion document is planned in 1981.

G.  A discussion memorandum on 'Reporting Earnings' was issued in July 1979, and public hearings were held in November and December 1979. Both 'concepts' and 'standards' statements may result from the project. The Board hopes to reach exposure draft stage in 1981 and an exposure draft will be issued after the public hearing on area H (which has been held in May 1981) covering both areas.

H.  A Discussion Memorandum on 'Reporting Funds Flow, Liquidity and Financial Flexibility' was issued in December 1980.

In summary, statements have been finalized on the 'objectives' of financial reporting by business enterprises, on the 'qualitative characteristics' of accounting information and on the 'elements' of the financial statements of business enterprises, while the accounting standards on 'changing prices' cover some of the measurement issues. There is also a standard on the 'objectives' of financial reporting by nonbusiness organizations. The areas of 'reporting earnings'; the distinction between 'financial statements' and other means of 'financial reporting'; and 'flow of funds, liquidity and financial flexibility' are presently still at the 'discussion' stage. In the remaining area, 'recognition criteria', so far only research studies have been issued. The Board is also considering what other topics in the area of nonbusiness reporting may need examination.

There follows an outline of some of the main publications in the development of the Board's 'conceptual framework'. Convenient summaries of the development of the project so far also appear in the Board's own 'Invitation to Comment' on 'Financial Statements and Other Means of Financial Reporting' (particularly at pages 1-16 and Appendix B), and in the background papers for the conceptual framework symposium held in June 1980.

## Area A

SFAC1: *Objectives of Financial Reporting by Business Enterprises.*
The statement deals with 'general purpose external financial reporting by business enterprises' (para.28) (called 'financial reporting' for short), i.e. the financial reports provided by the management/directors of businesses to 'external users'. In particular it addresses 'the informational needs of external users who lack the authority to prescribe the financial information they want from an enterprise, and therefore must use the information that management communicates to them' (para.28). 'The function of financial reporting is to provide information that is useful to those who make economic decisions about business enterprises and about investments in or loans to business enterprises' (para.16), or who 'base economic decisions on their relationships to and knowledge about business enterprises' (para.24). The information provided 'should be comprehensible to those who have a reasonable understanding of business and economic activities and are willing to study the information with reasonable diligence' (para. 34).

The potential external users identified are listed in paragraph 24 in no particular order, but in Figure 3(a) I have categorized them into main groups. The list is apparently not intended to be exhaustive.

These groupings I have used are of course not mutually exclusive. Investors read the financial press, the government is the owner (in the UK, if not in the USA) or main customer of many businesses and so on, but the groupings may help to show the basic similarity of approach to that adopted in other reports (see Figure 3(c)).

The financial information about a business that these potential users are considered to be interested in is its future cash flow 'because their decisions relate to amounts, timing, and uncertainties of expected cash flows' (para.25). The particular case of the decisions that have to be made by investors and creditors (existing and potential) is analyzed, and how cash flows to them ultimately depend on the cash flows to the businesses in which they have an interest. But the information they need 'is likely to be generally useful to members of other groups who are interested in essentially the same financial aspects of business enterprises as investors and creditors' (para.30). The prime objective is therefore identified in terms of 'financial reporting should provide information to help investors, creditors, and others assess the amounts, timing, and uncertainty of prospective net cash inflows to the related enterprise' (para.37). In other words, the criterion for selecting the contents of financial reports (i.e. for deciding what to disclose, how to measure and present the contents of the report, and at the end of the day, how to settle 'accounting standards') should be that the prescribed accounting procedures produce information that is useful in helping people predict the future cash flows of business enterprises.

The statement proceeds by arguing that what is needed to help people predict future cash flows is:

i) Information about an enterprise's economic resources, obligations and owners' equity, and 'the effects of transactions, events, and circumstances that change resources and claims to those resources' (para.40).

ii) (The 'primary focus of financial reporting') 'Information about an enterprise's performance provided by measures of earnings and its components', because investors and creditors often use evaluations of past performance in assessing the prospects of the enterprise (paras. 42-43). They find information about past earnings provided by accrual accounting a better indicator of an enterprise's performance than information about the past cash flows, although these may also be useful in 'understanding the operations of an enterprise, evaluating its financing activities, assessing its liquidity or solvency, or interpreting earnings information' (para.49). They may use reported earnings 'in various ways and for various purposes in assessing their prospects for cash flows from investments in or loans to an enterprise', e.g. to help them:

a) evaluate management performance (including
   'stewardship'),
b) estimate the 'earning power' of the enterprise,
c) predict future earnings, or
d) assess risk.

The information may help them confirm or revise their own or others' earlier predictions or assessments (para.47).

iii) The usefulness of financial information may be enhanced by management's explanations (para.54).

The statement ends by pointing out that the next phase of the Conceptual Framework project pertains to the 'elements of financial statements' (para.56).

It should be noted that subsequently the term 'comprehensive income' has been adopted for the concept called 'earnings' in this statement, as 'earnings' may be used for some part of 'comprehensive income' at a later stage of the project.

## *Area A*

SFAC4: *Objectives of Financial Reporting by Nonbusiness Organizations.*

This statement deals with 'general purpose external financial reporting by nonbusiness organizations' (para.10) (called 'financial reporting' for short) i.e. the financial reports provided by an organization to 'external users'. In particular, it focuses on the provision of 'information to meet the common interests of external users who generally cannot prescribe the information that is communicated to them by the organization' (para.10). 'Financial reporting by nonbusiness organizations should provide information that is useful to present and potential resource providers and other users in making rational decisions about the allocation of resources to those organizations. The information should be comprehensible to those who have a reasonable understanding of an organization's activities and are willing to study the information with reasonable diligence' (para.35).

Potential external users identified are listed in paragraph 29 of the statement, and again I have classified them in Figure 3(b). The classifications are again neither exhaustive nor mutually exclusive. Paragraph 29 identifies three groups (apart from managers) with a particular interest in financial reports: 'resource providers', 'constituents' and 'governing and oversight bodies'. The statement focuses on resource providers and their decisions in allocating resources to nonbusiness organizations, but argues that the information they want should be useful to other users as they 'share a common interest in information about the services provided by the nonbusiness organization, its efficiency and effectiveness in providing those services, and its ability to continue to provide those services' (para.38), and in information 'that is useful to present and potential resource providers and other users in assessing how managers of a nonbusiness organization have discharged their stewardship responsibilities and about other aspects of their performance' (para.40).

Therefore it is argued that what is needed is:

(i) 'Information about the economic resources, obligations and net resources of an organization and the effects of transactions, events and circumstances that change resources and interests in those resources' (para.43).

(ii) 'Information about the performance of an organization during a period. Periodic measurement of the changes in the amount and nature of the net resources of an organization and information about the service efforts and accomplishments of an organization together represent the information most useful in assessing its performance' (para.47). Information about resource flows 'measured by accrual accounting generally provides a better indication of an organization's performance than does information about cash receipts and payments' (para.50), although information about these should also be provided as they may be useful in 'understanding the operations of an enterprise, evaluating its financing activities, assessing its liquidity, or interpreting performance information provided' (para.54).

(iii) The usefulness of financial information may be enhanced by managers' explanations (para.55). It is also noted that as the ability to measure service accomplishments (particularly program results) is generally undeveloped, and research is needed to determine if satisfactory measures can be developed, then in their absence, information about service accomplishments may be furnished by managers' explanations and sources other than financial reporting. (The Research Report 'Reporting of Service Efforts and Accomplishments' surveys current practice in this area).

Overall, the statement comes to much the same conclusions as SFAC1 on the type of information that is wanted in financial reports. There is less emphasis on 'future cash flows' and 'earnings' (or 'comprehensive income'), and more on information about management stewardship. In addition there are the suggestions for inclusion of service output indicators (e.g. numbers of patients treated, fire alarms answered etc.) and measures of program results (i.e. the effectiveness of actions in achieving the goals of the organization in relation to its beneficiaries, or the problems it is attempting to deal with), which may include non-financial and non-quantified information.

The statement includes a comparison of the objectives for nonbusiness organizations with those in SFAC1 (para.67) and points out the difference in motive of resource providers to business organizations (who look for an economic benefit in return) and of resource providers to nonbusiness organizations, many of whom either expect no economic benefits in return or expect benefits that are not proportional to the resources provided, but are concerned rather with the efficiency and effectiveness of the organizations' activities.

Other important features of nonbusiness organizations that are normally of less significance in business organizations are the use of formal budgets and restrictions by donors in order to mandate spending on particular activities (so that compliance with these mandates is part of management's stewardship) (paras. 21-22). The statement does not, however, comment on any of the particular issues that often arise in applying accrual accounting to nonbusiness organizations, e.g. whether outflows of resources should be measured as expenses or expenditure; whether depreciation should be recorded; when resource inflows, such as taxes, grants and gifts should be recognised; or the extent to which 'restricted funds' should be accounted for separately. These are presumably 'recognition' matters that will be dealt with at a later stage of the conceptual framework project.

The Board's general conclusion is that 'it is not necessary to develop an independent conceptual framework for particular categories of entities'. 'Rather, its goal is to develop an integrated conceptual framework that has relevance to all entities and that provides appropriate consideration of any reporting objectives and concepts that may apply to only certain types of entities' (para.1).

## Area B
SFAC2: *Qualitative Characteristics of Accounting Information.*
This describes the characteristics or qualities of 'useful' information, (relevance, reliability, neutrality, understandability etc.) so as to provide criteria for choosing between alternative accounting and reporting methods or disclosure requirements. Other things being equal, the alternative which offers more of one of these desirable qualitative characteristics is to be preferred. However, it is recognised that this still leaves at least three types of problem:

1.   Where one alternative offers more of one desirable quality but less of another than the other alternative, so a 'trade-off' is needed (e.g. para.42).

2.   Where the importance of the characteristics to different users depends on their individual circumstances or preferences so that different users (or the same users in different circumstances) may find different alternatives more attractive. The Board has somehow to try and balance the needs of all the users of accounts (e.g. paras. 36-45).

3.   Where the benefits identified for the proposed method or disclosure may be outweighed by the costs imposed by requiring it. The assessment of such costs and benefits, and who will bear and enjoy them, is extremely complex and subjective, but the Board must recognize the need to undertake the discipline of attempting the assessment (para.144).

The statement develops a hierarchy of information qualities (see Figure 4(a)) with usefulness for decision making at its head. The two primary qualities are 'relevance' and 'reliability' and, subject (i) to the requirement that the benefits exceed the costs, and (ii) that the information is material (the two 'bands' across Figure 4(a)), the more relevant and reliable is the information, the more desirable it is. The statement then elaborates on what is meant by 'relevance' and 'reliability' and their subsidiary aspects which include timeliness, verifiability, representational faithfulness etc.—the list of qualities is broadly similar to those in other studies (see Figure 4(b)).

The statement argues that 'predictive value' and 'feedback value' are above all what distinguish relevant from irrelevant information, because what is needed to be useful for decision making is that the information improves decision makers' capacities to predict, or confirms or corrects their earlier expectations (para.51). Whether the information serves to confirm or change expectations, its value lies in altering the degree of uncertainty about the future that the decision maker faces (para.52). So relevant information is data, whether about the past, the present, or about other people's forecasts of the future, that the decision maker can use to improve his own forecasts about the future (para.48). Here is where the links between this statement and the view of the objectives for financial reporting set out in SFAC1 and SFAC4 are most strongly made.

The statement not only describes the desirable characteristics of accounting information (and the Board has tentatively concluded that they apply to nonbusiness organizations too (para.4)), but also mentions many of the difficulties in achieving or assessing these characteristics e.g. the need for experiment in finding out what may be useful information (para.50), despite the difficulties of assessing 'predictive value' in relation to human behavior (paras.54-55); the difficulties of achieving or assessing 'representational faithfulness' when one is dealing with amounts that require allocations (paras.65-67) or averaging (para.70), or that may be used in different contexts and at different levels of aggregation (para.71); and the difficulties of achieving or assessing reliability in an environment of uncertainty (para.97).

The statement also sets out, *inter alia*, the following guidelines for the Board's policy:

a)     'Conservatism' is a 'prudent reaction to uncertainty to try and ensure that uncertainties and risks inherent in business situations are adequately considered' (para.95). It should no longer connote 'deliberate, consistent understatement of net assets and profits' which is not consistent with the desirable characteristics described in this statement ('however well-intentioned'). But on the other hand, 'imprudent reporting, such as may be reflected for example in overly optimistic estimates of realization, is certainly no less inconsistent with those characteristics'. Thus, 'unjustified excesses in either direction' are unacceptable (paras.93 and 96).

b)     The concept of 'materiality' (essentially related to the size of an item) is strongly intertwined with those of 'relevance' and 'reliability' in individual circumstances, and the Board does not propose to issue any general quantitative materiality guidelines for broad application, although quantitative materiality criteria for individual standards may continue to be given where appropriate (para.131).

c)     The Board considers it important that accounting information should be 'neutral' (i.e. free from bias, and not chosen to favor some predetermined result, to encourage some particular type of behavior, or to promote the interests of some particular group). The Board seeks to be impartial in order to maintain the general credibility of financial reports (paras.98-110). Although it is important that they attempt to assess the likely economic impact of a proposed standard and try to monitor the impact of existing standards (extremely difficult though this is), they will not be aiming to promote any particular economic goals in selecting accounting methods and disclosure requirements (para.106).

d) Given the difficulties of assessing the costs and benefits of proposed standards, then 'before a decision is made to develop a standard, the Board needs to satisfy itself that the matter to be ruled on represents a significant problem and that a standard that is promulgated will not impose costs on the many for the benefit of a few' (para.143).

## *AREA C*

SFAC3: *Elements of Financial Statements of Business Enterprises.*
The statement gives definitions of ten elements of financial statements—'assets', 'liabilities', 'equity', 'investments by owners', 'distributions to owners', 'revenues', 'expenses', 'gains', 'losses' and 'comprehensive income'—all at a high level of generality (see Figure 5). The definitions are regarded as 'a significant first screen in determining the content of financial statements' (para.17), but they will need to be supplemented in two ways to become fully operational.

First, although the definitions describe characteristics which are necessary if things and events are to be represented in financial statements as assets, revenues etc., these characteristics are not sufficient to require inclusion. Thus, for example, assets are defined as 'probable future economic benefits obtained or controlled by a particular entity as a result of past transactions or events' (para.19). So anything which does not embody a probable future economic benefit etc. cannot be an asset—but not everything which does embody a probable future economic benefit etc. has to be shown as an asset. For this depends also on the rules and conventions for accounting 'recognition' (para.17), which will have to deal, *inter alia*, with questions about when the probability of economic benefit is sufficiently high for an asset to be included (para.40). Such 'recognition criteria' are to be dealt with in a later phase of the conceptual framework project. Similarly, the definition of an asset is not to be taken to imply anything about the way in which it is to be measured (whether at historical cost, current value etc.) as 'measurement' considerations too are dealt with in a separate phase (para.17)

Second, the definitions of revenues, expenses, gains and losses 'give broad guidance but do not distinguish precisely between revenues and gains or between expenses and losses. Fine distinctions . . . are principally matters of display in reporting' (para.73).

In the discussion of 'comprehensive income' no decision is reached about the appropriate 'capital maintenance concept', which may be chosen in relation to a definition of 'earnings' as part of the 'Reporting Earnings' phase of the project (para.58).

A number of related concepts and terms are also discussed and defined, and an appendix to the statement considers a number of examples from present practice and shows how the definitions apply to them. 'The Board emphasizes that the definitions . . . neither require nor presage upheavals in present practice, although they may in due time lead to some evolutionary changes in practice or at least in the way certain items are viewed' (para.102).

The Board also expects the definitions to be suitable for both business and nonbusiness organizations but expects to consider and to solicit views about what adaptations are needed, and whether other elements are needed, for financial statements of nonbusiness organizations (para.2).

## AREA D
Only preliminary Research Reports have been published as yet.

## AREA E
Statement of Financial Accounting Standards No.33: *Financial Reporting and Changing Prices.*
The standard was issued in September 1979. Its basic proposals are:
  i)   No change is to be made in the basic financial statements.
  ii)  Supplementary information is to be given on the following items:
       a) The income from continuing operations—both
          i) on a historical cost/constant dollar (general purchasing power) basis (i.e. similar to the CPP approach of the U.K.'s PSSAP7) and
          ii) on a current cost basis.
       b) The purchasing power gain or loss on net monetary items.
       c) Holding gains and losses (net of inflation).
       d) The current cost of inventory and of property, plant and equipment at the end of the accounting year. The current cost basis of these assets is essentially that of 'value to the

business' or 'deprival value' as recommended in SSAP16
in the U.K.

e) Five years' summaries of selected data are required,
restated into some common purchasing power.

The requirement for disclosure of this information applies only to
large public enterprises whose basic accounts show inventories and
property, plant and equipment (before depreciation) of 125 million
dollars or more, or total assets (after depreciation) of one billion
dollars or more. Other enterprises are encouraged to disclose it.

The relationship of the proposals to SFAC1 is discussed in the
introduction to the standard and its appendix C, which sets out the
basis for the conclusions arrived at. The main link is that 'deprival
value' in balance sheets, and the reporting of income on a current cost
basis (splitting operating profit and holding gains), is likely to improve
the prediction of future cash flows. The reasons for thinking this are
set out in appendix C, especially at paragraphs 116-123: thus the use
of current margins in the operating profit calculation may aid the
prediction of future margins, and a separate disclosure of holding
gains may improve the prediction of this element of income which
arises from the effect of different economic forces. Separation of
income into these two elements may therefore help the prediction of
future income.

Again current cost income may assist in assessing the extent to
which operating capacity has been maintained to earn future cash
flows. Similarly, it is argued that deprival values of assets are likely to
be more closely related to the value of future cash flows than are past
historical costs and generally that information about current costs
provides a more up to date basis for estimating future costs.

I do not propose to evaluate these arguments here—the disputes
over many of them are familiar from the debate on current cost
accounting in the U.K. It is however interesting to observe how the
current cost income measures and asset valuations are justified in
terms of their usefulness for predictive purposes i.e. in terms of the
objective identified in SFAC1.

Similarly, constant dollar (CPP) measures may provide a useful
basis for users to assess the impact of changes in the general price
level, and how these changes may affect the purchasing power of the
returns from their investment in the future (para.140).

However, it would be misleading to give the impression that all the explanations given for the recommendations made are based on such specific assumptions about the relationships between the required information and the prediction of future cash flows. Many of the arguments are the more general ones that are commonly used by supporters of the various methods of inflation accounting, such as the need for a common unit of measure and the need to show the effect of inflation on borrowing and monetary assets.

Indeed it is acknowledged that while many people regard relevance for the assessment of future cash flows as an argument favoring the use of current cost data, an important strength of historical cost/constant dollar (i.e. like PSSAP7) is its relative simplicity and its verifiability. The Board therefore hopes that the experiment of requiring both types of data will provide 'evidence of users' trade-off between relevance and reliability' (para. 149). It may be noted that the Board has not decided whether the 'financial capital maintenance concept' or the 'physical capital maintenance concept' is to be preferred (para. 104)—consideration of this question is now included in the project on 'Reporting Earnings' (Area G).

The decision to limit the 'changing prices' disclosures to supplementary data is explained in appendix C to the statement. It is argued that because people are familiar with historical cost accounting, and unfamiliar with inflation accounts, a change in the basic financial statements would be confusing and disruptive while the 'supplementary' approach allows for comparison between the new information and more familiar information and avoids the need to be so rigorous about specifying what is to be the 'standard' practice in the inflation accounts (para. 108).

Generally, the standard shows an 'experimental' attitude. It is recognized that there is a strong division of opinion on which type of reform is most useful (current cost or historical cost/constant dollar), and therefore requiring both will allow a better evaluation of the merits of the two methods. The Board intends 'to carry out research to answer questions such as the following: Which supplementary information is used? By whom it is used? How is it used?' They intend to allow up to five years to make these evaluations, but 'will amend or withdraw requirements whenever that course is justified by the evidence' (para. 115).

Two of the seven Board members dissented from the statement. Both were unhappy with the requirement to provide data on more than one basis—but one preferred current cost, while the other suggested historical cost/constant dollar (pages. 25-28).

## AREA F

Invitation to Comment on *Financial Statements and Other Means of Financial Reporting*.

An 'invitation to comment' on 'Financial Statement and Other Means of Financial Reporting' was issued on 12 May 1980. The bulk of it in fact comprises a useful summary of the development of the conceptual framework project to date; but the particular issues it raises are mainly concerned with the criteria for deciding *where* information should appear, and in particular whether an item should appear in the notes to the articulated financial statements or in supplementary information, and if the latter whether the supplementary information should accompany the financial statements or be available only on request.

It is pointed out that the work on elements of financial statements and the criteria for their recognition, when completed, will determine what appears in the articulated financial statements. As a consequence, the notes will then contain the additional and explanatory information needed to 'fill the gaps', such as explanations of accounting policies, details of aggregated items etc.

In addition, there may be other supplementary information required, depending on the criteria of 'relevance, reliability and cost' outlined in SFAC2.

Two main alternative approaches to demarcating 'notes' from 'supplementary' are suggested for discussion.

i) Recognizing that the methods chosen for preparing financial statements will reflect a particular 'perspective' (e.g. a historical cost approach to income and resource measurement), then the notes should contain the additional information needed to complete that picture, while supplementary information would include information from a different perspective such as current cost information. Or if financial statements contain the entity's own accounts, supplementary information could contain consolidated or segment reports.

ii) Alternatively, supplementary information could be regarded as the place for information that it would be too costly to include in financial statements, e.g. because the requirement for audit of its reliability would be inappropriate or too expensive. An example might be 'fair value of oil and gas reserves'.

The Board seeks comment on whether it should now attempt to prescribe what are to be the contents of financial statements and notes as opposed to supplementary information, or rather just lay down guidelines for dealing with particular items as they arise (and what these guidelines should be), and on whether a concepts statement is needed on this topic.

In general, the discussion paper is at an abstract level. It does not deal with any particular questions about what supplementary information is required in relation to individual matters, nor for example with how much should be given by way of management explanation of the accounts, as suggested in SFAC1 (para. 54).

## Area G

Discussion Memorandum on *Reporting Earnings*.

The memorandum raises issues for public discussion about the form and content of earnings reports, and points out that users are concerned because they 'perceive a need for additional information about the regular and irregular components of earnings as a basis for improved assessments of future earnings' (para.30). The document suggests a number of possible ways of giving more information about the various components of earnings (revenues, expenses, gains and losses), that might help users in assessing the 'regular' and 'irregular' elements and in understanding how earnings have varied under different conditions and are likely to vary in the future. Consideration is given to different ways of analyzing total earnings (including extension of segmental analysis for different lines of business), different ways of grouping items into sub-totals in the earnings statement and whether some items should be reported separately from current earnings, or as adjustments to retained earnings. The use of various ratios, percentages and of five-year summaries is also discussed, and comment is invited on whether the Board should undertake a project on the possibility of requiring the publication of managements' earnings forecasts.

In chapters 1 and 2 of the memorandum, there is an introductory exploration of the relationship between the need to improve the usefulness of earnings statements, and the prime objective for financial reporting identified in SFAC1, namely to help investors, creditors and others assess the amounts, timing and uncertainty of prospective net cash inflows to the enterprises in which they are interested. It is suggested that users could try and assess future cash flows from reports of past results either:

      a) by assessing them directly from a study of past cash flows, or

      b) by studying past earnings.

The memorandum argues that b) may be preferable because earnings reports attempt to relate the revenue of a period to the relevant expenses, which a statement of cash flows for a period does not. If b) is followed, a two-stage process is envisaged:

      i) reports of past earnings are used as a basis for the assessment of future earnings,

      ii) an adjustment is then made to the assessment of future earnings to derive an assessment of future cash flows.

Stage i) is the focus of this discussion memorandum. Stage ii) is to be considered in the project on funds flows and liquidity. A preliminary examination of the ways which the presentation of funds flow information might be improved, to assist users in understanding the relationship between the reporting of earnings and the timings of cash flows, is given in chapter 10.

Chapter 2 also argues that 'assessment of enterprise performance' is essentially a matter of estimating likely future cash flows. For measuring 'performance' really boils down to attempting to measure the increase achieved in the value of a business enterprise to the investors who own it—and the ideal measure of the value of an enterprise is the present value of its expected future cash flows. In a listed company, the return to its owners comes from the dividends they receive and the changes in the price of their shares. But the prices at which shares are quoted on the market may be regarded as estimates of the present values of future cash flows, based on information that is available to the public. In this context, 'the task of financial reporting may be seen to be the provision of information to enable the stock market values to be based on as efficient as possible an assessment of future cash flows' (para.48).

## AREA H

Discussion Memorandum on *Reporting Funds Flow, Liquidity and Financial Flexibility.*

The memorandum raises issues for public discussion concerning the provision of useful information about past funds flows, about liquidity (the 'nearness to cash' of assets and liabilities) and about 'financial flexibility' ('the ability of an enterprise to take effective action to alter the amount and timing of future cash flows so that it can respond to unexpected needs and opportunities' (para. 6)).

The potential usefulness of reports of past funds flows is discussed in terms of assisting the prediction of future cash flows and the identification of the relationship between income and cash flows; of providing 'feedback' for comparison with previous estimates of cash flows and of their relationship to income; and of providing more objective, comparable data about companies' performance than is provided by reporting income alone.

The document reviews current practice in presenting 'flow of funds' statements, and notes criticisms that confusion is caused by the compression of too much information into one statement and by the lack of a specific definition of the 'funds' on which the statement should focus. Alternative definitions of funds and alternative layouts and ways of analyzing and grouping flows (including possible extensions of segmental analysis for different activities; increased information about subsidiary and associated companies; the provision of summary ratios and percentages; and information about changes in asset or financial structure) are suggested.

The question of analyzing investment flows between expenditure for the maintenance and the expansion of operating capability is considered, and there is discussion of the impact of changing prices on operating, investing and financing flows. Their impact on the measurement of income has been dealt with in FAS33, but it is suggested here that there are also questions which arise in relation to flow of funds reporting. To use British terminology, questions of 'backlog depreciation', 'monetary working capital adjustments', 'gearing adjustments' and changes in the nature of replacement assets due to economic and technological change arise in assessing the funds needed for the maintenance of operating capability and the funds available for expansion and distribution.

Thus a number of topics familiar from the British debate on current cost accounting (but which are not reflected in FAS33) are dealt with here. It is noted that any possible new requirements to report the effects of changing prices on funds flows will only be considered in the context of reviewing the experimentation called for by FAS33.

In relation to liquidity, the memorandum asks whether changes are needed in the ways in which different classes of assets and liabilities are defined, grouped and presented, in order to give a better indication of the timing of cash flows associated with them, and what additional information (e.g. details of maturity dates and commitments; information about subsidiary and associated companies; and various ratios) might be given. The results of some empirical studies relating to the usefulness of ratios, and of other indicators obtained from existing reports, in predicting business failures are briefly described.

In relation to assessing 'financial flexibility' (a crucial determinant of the risk attaching to future cash flows) the memorandum identifies four key factors:

a)   the nearness to cash of investments
b)   the ability to obtain additional financing
c)   the amount of non-operating assets
d)   the ability to increase short-term funds flow by modifying operating and investing activities, including the ability to discontinue operations or sell operating assets (para.270).

A number of possibilities for giving information that would assist in assessing financial flexibility (and variations in it during the year) are suggested for comment, including information about borrowing facilities (and maximum and average borrowings outstanding during the year), credit ratings, and the separability and market values of assets; segregation of discretionary and non-discretionary expenses; and management comment and discussion of policy and plans.

Finally, some special matters relating to banks and insurance companies are considered.

## REFERENCES—APPENDIX I

1. M. Moonitz, Obtaining Agreement on Standards in the Accounting Profession, *op.cit.*

2. See the reference to SEC requirements in FASB documents:

   FAS33, 'Financial Reporting and Changing Prices', September, 1979.

   Invitation to Comment on 'Disclosures about Oil and Gas Producing Activities', May 13, 1981.

   Discussion Memorandum on 'Reporting Funds Flows, Liquidity and Financial Flexibility', December 15, 1980, chapter 10.

3. See for example A.J. Briloff, More Debits than Credits, New York: Harper & Row, 1976; The Truth about Corporate Accounting, New York: Harper & Row, 1980.

# Appendix II: Conceptual Framework Project

## PUBLICATIONS, TO 30 APRIL 1981, OF THE
## FINANCIAL ACCOUNTING STANDARDS BOARD

| | | |
|---|---|---|
| Jun 1974 | Discussion Memo. | Conceptual Framework for Accounting and Reporting: Consideration of the Report of the Study Group on the Objectives of Financial Statements. (20pp) |
| Dec 1976 | Discussion Memo. | Scope and Implications of the Conceptual Framework Project. (24pp) |
| | Discussion Memo | Tentative Conclusions on Objectives of Financial Statements of Business Enterprises (78pp) |
| | Discussion Memo | Conceptual Framework for Financial Accounting and Reporting: Elements of Financial Statements and Their Measurement. (360pp) |
| Dec 1977 | Exposure Draft | Objectives of Financial Reporting and Elements of Financial Statements of Business Enterprises. (v + 44pp) |
| May 1978 | Research Report | Financial Accounting in Nonbusiness Organizations: An Exploratory Study of Conceptual Issues, by Robert N. Anthony. (xviii + 205pp) |
| | Research Report | An Overview of the Research Report on Financial Accounting in Nonbusiness Organizations. (7 pp) |
| Jun 1978 | Discussion Memo. | Conceptual Framework for Financial Accounting and Reporting: Objectives of Financial Reporting by Nonbusiness Organizations. (10pp) |
| Jul 1978 | Research Report | Economic Consequences of Financial Accounting Standards, Selected Papers. (ix + 278pp) |
| Nov 1978 | Statement of Financial Accounting Concepts | No.1: Objectives of Financial Reporting by Business Enterprises. (x + 31pp) |

| Dec 1978 | Exposure Draft | Financial Reporting and Changing Prices. (v + 72pp) |
| Mar 1979 | Supplementary Draft | Constant Dollar Accounting (24pp) |
| Jun 1979 | | Financial Reporting and Changing Prices: The Conference, ed. P.A. Griffin. (ix + 242pp) |
| Jul 1979 | Discussion Memo. | An Analysis of Issues Related to Reporting Earnings. (v + 105 pp) |
| Aug 1979 | Exposure Draft | Qualitative Characteristics: Criteria for Selecting and Evaluating Financial Accounting and Reporting Policies. (viii + 53pp) |
| Sep 1979 | Statement of Financial Accounting Standards | No.33: Financial Reporting and Changing Prices. (iii + 127pp) |
| Dec 1979 | | Illustrations of Financial Reporting and Changing Prices: Statement of Financial Accounting Standards No.33. (iii + 112 pp) |
| | Exposure Draft (Revised) | Elements of Financial Statements of Business Enterprises. (x + 99pp) |
| Mar 1980 | Exposure Draft | Objectives of Financial Reporting by Nonbusiness Organizations. (x + 27pp) |
| Apr 1980 | Exposure Draft | Financial Reporting and Changing Prices: Specialized Assets. (57pp) |
| May 1980 | Invitation to Comment | Financial Statements and Other Means of Financial Reporting. (49pp) |
| | Statement of Financial Accounting Concepts | No.2: Qualitative Characteristics of Accounting Information. (xvi + 73pp) |
| Oct 1980 | Statement of Financial Accounting Standards | No.39: Financial Reporting and Changing Prices: Specialized Assets—Mining and Oil and Gas. (30pp) |
| Nov 1980 | Statement of Financial Accounting Standards | No.40: Financial Reporting and Changing Prices: Specialized Assets—Timberlands and Growing Timber. (11pp) |
| | Statement of Financial Accounting Standards | No.41: Financial Reporting and Changing Prices: Specialized Assets—Income-Producing Real Estate. (13pp) |
| | Special Report | Examples of the Use of FASB Statement No.33, Financial Reporting and Changing Prices. (vi + 167pp) |
| | Research Report | Reporting of Service Efforts and Accomplishments, by P.K. Brace, R. Elkin, D.D. Robinson, and H.I. Steinberg, of Peat, Marwick, Mitchell & Co. (xii + 114pp) |

| | | |
|---|---|---|
| Dec 1980 | Statement of Financial Accounting Concepts | No.3: Elements of Financial Statements of Business Enterprises. (xiii + 80pp) |
| | Statement of Financial Accounting Concepts | No.4: Objectives of Financial Reporting by Nonbusiness Organizations. (xiv + 37pp) |
| | Discussion Memo. | Reporting Funds Flows, Liquidity and Financial Flexibility. (vi + 141pp) |
| | Research Report | Recognition of Contractual Rights and Obligations: An Exploratory Study of Conceptual Issues, by Yuji Ijiri. (vii + 92pp) |
| Jan 1981 | Research Report | Survey of Present Practices in Recognizing Revenues, Expenses, Gains and Losses, by Henry R. Jaenicke. (vii + 165pp) |
| Feb 1981 | Exposure Draft | Financial Reporting and Changing Prices: Motion Picture Films. (3pp) |
| Mar 1981 | Statement of Financial Accounting Standards | No.46: Financial Reporting and Changing Prices: Motion Picture Films. (3pp) |

The Board also publishes 'Public Records' (in bound volumes or on microfiche) which contain copies of the comment letters it has received, or transcripts of the public hearings it has held. The volumes published specifically in respect of the Conceptual Framework project are:

1974 Volume VIII—Discussion Memorandum on Conceptual Framework for Accounting and Reporting (in two parts).

1977 Volume VIII—Discussion Memorandum on Conceptual Framework for Financial Accounting and Reporting: Elements of Financial Statements and Their Measurement (in four parts).

— Transcript of the conceptual framework symposium held in June 1980, and of the background paper prepared for symposium participants.

# Appendix III: The Corporate Report

This discussion paper was prepared for ASC (then the Accounting Standards Steering Committee) by a study group under the chairmanship of Derek Boothman, FCA, with the assistance of members of the International Centre for Research in Accounting at Lancaster University, and of the technical directorate of ICAEW, and published for comment in July 1975. It runs to 103 pages (including appendices).

The paper itself contains a clear five-page summary of its main conclusions and proposals and as these are now very well known, this appendix gives only a brief overview of the way in which the arguments are developed.

The study is concerned with 'the fundamental aims of published financial reports and the means by which these aims can be achieved' (para.0.1) and uses the term 'corporate report' to indicate that it is concerned not just with the 'basic' financial statements (such as the audited balance sheet, profit and loss account and flow of funds statement) but with the 'comprehensive package' (including other statements and illustrative material) which describe an organisation's 'economic activity' (para.0.2). Consideration is given to three main areas: the types of organisation that issue the reports; the main users of that information and their needs; and the form and frequency of the reports that will best meet those needs.

In Part I, the study begins by stressing the need for corporate reports to be useful to users and argues that there is an implicit responsibility to report publicly ('public accountability') incumbent upon every economic entity whose size or format renders it significant. This would extend public accountability for example to 'significant' partnerships and unincorporated businesses (and suggested tests of significance are offered in Appendix I to the paper). Further research is recommended in the area of public sector accounting. The type of reporting being considered is general purpose reporting for general purpose uses (i.e. not special purpose reports that those with a right to obtain specialised information can call for). Users are those with 'a reasonable right to information concerning the reporting entity' and the groups of users are identified. It is acknowledged that it is impractical to suggest that all needs of users could be entirely met by such general purpose reports, and that judgment will be needed in balancing conflicts of interest (e.g. where confidential information is involved).

The paper proceeds by discussing the basis of the rights of different user groups and their information needs (see Figure 3(c)). Considerable overlap of interest is identified and the list of needs given includes items like evaluating the performance of an entity; assessing the achievement of its objectives; assessing its economic stability and vulnerability; assessing its liquidity and flexibility; estimating its future prospects; making economic comparisons over time or with other entities; estimating the economic performance, position and prospects of its individual establishments and/or constituent companies; estimating the value of users' interests in the entity; estimating the economic performance of the entity in relation to society and the national interest; ascertaining details about its ownership and control, its management and its products; and assessing compliance with appropriate laws and regulations (Section 2).

On this basis the conclusion is reached that 'the fundamental objective of corporate reports is to communicate economic measurements of and information about the resources and the performance of the reporting entity useful to those having reasonable rights to such information' (para.3.2). To achieve this purpose they must be relevant, understandable, reliable, complete, objective, timely and comparable (para.3.3) (see Figure 4(b)) and the meaning of these characteristics is discussed. Practical constraints include the cost of providing them and confidentiality. 'The interests of users in general are unlikely to be served if information is published which is against the national interest or seriously prejudicial to the continued existence of the reporting entity' (para.3.15).

The study then reviews existing requirements and trends in recent legislation, and points to evidence that the chairmen of the U.K.'s largest companies no longer think of corporate objectives solely in terms of 'earning profits' or even mainly in terms of 'profit for shareholders'. Given this acceptance of multiple responsibilities, it is suggested that additional performance indicators are needed, in particular 'non-monetary' indicators of performance of non-commercially oriented concerns and information that would give insight into entities' employment policies, use of human resources, and contribution to national efficiency (Section 4).

Part II of the study considers the 'measurement and method' aspects of achieving these aims, discusses ways to improve communication and publication methods and considers frequency and distribution of reports (Section 5). Additional statements are proposed beyond those currently provided including a statement of value added, an employment report, a statement of money exchanges with government, a statement of transactions in foreign currency, a statement of future prospects (showing likely future profits, employment and investment levels) and a statement of corporate objectives. In addition, research into methods of 'social accounting' is called for and an extension to disaggregated reporting of different classes of activity within an entity (Section 6).

Finally, consideration is given to the concepts and measurements employed in the 'basic financial statements'. Their likely contribution to the user needs previously identified is commented on, and the two main aspects of difficulty in preparing them are discussed. First, there is consideration of the purpose and nature of profit measurement. It is argued that the main concern should be 'measurement of performance' but a second purpose is that of 'capital maintenance and income distributability' and that it is 'important to appreciate that these are distinct aspects', given the absence of perfect measures of wealth due to the risk and uncertainty involved in the treatment of uncompleted transactions. This often leads to conflict in the application of accounting concepts, in particular, conflict between the concepts (as set out in SSAP2) of 'matching' or 'accruals' (which is performance oriented) and of 'prudence' (which is orientated towards the needs of those, e.g. loan creditors, concerned with assessing the economic stability and vulnerability of entities). In cases of conflict, 'prudence' prevails. it is therefore suggested that these two different needs would each be better met by having a more rigorous application of the relevant one of these two principles. The performance measures would be improved if 'realities were not distorted by the need to observe cautious accounting precepts' (para.7.14).

Second, measurement bases are discussed together with the inadequacies of historical cost accounts in a period of rapidly changing prices. It is considered essential that a standard unit of measurement is used, so that general purchasing power adjustments are required (para.7.16). A brief examination is then given of historical cost, CPP and various current value approaches to accounting i.e. replacement cost, net realisable value, net present value and value to the firm, and Appendix 5 to the paper contains a matrix giving assessments of the usefulness of these different approaches for different purposes. The conclusion is that a number of different bases are likely to be useful and therefore that research should be undertaken into the feasibility of 'multi-column' reporting (particularly the presentation problem) to supplement the basic historical cost accounts (para.7.40), and into a workable and standardised system of current value accounting (para.7.43).

# Appendix IV: The Sandilands Report

This Report was prepared by a Committee of Enquiry, appointed by the Chancellor of the Exchequer and the Secretary of State for Trade and Industry and chaired by Francis Sandilands (later Sir Francis Sandilands). It was submitted on 25 June 1975 and published in September that year, running to xvi + 364 pages (including appendices). The committee's principal term of reference was 'to consider whether, and if so how, company accounts should allow for changes (including relative changes) in costs and prices'. It was also asked to consider the likely economic consequences of changing accounting methods, in various areas such as investment and management decisions and company efficiency, the allocation of resources through the capital market, the implications for taxation and the need to restrain inflation. In undertaking this study, the committee carried out a wide ranging review of the function of published accounts and, for present purposes, the main aspects of interest in the Report (the recommendations of which are well known), seem to be the following :

1)   The introduction comments that 'accounting . . . is essentially concerned with events that are past, and while it may form a basis for assessing what may happen in the future, it is not its function to make direct predictions about future events' (para.27).

2)   'The task of accounting is to measure a company's 'net assets' at a particular date and its gain or loss during a particular period. In order to be meaningful these measurements need to be expressed in terms of a common unit' (para.62). 'An accounting system . . . is intended to measure the extent to which resources or income have been created by the activities of a company. There are many different ways of measuring the assets and liabilities of a company at a particular date, or the income arising during a particular

period . . . but some ways of measurement may be more useful than others from the point of view of meeting the requirements for information of different users of accounts' (para.64).

3) 'No clear cut distinction exists between those gains which may be regarded as profit and those that may not. 'Profit for the year' is a practical business concept used as a guide for prudent decision making by companies. It may usefully be defined as the amount of the total gains arising in the year that may prudently be regarded as distributable. It is thus a subjective concept . . . ' (para.95). 'The practical purpose of the concept of profit is to ensure a company does not prejudice its future by distributing too much of the gains arising during the year . . . Thus any definition of profit . . . implies a consequent concept of capital which the company considers should be maintained intact' (para.96). Hicks's well known definition of income is examined. A measure of this that is believed to be ideal in a world of certainty (the change in the discounted net present value of future cash flows arising during a period) is considered and various possible 'approximations' that can be made in a world of uncertainty are discussed (paras.97-143) ' . . . they are all equally 'correct' . . . Some will be more useful than others in certain circumstances . . . ' (para.137).

4) 'The requirements of users of accounts should be the fundamental consideration in deciding the information to be disclosed in company accounts' (para.144). Following examination of the needs of a number of user groups (see Figure 3(c)) and consideration of their particular interests in assessing a company's performance and its future prospects and in making comparisons over time and with other companies, the general conclusions are drawn that in a useful accounting system:

i) The unit of measurement used as the basis for company accounts should as far as possible meet certain specified criteria set out in para.149. It is argued that the monetary unit is preferable to the 'purchasing power unit' on these grounds (paras. 207 and 409-415).

ii) 'There is a requirement for information on the historic cost of net assets and on their current 'value' on a number of different bases. The dominant requirement is probably for information on the 'value to the business' of net assets' (para.199). 'In the majority of cases, this will be their written down current replacement cost (or current purchase price) but may in some cases be their net realisable value or 'economic value'.' (para.201).

iii) 'Liabilities should be measured generally on the same basis as assets, although in practice this may cause difficulties' (para.201).

iv) ' . . . a concept of 'operating profit' . . . appears to be more useful to many users of accounts than other concepts of profit . . . Nevertheless, information on the extent of holding gains and extraordinary gains made during the year is useful to many users of accounts and should be shown' (para.199).

v) 'There is a common requirement by most users of accounts for information on a company's liquidity position' (para.199). 'A cash flow statement for the year should be attached to the accounts. It is essential for cash flow forecasts to be prepared for internal purposes although they need not be published' (para.201).

vi) 'Accounting statements, as far as possible, should meet seven general qualifications: objectivity, realism, prudence, comparability, consistency, intelligibility and ease and economy in preparation' (para.201). (See Figure 4(b).)

In arguing for the usefulness of 'operating profit' for shareholders and investors, it is noted that 'the stock market value of the company's shares is . . . affected by a large number of different factors which may be either inside or outside the company's control.

'Accounts cannot tell shareholders what these factors are, nor help to quantify them. These are matters for shareholders to judge for themselves and it is the essence of the stock market that different investors will make their individual assessments of the future and will act accordingly. However, in making such assessments of the future, the results of past periods given in a company's accounts are potentially a useful source of information. Investors would undoubtedly like to see accounts drawn up in a form which provides the most satisfactory basis for assessing the future prospects of a company—a quality which has been described to us as 'predictive ability'.

'No accounting system can predict the company's future prospects. However, an accounting system can at least ensure that a profit figure reported is such that, if the profit for the year were fully distributed, it would not prejudice the ability of the company to continue to generate the same profit in future years if revenues earned and costs incurred in future years were the same as in the year of account. Such a form of presentation of information is useful in any situation where future possibilities need to be forecast . . .

'This concept of profit is identical to operating gains' (as defined) (paras.164-167).

5)   On this basis, proposals for current cost accounting are then developed. First, there is a review of 'historic cost accounting' which notes, *inter alia*, that depreciation charges, although usually based on a known and very reliable figure (the historic cost of the assets), depend on three variable factors: the estimated residual value, the estimated useful life and the particular depreciation convention chosen (para.258); that there may be allocation problems in arriving at historic costs of individual assets (page 73, footnote 2); that there is considerable scope for the exercise of subjective judgment and alternative bases of accounting in other areas; and that the ASSC has begun studying the need to introduce greater standardisation (para.268), but that 'Despite the significant element of subjectivity in historic cost accounts, they provide a sound basis for comparing different companies when prices are stable . . . and the ability to compare the results of different periods in a meaningful way . . .' (para.270). They are intelligible and cheap (para.271). But with steeply rising prices 'the effect on historic cost accounts is so significant that the question arises whether their advantages are outweighed by their disadvantages' (para.274).

6)   Possible modifications to historic cost accounts are considered and rejected, as is the CPP method. Here it is noted that the evidence submitted to the committee 'revealed more support for the CPP method than for any other method of inflation accounting' (para.400) and that 'surveys of opinion among companies have shown a majority in favour of the CPP method' (para.401). However, this result is attributed at least in part to the fact that the CPP method is the only one 'defined in a single readily available document (SSAP7)' and the committee notes

increasing opposition to the proposals since the date of its own questionnaire (para.404).

7)   Various value methods are reviewed, and it is noted that 'the difficulties involved in the process of valuation should not be underestimated. A significant difficulty arising is that the value of an asset considered in isolation may be different from its value considered as part of a group of assets with which it operates' (para.462). A footnote here points out 'The practical problems arising in estimating the value of an asset are often related to such problems of aggregation, while problems associated with the ascertainment of historic cost are typically associated with disaggregation (see footnote 2 to page 73)'.

8)   Next, consideration is given to the fact that, although so far the study has been considering income measurement, there are some 'who take the view that the debate over the years between these various methods has merely emphasised that there is no such thing as an objective 'correct' measure of income and financial position appropriate to all companies, and that any accounting system based on a particular definition of business income will inevitably allow scope for arbitrary and subjective judgment and lead to inconsistencies between the accounts of different companies. It is argued that as a result of these difficulties the concept of 'income' or 'profit' is unsuitable as a basis for attempting to assess the financial position of a company. Support has, therefore, grown . . . for a return to a system of accounting . . . in terms of cash' (para.512).
        Certain attractive features of reporting past cash flows are considered (in particular objectivity and simplicity) but the committee feels constrained by the requirements of the Companies Acts to provide a balance sheet and a profit and loss account, observing that 'despite its subjectivity users of accounts still require a useful measure of the profitability of a company for practical purposes' and that the thesis of the Report is that 'historic cost accounts do not meet this requirement at the present time and there is therefore a need for the profit and loss account and balance sheet of a company to be drawn up on a more useful basis'. Abandonment of these and the substitution of a statement of cash surplus or deficit for a period would not 'fully meet the requirements for information of users of accounts . . . In addition, to be of most use a cash flow accounting system would need to incorporate cash forecasts, possibly based on different assumptions about future

changes affecting the company. We doubt whether such a fundamental change would be acceptable to British companies at the present time' (para.517). However, the argument that the (past) cash flow statements could, at least initially, appear as supplementary is acknowledged (para.514) and in view of the vital need to consider liquidity, as well as profitability, the importance of stating the company's cash position and of preparing internal forecasts of cash flow for the following year is stressed (para.518).

9)   The Report then proceeds to the development of current cost accounts (recommending that these should become the basic accounts, with certain historic cost figures in notes) (para.519) and discusses some other topics relating to their introduction.

# Appendix V: The Stamp Report

The Canadian Institute of Chartered Accountants (CICA) published a research study in June 1980 on 'Corporate Reporting: Its Future Evolution' written by Professor Edward Stamp, FCA, Director and Endowed Research Professor at the International Centre for Research in Accounting, Lancaster, England. It runs to 107 pages and is 'intended to provided a Canadian solution to the problem of improving the quality of corporate financial reporting standards' but it is hoped that it will be useful elsewhere too (ch.1, para.3). It is confined to the 'financial statements, subject to audit, that are published by Canadian public companies' (ch.1, para.19).

The final chapter 'examines some of the major implications of the Study—although readers are warned that it is in no sense a summary of the analysis and argument of the Study. It is necessary to read the whole of the Study in order to appreciate the significance of its proposals' (ch.1, para.11).

This makes it correspondingly more difficult to provide a précis that does justice to the author's intention, but the central pattern of development is I think fairly clear, although there are other themes and ideas that appear in various places in the study.

In chapter 1 the study begins by discussing the problems facing standard setters and notes the efforts currently being devoted to the 'conceptual framework' project by the FASB. 'The British have displayed some interest in the notion of establishing a conceptual framework but they have yet to make any material commitment of resources to such a project' (para.16).

The problems identified include the public criticisms voiced of individual standards and the relationship of standard setting to action by governments and international bodies (such as the UN, the OECD and the EEC). The need for accounts to be useful is stressed (para.22) and then attention is given to a number of problems about the purpose and nature of accounting which are to be discussed in the study.

i) How is 'economic reality' to be measured when the measurement of value is ambiguous, and it is the 'estimate of the benefits that we shall derive from an asset in the future (ultimately, in economic terms, in the form of cash flows) that determines its value to its owner today', so that it is 'impossible to divorce the past from the present and the future when the accountant attempts to measure past performance'? (paras.25 and 26).

ii) Should we therefore regard accounting as an art, a social science (like law), a natural science, an axiomatic discipline like mathematics or a language? (paras.27-32). (Chapter 9 later adds the possibility of a 'technology'). 'How best to develop accounting standards cannot be properly answered until we have considered the nature of accounting itself' (para.32) and asked whether indeed there are any permanent and universal underlying concepts in accounting (para.33).

iii) Considering the usefulness of accounting will require an assessment of user needs, establishing criteria for judging the quality of accounting standards and recognising the difficulties of calculating costs and benefits and of potential conflicts of interest between the preparers and users of accounts and between different user groups (which is why accounting standards and auditing are needed). Can standards resolve these conflicts of interest by achieving 'neutrality'? (paras.36-45).

iv) Criticisms of individual standards and of adequacy of disclosure are common but what are the implications of the 'efficient market' evidence about the importance of accounting disclosure and measurement to the stock market? Are published statements of any use at all for predictive purposes? Are they too complex so that they cannot be understood? (paras.48-50).

v) Should there be extensions to disclosure? Should these include forecasts? (paras.52-55).

vi) Given that accounting standards are generally regarded as necessary to 'narrow the areas of difference' in financial reporting, is such an increase in uniformity possible? If not, why not? If it is, how do we avoid stifling legitimate innovation, the risk of lack of response to changing conditions and the danger of substituting a 'book of rules' for professional judgment? (paras.56-59).

vii) Should indication be given of the 'margin of error' in preparing accounts, rather than the illusion of precision? (paras.60-62).

viii) Are 'general purpose reports' enough? Do we need more than one basis of valuation? Do we need supplementary information for different user groups? And should this be presented in the main financial statements (e.g. in additional columns) or in supplementary statements? (para.63). (Chapter 8 adds the possibility of reports available on request.)

ix) The need for standards to acquire sufficient consensus to be authoritative indicates that the process of standardisation is 'essentially a political one' which requires awareness of the attitudes of preparers and users to the quality of the standards. In addition, what means of enforcement are necessary? It is noted that Canada is unique in that the accounting recommendations issued by CICA effectively have the force of law under the provisions of the Canada Business Corporations Act (paras.64-66).

Having identified the important issues that are to be dealt with it is emphasised that it is impossible to produce final answers to many of them and that some previous solutions will be considered and rejected. Nevertheless 'Chapter 10 outlines what is believed to be a practical way out of the quagmire of doubt and confusion which now appears to surround the accounting standards program. But there is no final answer that can be reached in one fell swoop, and those who are looking for such an answer should read no further in this Study' (para.67).

Before developing his proposals, Professor Stamp sets out in chapter 2 some 'perplexing conceptual issues' which explain 'why it is that accounting, so often and so mistakenly thought of as an exact discipline, is frequently forced to make choices that would have taxed the judgment of Solomon. As argued later in this Study, accountants and those who read their reports might often be better off if the alternatives were openly displayed and the reader left to make his own judgment as to which of them best suits his needs.' (para.1). Under this head, he discusses:

a) Allocation problems—the process of chopping up into arbitrary periods the consequences of continuing business and financial operations; of disaggregating results to various activities; and of attempting to split joint costs in arriving at individual assets and liabilities; is 'arbitrary' or 'incorrigible' and the problems not only have not been solved, but are probably insoluble (paras.4-13). Nevertheless it is necessary 'to develop systematic and (as far as possible) rational methods of making allocations' for both internal and external reporting purposes (para.9).

b) Income problems—should profit be measured indirectly by comparing the net assets in two balance sheets or directly by matching costs and revenues? (paras.13-16).

c) Reporting focus—should the proprietorship concept (which 'looks at the financial affairs of an enterprise through the eyes of its owners') or the 'entity' concept (which views them 'from within, as it were') be used? (paras.17-23).

d) Problems of which capital maintenance concept is to be used e.g. 'financial' or 'physical' (it is argued that this is related to problem (c)) (paras.24-42).

e) What valuation basis is to be used for assets (e.g. historical cost, replacement cost, net realisable value or value to the firm)? (paras.33-37).

In relation to each of these problems it is argued that the suitable approach depends on the perspective and needs of the users and their circumstances and in relation to some of them that 'it is not either necessary or even possible to make an arbitrary choice that will be appropriate for all users' (e.g. para.32).

Finally,

f) The problem of 'what is economic reality' is raised again, emphasising here the impossibility that a balance sheet can ever measure the current worth of an enterprise. This is the 'goodwill' problem which is 'almost certainly irresolvable' (para.41).

In conclusion, it is pointed out that the main purpose of this review has been 'to indicate that many of the perplexing problems of accounting are indeed irresolvable in the sense that a unique solution is neither possible nor necessary' (para. 41).

The next chapter (Chapter 3) deals with the need for accounting standards and 'the central role played by accounting standards in the development and future evolution of a satisfactory system of corporate reporting' (para.1). The important factors that are mentioned include the separation of ownership and management and more generally the interests of many external groups in the affairs of a company and their concern with how the management reports these, and the confidence they need to have in the fairness and reliability of the financial statements on which they rely. 'Accounting standards deal mainly with the system of financial measurement and disclosure used in producing a set of fairly presented financial statements. They can thus be thought of as a system (and ideally an internally consistent system) of measurement and disclosure rules' (para.8). 'They also draw the boundaries within which acceptable conduct lies and in that, and many other respects, they are similar in nature to laws' (para.10).

It is argued that different users have competing economic interests and accounting standards are an important mechanism to help to resolve these conflicts. 'It follows that it is essential that accounting standards should command the greatest possible credibility among all of these different groups' (para.18), and strike the right balance between them (para.20).

Next, the 'overall purpose of published financial statements' is considered (para.22). While it is acknowledged that the information in annual reports may contain little that is not already known (at least to the stock market), the annual accounts and the rules for drawing them up provide 'financial benchmarks' against which other information can be assessed, confirmed and legitimised and also determine the form in which interim announcements and reports are made (paras. 23-26).

They are useful as a basis for decisions and actions by users, assisting them in formulating future expectations, e.g. for investment and lending decisions (para.27). Similarly, they are used for settling taxes and bonus payments; as an important part of the record of a company's progress and its management's stewardship; and influence many aspects of social and government policies e.g. taxation policy, government grants and subsidies etc. (paras.28-29).

The standards used in their preparation therefore must be of the highest possible quality (para.30) and will include not only disclosure requirements but 'of equal if not greater importance are the measurement standards that ensure that published financial reports 'tell what really happened' ' (para.31). It is noted, however, that 'predictive ability' is not a criterion for judging the quality of measurement standards—this point is to be discussed later in detail (paras.32-33). 'The function of good accounting is to provide, as input, the most reliable and accurate measures of the results of what has happened in the past' (para.32).

The need for enforcement and the analogy of law is referred to again (para.36) and then some consideration is given to 'the fact that there are certain elements in the community who object to, or question the need for, such standards' (para.39), citing first managements' concern for freedom to report in the way they think best and their fears that standards may threaten the competitive position of their company or be unduly costly to implement (so consideration of cost/benefit aspects is crucial in setting standards) (paras.40-47); second, resistance of accountants to the tendency to substitute 'books of rules' for professional judgment and the danger of stifling innovation (so that standards should be 'floors' not 'ceilings') (paras. 48-50); and third, the implications of the evidence of research into the U.S. stock market on the 'efficiency' with which new information is impounded into stock prices, which is interpreted as showing firstly that the market has already discounted the effects of any new information in published accounts by the time they reach investors, and secondly that the market 'cannot be fooled by changes in accounting methods' (such as switching depreciation methods) 'provided that sufficient information is provided in the form of notes, etc., so that adjustment can be made by readers to the non-reported method.' This suggests at first sight that it is a waste of time to develop standards designed 'to narrow the areas of difference' in accounting methods (paras.51-55). But, it is argued, full disclosure could just mean swamping people with material that they could not make use of; that there are other users beside investors in efficient stock exchanges and they need 'an expert determination of income and value figures for the enterprises in which they are interested'; and anyway that 'it is now recognised that the validity of the ['efficient markets'] hypothesis is dependent upon a general disbelief in it' and that though it may be shown that share prices are quick to respond to information 'it is impossible to say whether the response is reasonable' and thus whether share prices are at their 'real value'. So without sufficient explanation of the behaviour of the stock market, it is impossible to use the 'efficient markets hypothesis' 'to make any rational correlation between its findings and the problem of deciding how much (or how little) standardisation is really necessary in the published financial reports of corporations' (paras.56-62).

So following the first three chapters, which have given an introductory survey of the problems of, but need for, standard setting, the following five chapters undertake the development of the main theme of the study's recommendations, considering in turn objectives, users, user needs, criteria for the quality of accounting and how to cope with differences between the needs of different users and changes in them. This leads to two further chapters covering the appropriate means for developing a conceptual framework and the proposed framework that the study itself offers. Two final chapters form a 'coda' in which are discussed possible extensions of disclosure and the major implications of the study.

In relation to objectives, 'the first thing to be emphasised is that it is not possible to define the objectives of corporate financial reporting in one sentence, or even in a single paragraph, and the attempt will not be made in this chapter' (ch.4. para.4). However, chapter 5 (para.1) offers 'the primary if not sole objective of such standards—namely to ensure that the legitimate needs of users are properly met.' It is thought that the objectives of reporting apply to all users and will not change radically as users or their needs change (ch.4 para.6) but they may vary as between countries because the usefulness of measures derived from markets will vary with the economic system that prevails (para.7). It is pointed out that the main reason for defining the objectives is 'to assist in the process of devising adequate means for achieving them' (para.10) and then the importance of accounts (along the lines of previous chapters) is reaffirmed, as is the need for 'credibility' which will depend in part on meeting the qualitative criteria that are to be specified and on achieving a consensus or general acceptability (paras.11-16). Given an environment of uncertainty and risk it is an objective of good financial reporting to 'minimise uncertainty about the validity of the information, and to enable the user to make his own assessment of the risks associated with the enterprise' (para.19). Cost/benefit factors must be considered. Sufficient accommodation to innovation and change must be allowed for, and financial reports must, as far as possible, show the 'underlying economic reality' (paras.21-25). The objectives also need to specify the authoritative backing needed to ensure compliance (para.26). Given the complexity of the affairs with which accounts deal, they cannot be expected to be comprehensible and explicable to 'laymen' without misrepresenting reality and oversimplifying complexity, so they should be aimed at sophisticated users or expert advisers (paras.27-35).

In chapter 5, attention is next given to the users, and to general consideration of the legitimacy of their claims for information (and therefore to the 'accountability' of management) and the need for balancing on the other side rights to and needs for privacy (for example where information might put a company at a competitive disadvantage) (paras.1-23). A range of fifteen user groups is proposed for consideration which 'is much broader than that being considered by the FASB in the United States in its efforts to develop a Conceptual Framework' (para.24) (See Figure 3(c).) In chapter 6, there is discussion of their needs in similar terms to those set out in the Corporate Report and the Sandilands Report (see Appendices III and IV). It is emphasised that 'one of the most difficult problems in developing accounting standards arises from our ignorance about . . . the rational (and often irrational) mental processes that users go through in reaching their decisions' (para.5).

Chapter 7 then develops and defines qualitative criteria (see Figure 4(b)) as 'yardsticks whereby standard setters, as well as preparers and users of published financial statements, can decide whether . . . published financial statements are indeed meeting the needs of users and the objectives of financial reporting' (para.4). It is recognised that the criteria may conflict, that some are more important than others and that, being qualitative, judgement is needed in assessing both the extent to which some proposed procedure meets any given criteria, and their relative importance (paras.8-10). In using them a standard setter should first decide (and announce in the published standards) 'which user groups the standard is intended to cover, and it should then use the . . . criteria in order to satisfy itself that the standard is in fact compatible with the various users' needs and is optimal in the way in which it steers a path between the often opposing requirements of the various criteria' (para.7). 'Because of the qualitative and essentially subjective nature of many of the decisions that have to be made, it is essential to stress at this stage the fact that even the criteria developed below cannot be expected to produce final answers to all of our difficulties in standard setting. It is futile to look for some sort of accountant's philosopher's stone that will miraculously produce golden answers to all our questions' (para.13).

Thus, it hoped that the standard setters will use the criteria when deciding on the best solution in developing an inflation accounting standard, but users' satisfaction will be determined by their own individual (and therefore different) assessments of the importance of the various criteria and in fact 'it is largely because different user groups do have different needs and different criteria that a consensus in favour of a move by the profession towards inflation accounting tends to break up once a specific solution has been proposed' (paras.14-15). Hence 'general acceptance' is necessary too, which requires, *inter alia*, leadership, education and training (paras.73-75).

It is also noted that any information which does not conform to the criteria should be 'excluded' (para.16).

Chapter 8 then considers the problem of the different needs of different users and first suggests that improvements in computer technology may enable users to have direct access to company data, but then argues that accounting standards will still be needed to govern the way in which the data is organised, measured and presented, and similarly accountants will be needed to guide users as to what data they need and how to interpret it (paras.4-7). It is then argued that different measures (particularly different bases of valuing assets) seem to be relevant for different users and different needs so consideration needs to be given to providing them all (in the light of the qualitative criteria) which raises the question of whether, as there are correspondingly several different useful measures of income 'one is correct in some absolute sense and the others merely variants, or whether each measure is of roughly equal validity' (para.21). 'The short answer to this is that it depends entirely upon user needs, and the decision models users employ (that determine their needs). So little is known about these matters at present that it is impossible to give an unequivocal answer to the question. What is, however, quite certain is that it is the profession that should deal with the problem of defining income, since the alternative will be for the government to step in with arbitrary definitions (as already exist in determining taxable income). Such arbitrariness will certainly not provide an optimal response to the various criteria defined in the previous chapter' (para.22), so the private sector standard setters must develop acceptable standards and 'it is the function of this Study to aid the standard setters in performing their function (not to usurp their responsibility for doing so)' (para.23).

More generally it is argued that 'accountants must cease to believe that all of the financial complexities of a modern public corporation can be captured and portrayed by one set of figures prepared on what would necessarily be an arbitrarily selected measurement basis' (para.28). There is a need for more supplementary information and the 'efficient market' evidence indicates that the market would not be swamped or unable to absorb it. There can be multi-column presentation, supplementary statements, supplementary reports available on request (which may be better in avoiding confusion for unsophisticated readers, although against this is the convenience and cheapness of putting everything under one cover)—experiment is needed to find what is best and how far standards should apply to the supplementary information (paras.29-44). It may well be worth producing a 'benchmark' statement that is based on the aims of precision, uniformity and objectivity to satisfy users whose main need is for these qualities and also to show that these qualities are often only obtainable at the expense of relevance and reality (paras.37-39).

Chapter 9 then turns aside briefly to ask what the nature of accounting is and in particular to discuss the underlying economic reality with which it has to deal; the extent to which a more scientific approach might be useful in developing accounting standards; and the shortcomings of current efforts (particularly by FASB) to develop a conceptual framework.

The similarities and dissimilarities of accounting to a number of other intellectual disciples are described (as outlined at (ii) under chapter 1 above), and further consideration is given to 'what we mean by economic reality which presumably is what accounting attempts to measure and interpret' (para.15). Observations made earlier are reviewed again—thus it is pointed out that almost all measurements of economic reality (apart from cash itself) are of abstract ideas and require subjective assessment; that the allocations made in accounting measurements are arbitrary and therefore may or may not reflect user needs: and that although accountants are concerned with measuring the past and the present, as all values ultimately reside in the future, their measurements require assessments about the future. It is argued that laying down rules for systems of measurement in an authoritative fashion is unlikely to be successful as the rules will be arbitrary and fail to meet user needs. It would be better to offer several different measures to reflect the variety and complexity of economic reality.

It is also pointed out that there is 'behavioral feedback'. For example, values depend on people's expectations which are in turn influenced by, *inter alia*, the making of accounting measurements so that a measurement of value may itself alter people's expectations and thus the value it seeks to measure (paras.15-32).

There is also a discussion of the extent to which accounting can be 'scientific' and the role of 'prediction' (paras.10-12 and 33-45). Professor Stamp's conclusion seems to be that scientific method is inapplicable in accounting and one cannot use 'predictive ability' as a criterion for judging the usefulness of accounting standards.

In the remainder of this chapter, consideration is given to the manner in which a conceptual framework for accounting should be developed, and reference is made to the FASB's project. It is argued that such a framework 'must proceed from a set of definitions of the basic consistuent elements of the set of financial statements (assets, liabilities, revenues, expenses etc.)'. But, given different user needs, which may require different approaches to reporting these elements, the definitions have to be at a very high level of generality to accommodate all legitimate user interests and thus run the risk of being 'so nebulous as to be of little value in producing or deducing answers to specific problems' (paras.46-48). It is noted, *inter alia*, that for definitions, say of assets, to be complete they must state not only the necessary qualities for something to be an asset, but also what collection of qualities is sufficient to make it in asset; and again, that definitions such as those being adopted by FASB (e.g. for assets) are inadequate because they do not explain whether an asset must be severable from the enterprise or not (which will affect for example the treatment of goodwill and research and development expenditures) nor the level of aggregation at which an asset is to be identified (a separate 'dry hole' is not an asset to an oil company but the whole exploration programme taken together, which may include the digging of what prove to be dry holes, is). Alternatively, there is considerable danger that definitions will merely 'define away' the main accounting controversies, and then the arguments over standards will just shift from arguing about the specific accounting problems to arguments about the definitions from which the particular standards are deduced, so that the promise of 'consistency' that is held out by those who argue for the need to settle definitions first is illusory. Alternatively, they may become authoritarian and arbitrary, and thus lose their utility in relation to the aim of measuring economic reality (paras.51-64).

What is needed, rather, is an approach to a conceptual framework that is based on 'utilitarianism' rather than 'authoritarianism' (paras.64-68).

Then, in chapter 10, it is argued that while FASB's approach may be suitable for the U.S.A., it is not for Canada. It is too normative (if not axiomatic) and too narrow in its scope (as its primary concern is with investors) (para.1). So after a comparison of some aspects of the history of the U.S.A. and Canada (paras.2-8) the study offers a conceptual framework for Canada (and elsewhere) which it is argued exhibits an evolutionary (rather than revolutionary) approach to standard setting and is based on the objectives of financial reporting— 'the primary consideration being to ensure that the contents of financial reports meet all the reasonable needs of the legitimate users of such reports' in accordance with the qualitative criteria that have been developed. In addition, there must be public justification and explanation of the basis of standards to win general acceptance and the proposals must be based on intelligent thinking, against a respected conceptual background, supported by adequate research, and with adequate arrangements for monitoring implementation and ensuring responsiveness to the needs of preparers and users (paras.9-11).

A number of practical considerations are mentioned and it is suggested that this evolutionary approach will minimise the danger of the 'rule book' attitude, and also reflect the need for accounting standards to be more than a technical matter as their role is in resolving conflicts. They are therefore more like the Law, and it is argued that the approach being recommended is similar to that of the evolution of the Common Law, so that consideration needs to be given to setting up a kind of accounting court ('a Board of Review') to whom auditors could turn to establish precedents (and possibly some system whereby businesses could appeal from a decision) (paras. 17-46).

Chapter 11 then considers areas where disclosure might be extended, including accounting for price changes; forecasts; the need to explain which capital maintenance basis is being used and whether the proprietorship or entity concept has been adopted; the possibility of indicating 'margins of error' in the accounts; and of providing statements of cash flow. It is also noted that anything which is 'not useful' should be dropped from existing accounts.

Chapter 12 ('major implications of this study') highlights again some of the points that have already been made about the way in which the standard setting body should use the conceptual framework that the study offers, and concludes by recommending further research a) to monitor changing user needs; b) to assess the extent to which some of the suggestions for further disclosure are useful; c) to investigate and experiment with multi-column reporting; and d) to attempt to develop knowledge of user decision processes.

## FASB CONCEPTUAL FRAMEWORK
## FOR FINANCIAL ACCOUNTING AND REPORTING

*ACCOUNTING*          *REPORTING*

ELEMENTS [C]          FINANCIAL
STATEMENTS
FINANCIAL
REPORTING [F]

*OBJECTIVES*
[A]

RECOGNITION [D]          EARNINGS [G]

MEASUREMENT [E]          FUNDS FLOW,
LIQUIDITY
AND FINANCIAL
FLEXIBILITY [H]

*QUALITATIVE CHARACTERISTICS* [B]

Source:
Based on Figure 6 in FASB Discussion Memorandum, 'Financial Statements and Other Means of Financial Reporting' (May 12 1980).

Figure 1

# FASB TECHNICAL PLAN
## As of April 1, 1981

| | 1981 by Quarter | | | 82 | 83 |
|---|---|---|---|---|---|
| | 2 | 3 | 4 | | |
| **MAJOR PROJECTS \*** | | | | | |
| | | | | | |
| Conceptual Framework | | | | | |
|   Accounting Recognition Criteria for Elements | | M | | | |
|   Measurement of the Elements of Financial Statements | | | | | |
|   Reporting Earnings | | E | | F | |
|   Funds Flows, Liquidity, and Financial Flexibility | H | E | | F | |
|   Financial Statements and Other Means of Financial Reporting- | | | | | |
|     Small and Closely Held Business Enterprises | | M | | | |
|   Reporting the Performance of Nonbusiness Organizations | | | | E,H | F |
| Foreign Currency Translation | E | | F | | |
| Employers' Accounting for Pensions- | | | | | |
|   Phase One | | H | T | | |
|   Phase Two | | | | M,E,H | F |
| Rate Regulation | | E | | F | |
| Disclosures about Oil and Gas Producing Activities | M | E | H | | |
| Specialized Principles- | | | | | |
|   Entertainment Industry | E | | F | | |
|   Insurance Industry | | E | | F | |
|   Real Estate Industry | | E | | F | |
|   Mortgage Banking Industry | | E | | F | |
|   Investment Companies | | E | | F | |
|   Revenue Recognition When Right of Return Exists | | F | | | |
|   Product Financing Arrangements | | F | | | |
| | | | | | |
| **IMPLEMENTATION AND PRACTICE PROBLEMS\*** | | | | | |
| | | | | | |
| FASB Statement 19 (Oil and Gas) | | | | | |
|   Exploratory Wells | F | | | | |
| FASB Statement 33 (Changing Prices) | | | | | |
|   Mutual Funds | B | | | | |
| FASB Statement 34 (Interest Cost) | | | | | |
|   Equity Method Investees | E | | F | | |
| APB Opinion 18 (Equity Method) | | | | | |
|   Criteria for Applying the Equity Method | F | | | | |
| Other Issues | | | | | |
|   Shared Appreciation Mortgages | E | | F | | |
|   Transfers of Receivables with Recourse | E | | F | | |
|   Related Party Transactions | B | | | | |

Figure 2

*Background and additional information regarding plans for each project is provided on pages 3-7. Next steps on projects for which future plans have not yet been determined also are discussed on those pages. Additional issues that are presently under consideration by the staff are listed on page 7.

Codes
B — Board to consider adding project to its agenda
E — Exposure Draft of a Statement or of an Interpretation
F — Final Statement or final Interpretation
H — Public hearing
M— Discussion Memorandum or other initial document, such as an Invitation to Comment
T — Tentative Board conclusions on issues in the first Discussion Memorandum

Source: FASB STATUS REPORT No. 114, April 1981

Figure 2 (cont.)

USERS (other than management)

SFAC1 (para.24)

*Suppliers of Capital and their Representatives or Advisers*
Owners
Lenders
Potential Investors
Creditors
Financial Analysts and Advisors
Brokers
Underwriters
Stock Exchanges

*Suppliers of Labor and their Representatives or Advisors*
Employees
Labor Unions

*Business Contacts*
Suppliers
Customers
Trade Associations

*Government Agencies*
Taxing Authorities
Regulatory Authorities
Legislators

*Others*
Lawyers
Economists
Financial Press and Reporting Agencies
Business Researchers
Teachers and Students
The Public

Figure 3(a)

USERS (other than management)

SFAC4 (para.29)

*Resource providers and their Representatives or Advisors*
Members
Contributors
Grantors
Taxpayers
Lenders
Suppliers
Creditors
Employees
Financial Analysts and Advisors
Brokers
Underwriters
Trade Associations
Labor Unions

*Constituents*
Service Beneficiaries

*Governing and Oversight Bodies*
Directors and Trustees
Regulatory Authorities
Legislators

*Others*
Taxing Authorities
Lawyers
Economists
Financial Press and Reporting Agencies
Researchers
Teachers and Students

Figure 3(b)

## USERS (other than management)

| *CORPORATE REPORT* (para.19) | *SANDILANDS REPORT* (para.147) | *STAMP REPORT* (Table 1: p.44) |
| --- | --- | --- |
| Equity Investor Group | Shareholders | Shareholders |
| Loan Creditor Group | Investment Analysts | Creditors, long and short-term |
| Employee Group | The City (Stock Exchange, etc.) | Analysts and Advisers |
| Analyst - Adviser Group | Creditors and Lenders | Employees |
| Business Contact Group | Other Companies | Non-Executive Directors |
| Government | Employees | Customers |
| Public | The Government and official bodies | Suppliers |
|  | The general public | Industry Groups |
|  |  | Labour Unions |
|  |  | Government Departments and Ministers |
|  |  | Public |
|  |  | Regulatory Agencies |
|  |  | Other Companies |
|  |  | Standard Setters and Academic Researchers |

Figure 3(c)

## QUALITATIVE CHARACTERISTICS - SFAC2

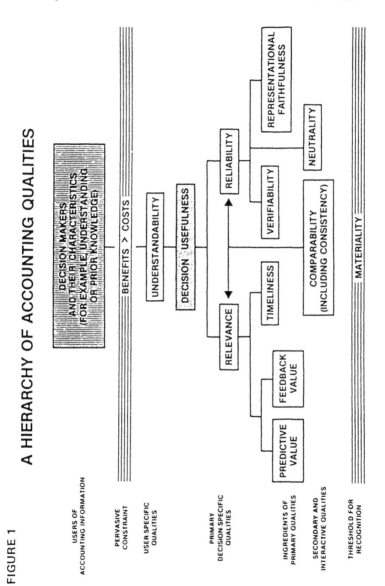

FIGURE 1

A HIERARCHY OF ACCOUNTING QUALITIES

USERS OF ACCOUNTING INFORMATION

PERVASIVE CONSTRAINT

USER SPECIFIC QUALITIES

PRIMARY DECISION-SPECIFIC QUALITIES

INGREDIENTS OF PRIMARY QUALITIES

SECONDARY AND INTERACTIVE QUALITIES

THRESHOLD FOR RECOGNITION

DECISION MAKERS AND THEIR CHARACTERISTICS (FOR EXAMPLE, UNDERSTANDING OR PRIOR KNOWLEDGE)

BENEFITS > COSTS

UNDERSTANDABILITY

DECISION USEFULNESS

RELEVANCE

RELIABILITY

PREDICTIVE VALUE

FEEDBACK VALUE

TIMELINESS

VERIFIABILITY

REPRESENTATIONAL FAITHFULNESS

NEUTRALITY

COMPARABILITY (INCLUDING CONSISTENCY)

MATERIALITY

Figure 4 (a)

## QUALITIES

| *CORPORATE REPORT* (para 3.3) | *SANDILANDS REPORT* (para.231) | *STAMP REPORT* (Table 3, p.55) |
|---|---|---|
| Relevance | Objectivity | Relevance |
| Understandability | Realism | Comparability |
| Reliability | Prudence | Timeliness |
| Completeness | Comparability | Clarity |
| Objectivity | Consistency | Completeness (full disclosure) |
| Timeliness | Intelligibility | Objectivity |
| Comparability | Ease and economy in preparation | Verifiability |
| | | Precision |
| | | Isomorphism |
| | | Freedom from bias |
| | | Rationality |
| | | Non-arbitrariness |
| | | Uniformity |
| | | Substance over form |
| | | Materiality |
| | | Cost/benefit effectiveness |
| | | Flexibility |
| | | Data availability |
| | | Consistency |
| | | Conservatism |

(Subject to cost and
confidentiality,
para.3.15)

Figure 4(b)

# SFAC3—ELEMENTS OF FINANCIAL STATEMENTS OF BUSINESS ENTERPRISES

## *HIGHLIGHTS*

### *[Best understood in context of full Statement]*

Elements of financial statements are the building blocks with which financial statements are constructed—the classes of items that financial statements comprise. The items in financial statements represent in words and numbers certain enterprise resources, claims to those resources, and the effects of transactions and other events and circumstances that result in changes in those resources and claims.

This Statement defines 10 interrelated elements that are directly related to measuring performance and status of an enterprise. (Other possible elements of financial statements are not addressed).

Assets are probable future economic benefits obtained or controlled by a particular entity as a result of past transactions or events.

Liabilities are probable future sacrifices of economic benefits arising from present obligations of a particular entity to transfer assets or provide services to other entities in the future as a result of past transactions or events.

Equity is the residual interest in the assets of an entity that remains after deducting its liabilities. In a business enterprise, the equity is the ownership interest.

Investments by owners are increases in net assets of a particular enterprise resulting from transfers to it from other entities of something of value to obtain or increase ownership interests (or equity) in it. Assets are most commonly received as investments by owners, but that which is received may also include services or satisfaction or conversion of liabilities of the enterprise.

Distributions to owners are decreases in net assets of a particular enterprise resulting from transferring assets, rendering services, or incurring liabilities by the enterprise to owners. Distributions to owners decrease ownership interests (or equity) in an enterprise.

Comprehensive income is the change in equity (net assets) of an entity during a period from transactions and other events and circumstances from nonowner sources. It includes all changes in equity during a period except those resulting from investments by owners and distributions to owners.

Revenues are inflows or other enhancements of assets of an entity or settlements of its liabilities (or a combination of both) during a period from delivering or producing goods, rendering services, or other activities that constitute the entity's ongoing major or central operations.

Expenses are outflows or other using up of assets or incurrences of liabilities (or a combination of both) during a period from delivering or producing goods, rendering services, or carrying out other activities that constitute the entity's ongoing major or central operations.

Gains are increases in equity (net assets) from peripheral or incidental transactions of an entity and from all other transactions and other events and circumstances affecting the entity during a period except those that result from revenues or investments by owners.

Losses are decreases in equity (net assets) from peripheral or incidental transactions of an entity and from all other transactions and other events and circumstances affecting the entity during a period except those that result from expenses or distributions to owners.

Figure 5

(III)

# THE FASB'S CONCEPTUAL FRAMEWORK—VISION, TOOL OR THREAT?

Richard Macve

Rice University and the University College of Wales, Aberystwyth

Presented at the Arthur Young Professors' Roundtable, May 7, 1983

# The FASB's Conceptual Framework— Vision, Tool or Threat?

## INTRODUCTION[1]

It is difficult to get a grip on the "conceptual framework," so I was grateful that when Sandy Burton invited me to give this paper he also suggested the title. The paper is divided into the following sections:

(A) VISION. Here I first present the conclusions of my study [Macve, 1981] for the British Accounting Standards Committee (ASC)[2] , and then ask what drives the Financial Accounting Standards Board (FASB) to expend so much more effort on this type of project than do the standard setting bodies in other countries. I review some developments elsewhere and then concentrate on two "imperatives"— the major intellectual tradition in U.S. accounting and the strength of the political pressures to develop "accounting principles." I argue that together they have diverted attention from the major problems of achieving comparability in accounting.

(B) TOOL. Here I look at how the FASB's project has been, and may be, used in tackling problems of standard setting, in stimulating research, in influencing education, and in reinforcing the authority of the FASB.

(C) THREAT. Here I comment on some dangers that may lurk in the attempt by an "official" body like the FASB to develop a conceptual framework, in so far as it tries to go beyond the rather modest aims discussed under (B). I argue that it is important, now that the project is tackling recognition and measurement issues, to develop understanding of why the objectives and concepts that have been adopted are not able to provide clear guidance on how to solve accounting problems.

(D) CONCLUSION.

# (A) VISION

The search for a conceptual framework for accounting has often been likened to the search for the Holy Grail [e.g., Watts, 1981]—the visionary quest that inspired the knights of King Arthur's Round Table.[3] The FASB's conceptual framework project has an able champion in David Solomons, one of the preeminent knights of the Arthur Young Roundtable, who has recently entered the lists again to persuade the laggardly British to spurn the doubters and defeatists (among whom he names myself) and devote much greater energy and resources to these fundamental issues [Solomons, 1983].

Solomons gives an authoritative perspective on developments in both the U.S.A. and Britain, and the kernel of his argument seems to be the following:

a) In making recommendations or setting standards, the professional bodies in the U.S.A. and Britain must have had at least an *implicit* conceptual framework, or else they would not have been able to issue series of statements exhibiting any consistency over time. If progress is to be made, it is important to try to make explicit this governing framework of thought—which Solomons characterizes "loosely" as the "recoverable cost" model. In the U.S.A. there has been far more effort to do this [Storey, 1964]. As Solomons occasionally expresses a preference for movement away from the present model to a model incorporating "current values," I infer that he sees one valuable consequence of making the present model explicit to be that it should bring about a fundamental reevaluation of its merits.

b) The development of a coherent theoretical basis for accounting standards is an important, even if not complete, defense against "political" interference in standard setting. Standards that can be shown to be consistent with an agreed set of objectives (objectives which, he accepts, may differ to some extent from country to country) and are thereby seen to be "neutral" (i.e. not biased in favor of any vested interests) are less vulnerable to manipulation to achieve particular political aims—manipulation which, in the end, can only undermine the credibility of financial statements.

I therefore view the search for a conceptual framework when undertaken by an "official" standard setting body like the FASB, from two perspectives:

(1) It is an intellectual inquiry—a process of exploring the rational foundations of accounting practice to suggest where and how improvements and developments may be made.

(2) It is a "legitimizing" process—a demonstration that the standard setting body does have a unique technical expertise which is necessary, if not sufficient, to justify its exercise of authority over those affected by its decisions. This may help to reduce opposition to its standards and the chances of their being overruled, or taken over, by a higher authority.

## The Macve Report

The ASC asked me for a kind of feasibility study [Macve, 1981] in order to decide how to respond to the demands it had received for research to be undertaken into developing a conceptual framework (some of these demands are quoted in Solomons [1983], Tweedie [1981] and Zeff [1981]).

The general conclusion of my study (which has not been adopted by the ASC as an official view) was that many people (at least in Britain, even if no longer in the U.S.A.) were probably expecting too much of what developing a conceptual framework might offer. This could distract attention from important questions that do need to be considered.[4]

I reviewed the difficulties of drawing clear conclusions for accounting practice either from attempts to refine the notions about income ("profit") and wealth ("net assets") that underlie present practice, or from examination of how financial reports can best provide "useful information." I urged the importance of identifying and considering accounting "problems" within a wide context of consideration of objectives and likely consequences, but doubted whether much could be said in general about the answers to the problems raised.

My conclusions as to the likely pay-off to the ASC of undertaking a conceptual framework project were, albeit in much simplified terms, essentially in line with the views of SOATATA [AAA, 1977] on the main lines of development of and the state of agreement on accounting theory; with those of Dopuch and Sunder [1980] on the discernible achievements of the FASB's project in relation to decisions on accounting practice; with those of Beaver [1981] on the ambiguities in relation both to the choice of information and to the role of regulation that are implied by the orientation of the FASB's conceptual framework to "providing useful information"; and with those of May and Sundem [1976] on the role of accounting theory and research in policy formation. I would claim nothing new for my study. However, like Peasnell [1978], I saw no need to call on the "paradigm conflict" adduced by SOATATA to explain the difficulties of reaching agreement on accounting theory. By Occam's Razor[5] explanations should be kept as simple as possible, and there seems to be a sufficient explanation for the difficulties in the ambiguities and ultimate subjectivity of the notions of "income" and "wealth"; and in the conflicts of view, conflicts of purpose, and conflicts of interest that arise in relation to providing "useful" information in an uncertain world of many individuals and organizations.[6] Moreover, many, if not all, of these difficulties were at least suggested, and often emphasized, in SFAC2 [FASB, 1980a].

It would be pointless now to attempt to go back to the early days of the project and try to assess what expectations were originally held by the Board or its constituents—but it seems clear that if there was any visionary quality to belief in its importance, it should have been dispelled by what the project has been able to achieve. The expectations that I consider can be realistically held, I will discuss in section (B).

The project has taken a large amount of resources—in my report (p. 95) I quoted Michael Alexander's comment in June 1980 that the project was occupying approximately 40% of the staff's effort, and noted that the Financial Accounting Foundation's annual expenditure was approaching US $8 million. (In 1982, the total was $8.5 million [FAF *et al.*, 1983, p. 13].) The resources applied elsewhere have been minuscule by comparison (e.g., my report cost the Institute of Chartered Accountants in England and Wales (ICAEW) about £2,500).

Dopuch and Sunder [1980] ended their review by suggesting that:

> "Perhaps we can achieve more progress by developing and testing theories regarding why a major part of the responsibility for standard setting continues to lie with a private agency, and why members of the profession and corporate managers continue to contribute time and money to the process of developing a conceptual framework. It is unlikely that a general fear of government regulation alone can account for the latter."

Their "latter" question is the question of interest to me here—and of course it is asked in the context of the U.S.A. Before sketching some tentative answers it is worth making some comparisons between the FASB's project and the development of related work in other countries.

## Other countries

Standard setting bodies outside the U.S.A. also face demands to develop a conceptual framework and have sponsored studies. In preparing my report for the ASC, I was able to look at the "Stamp report" prepared for the Canadian Institute [CICA, 1980] as well as the "Corporate Report" [ASSC, 1975] in Britain. Summaries of those reports are included in Chapter 8 and the appendices of Macve [1981]. My conclusion was as follows:

> "So far as the development of a 'conceptual framework' is concerned, it is difficult to see that the conclusions offered by these various reports (including FASB's project and the many other similar studies that have preceded them) go much beyond listing the conceptual problems and stating the common sense view that accounting must be useful; that it is about the financial affairs of individuals and organisations, whether business or 'nonbusiness', and that one must respect the interests and rights of the different individuals and groups who have an interest in their financial affairs, so that accounting policies and standards must be practicable and acceptable' [Macve, 1981, p. 71].

Since then a report has been published by the Australian Accounting Research Foundation (AARF) [Barton, 1982]. The author's preface notes that its origin dates back to 1975:

> "A watershed had been reached in the development of accounting standards by conventional pragmatic methods, and the need for a new approach using the normal analytical methods of the sciences was acknowledged. This recognition of the need for the development of a conceptual framework for accounting and financial reporting occurred at much the same time in Australia, the United States and the United Kingdom" (p. iv).[7]

There is not space in this paper for me to give an extensive review, but I have included a brief synopsis in Appendix II. Generally, the study adopts a structure similar to the FASB's project but places greater emphasis on the links between financial and management accounting, giving equal emphasis to the "decision making, control and accountability" functions of accounting. While it endorses the continued presentation of the familiar financial statements (income statement, balance sheet, and flow of funds statement), it rejects historical cost based systems and favors systems based either on current entry prices or current exit prices. It is too early to judge its impact, but it will surely be controversial.

With respect to the Canadian report,[8] Peasnell [1982] comments:

> "It is too early to form a view on the profession's reactions to Stamp's proposals. Initial reactions have focused, in the main, on the case made by Stamp that Canada needs a CF appropriate to its particular cultural and institutional needs; some commentators take the view that the most cost-effective line for the Canadian profession and business community to take is simply to adopt the FASB's standards except when clear and compelling local concerns dictate otherwise."

In Britain, the Corporate Report had limited impact.[9] This was partly because it was overshadowed by the Sandilands [1975] report (issued only a few months later), partly because it spent little time on "the fundamental problem of measurement of profit" which (as the foreword by the ASSC's chairman, Sir Ronald Leach, made clear) is *the* important problem in the eyes of accountants, and partly because it was regarded by some as "politically" suspect, as it proposed new criteria of accountability and extension of disclosure requirements beyond those of company law.

Since my report was published in 1981, the only explicit activity until now that I am aware of has been research conducted by Professor Stamp with the cooperation of the ASC to attempt to establish rankings of accounting systems based on ASC members' scoring of them in relation to the qualitative characteristics identified in CICA [1980] and members' rankings of these characteristics [e.g., Stamp, 1983]. However, ICAEW's Director of Research, Professor Bryan Carsberg (formerly on the FASB's staff), has recently announced a 2-3 year research program which is to include projects on "Needs of users of financial reports" and "Guidelines for decisions in financial reporting."[10]

In comparing the activity in the U.S.A. with that taking place elsewhere, it is important to remember that to many people the most important issue in the conceptual framework has been "Inflation Accounting." The debates over how to cope with changing prices have opened up many more fundamental questions. In the U.S.A., the FASB has always classified the work on FAS33 [FASB, 1979] in its Technical Plans (published in its "Status Report") as part of the conceptual framework project.

In several other countries, a major public examination of these issues has been undertaken by government-appointed committees. Britain had Sandilands, Australia the Mathews Report, and New Zealand the Richardson Report. In Canada the provincial government of Ontario also established a Committee on Inflation Accounting [Alexander, 1977]. All recommended current cost accounting disclosures (see Bell [1982] and Gynther [1982] for discussion and references). The resulting British standard permits the current cost accounts to be the main accounts [ASC, 1980, para. 28] (Sandilands had envisaged them replacing the historical cost accounts [1975, para. 541].)

In Britain, this standard is "experimental" and still highly controversial, so that research in this area has occupied the most effort related to the conceptual framework. As the FASB's project has not produced any statements since December 1980 (other than supplements to FAS33), there is probably a feeling in Britain that it is sensible for the ASC to "wait and see" before committing substantial further effort to other aspects of the conceptual framework.

The FASB's project is therefore unique in at least two respects:

a) Except for the area of inflation accounting, it is the only project where the standard setting body has gone beyond sponsoring research studies to adopting conclusions and issuing statements.

b) It is the only project of this kind that has been able to draw on such an extensive input from its "constituencies" in terms of comment letters, public hearings, conference participations, etc. It is doubtful whether one could expect a similar degree of participation in such matters elsewhere. Even though progress has been perceived to be slow, the Board has been able to find considerable support for its efforts [e.g., Kirk, 1981].

What inspires such a commitment? Why should the commitment be stronger in the U.S.A. than elsewhere? In drawing some contrasts which may be relevant I will deal mainly with Britain, in which I have direct experience, and try to distinguish "intellectual" from "political" influences.

## Intellectual tradition

Solomons [1983] comments on the disparity between the size of the academic accounting profession in the U.S.A. and in Britain as a factor in explaining why there has been little intellectual push so far on the ASC to develop a conceptual framework—British accountants do not have much intellectual tradition. Indeed, even now the great majority of new British accountants do not receive their accounting education in a university course, unlike the typical American accountant [Solomons, 1981, Appendix B] who may therefore be more amenable to the view that academic inquiry and debate can contribute to the resolution of accounting problems.

Moreover American accountants have long been educated to expect the profession to provide authoritative solutions to accounting problems. In the U.S.A. not only have there now been 10 years of the FASB to look back on—there have also been about 50 years of the "Search for Accounting Principles" [Storey, 1964; Zeff, 1972; Zeff 1982a]. There cannot be an accountant practising in the U.S.A. today who did not gain his professional certificate after the profession had undertaken a responsibility for issuing authoritative statements of accepted accounting principles. By contrast, in Britain, although professional "recommendations" began in 1942 with the formation of the Taxation and Financial Relations Committee of the ICAEW [Zeff, 1972, p. 8], we have had little more than ten years of mandatory accounting standards.

Furthermore the dominant academic tradition in which American accountants have received their education has been the "Paton and Littleton" tradition of historical cost accounting and "attaching and matching." There is no equivalent to Paton and Littleton [1940] in British accounting literature. The significance of this work lies in the way its authors were able to absorb the objective of "providing useful information to investors" that became dominant in the 1930s [Watts and Zimmerman, 1979] into the traditional accounting framework. They argued (and convinced the academic establishment) that the accountants' conventions for reporting realized income were the basis of what was needed to enable investors to assess the "earning power" of businesses.

By contrast the dominant academic tradition in Britain owes its intellectual origins to the "LSE tradition" [Gould, 1974; Baxter, 1978; Dev, 1980]. In examining the nature of information useful for investment and management decisions, writers there quickly came to the view [e.g., Edwards, 1937; Baxter, 1938; Coase, 1938; Edwards, 1938; Thirlby, 1946] that the accountants' "unexpired costs" (especially when loaded with overheads) were unlikely to be of much relevance either in financial or managerial accounting. At best, they could be justified only if they could be shown to be a cost-effective means of collecting information that gave some guidance about how the magnitudes which were relevant were likely to behave.

While it is true that, due to the different educational arrangements just described, these ideas have until recently had limited currency in the profession, at least British accountants have not had the beliefs that are ingrained through practice reinforced by academic blessing— except insofar as British accountants [e.g., Norris, 1946] have acquainted themselves with American authors such as Paton and Littleton [1940].

The degree of interest in the conceptual framework in the U.S.A. must, I think, be seen within the academic accounting tradition here. The difficulties of standard setters in making use of the historical cost, "matching" model as a framework for choosing a particular practice have always been considerable and in recent years have been exacerbated, *inter alia*, by rising prices, fluctuating foreign exchange rates, and the growth of massive future commitments by companies (e.g., leases, pensions, and, depending on your viewpoint, deferred taxation). But U.S. accountants have their education in the "Paton and Littleton" tradition to cope with too—which may help explain, for example, the APB's peremptory rejection of Moonitz [1961] and Sprouse and Moonitz [1962]. It may be all very well for the Securities and Exchange Commission (SEC) (which previously rigorously enforced the same attitude) to have changed direction in the 1970s to go for current costs, reserve recognition, forecast disclosures, and management discussions, but it is important for the intellectual sanity of practising accountants that either they do finally reconcile their accounting model with the demands of practical problem solving—or that they identify what is wrong with it and establish a replacement on a firm foundation. Storey [1981] expresses the view that the fundamental questioning involved in the FASB's project is an important but difficult attempt to re-educate the profession (academic as well as practising) from the modes of thought of the dominant historical cost "matching" model.

From this perspective the project may be seen as a tribute to the power of ideas. The fact that it carries no clear implications for practice is not a serious criticism. It is rather a triumph that the official standard setting body has been persuaded to endorse a framework that at least allows the possibility of developing practical recommendations far different from current practice.

But if one sees the conceptual framework as the final crowning of the "search for accounting principles" there is surely little reason to suppose that in its latest style it will be any more successful than it has been in the past. Paton and Littleton [1940] stirred the ingredients of usefulness to investors (and others); the qualities of "relevance" and "dependability"; the relevance of concepts from economics and law; the role of past exchanges, present prices, and estimates of the future; the distinction between recurring and non-recurring elements of income. In offering their own solution to the problem of measuring an income that would help readers assess "earning power," they justified the particular balance they proposed between what should go into financial statements and what else might usefully be disclosed and discussed as supplementary "interpretation." Many other writers have stirred the same pot since, and now it is the turn of the FASB. But for the reasons already given there is unlikely to be any conclusive answer to what is the right mix of these ingredients—as George O. May argued in 1932.

## Political pressures

The "search" itself is largely a response to political pressures placed on the profession. It is well known that George O. May's Special Committee on Co-operation with Stock Exchanges recommended in its letter of September 22, 1932, just over 50 years ago that it was advisable to

> "leave every corporation free to choose its own methods of accounting within the very broad limits to which reference has been made, but require disclosure of the methods employed and consistency in their application from year to year" [Storey, 1964, p. 10; Zeff, 1972, p. 240].

To May's disappointment the "disclosure" suggestion was not taken up [Zeff, 1972, p. 125].[11] Storey [1964, p. 13] comments that May's proposal was "essentially English practice modified to fit the American situation" and that "adoption of British accounting practice in its pure form was probably politically unfeasible in the United States in the early 1930s" (p. 15).[12]

It was the SEC's ultimatum in ASR 4 of 1938 [Zeff, 1972, p. 134) that compelled the profession to search for accounting principles, just as, much later, government pressure in Britain was applied (less publicly) to persuade British accountants to do the same [Zeff, 1972, p. 40]. It is interesting to speculate how differently things might have gone in both countries if there had earlier been full disclosure in accounts of the methods used; at least it would have helped to educate the public and legislators not to be surprised that two accountants can, in all honesty, justifiably produce different net asset and income figures in the "same" situation [Slimmings, 1981]. Of course, such an orientation would not have solved all the problems either—for example, how detailed should the disclosures be? Whether this extra information is in fact worth having is itself a substantial policy and research question, but at least one can see why it matters.

To the proper intellectual concern with the nature of accounting, and questioning of how far practice can be standardized, has therefore been added the political necessity of justifying what accountants do. The SEC, itself born of public disillusionment after the Stock Exchange crash of 1929, in turn saw the problem with accounting as the variety of acceptable practices. Ever since then the main intellectual effort of the profession has been devoted to standardizing practice.[13]

Moreover the SEC, whose concern until the 1970s has seemed to be more with preventing accounting abuses than with providing useful information for investors' decisions, has traditionally insisted that the solutions be found within the "historical cost" framework. This practical straitjacket has been interwoven with the intellectual and academic tradition to produce the viewpoint that the problems of accounting require solution by refining Paton and Littleton's [1940] basic ideas about income measurement in order to distill best practice.

As a result, the historical cost model has traditionally been adhered to much more strictly in U.S. practice than it has in Britain. While there are common factors influencing practice, including income tax law and the economic conditions in which the profession first arose [Zeff, 1982b], the British have generally been more flexible. They have often included selective revaluation of assets in accounts; they have tended to use current exchange rates for foreign currency items; they issue forecasts, on which accountants have (at least since 1969 [Zeff, 1972, p. 60]) been prepared to give opinions [ICAEW, 1978]. In a previous era they were high exponents of the art of secret reserve accounting (still legally permitted for some banks and insurance and shipping companies), which gave managements the power to use the accounts to tell investors what managers considered they ought to be told [Hastings, 1949]. I am aware of no official endorsement in the U.S.A. of any secret reserve accounting;[14] revaluations and forecasts have until recently been equally frowned on, so there has been less obvious scope for managements here to tell investors their own story.

The pressures on the profession to standardize practice have intensified, not diminished, as accounting and the consequences of accounting have become more public. They reached a peak of intensity in the 1970s. Moreover, a recurring criticism of the FASB's predecessor bodies was the lack of attention to fundamental principles as opposed to the *ad hoc* approach to particular problems as they arose [e.g., Burton, 1978].[15] In my previous study (p. 97) I set this out for a British readership as follows:

> "Many commentators see FASB as the 'last chance' for keeping standard setting 'in the private sector' and consider that its survival in this role depends to a large extent on how successful it is judged to be in developing its conceptual framework project, and in tackling, in particular, the controversial topics of inflation accounting and foreign currency translation. This perception of its role, as the only alternative to greater government regulation, probably explains why the Board generally seems to enjoy strong financial and moral support from the leaders of the financial and business community in the U.S.A. and why it has itself stressed the role of good accounting in assisting the functioning of the capital market in a free enterprise economy and emphasized the importance of public confidence in accounting for confidence in business as a whole. As it said in 'Scope and Implications of the Conceptual Framework Project' in 1976, 'skepticism about financial reporting . . . creates adverse public opinion, which may be the antecedent of

unjustified government regulation. Every company, every
industry stands to suffer because of skepticism about
financial reporting.' "

The profession has had to cope with Congressional investigations,
litigation, and increasing competition between firms. Accounting
standards may help in maintaining the quality of work and in defining
what is fair competition [Benston, 1981], so a conceptual framework
that promises to reinforce the standards program appeals strongly to
public accountants (the strongest demands in Britain too came from
the accounting firms).

Given the "trials" that the profession in the U.S.A. has gone
through during the first decade of the FASB [Olson, 1982] and the
innovative activity of the SEC during this period in spearheading an
"accounting revolution" of new disclosures of information [Beaver,
1981, Chapter 1], I think Dopuch and Sunder [1980] may have unduly
discounted the persistence of the "fear of Government regulation."

Similar, though less intense, pressures led to the creation of the
British ASC and its "statement of intent" to "narrow the areas of
difference in accounting practice" [Zeff, 1972, pp.33-40; Leach, 1981].
Yet there is less interest in developing a conceptual framework in
Britain.

Recently Peasnell [1982] has suggested that a conceptual
framework should be of most value to a standard setting body, like the
Canadian, which has full authority to set legally binding standards—
because it can help to justify the legitimacy of the body as acting in the
public interest rather than in some more narrow professional or client
interest. He sees little role for it in a *laissez faire* situation where the
task of the standard setting body is to arbitrate between conflicting
interests—here a conceptual framework may reduce the scope of
maneuvering to reach acceptable compromises. He argues that the
British ASC operates in this kind of environment, and developing a
conceptual framework might prove more of a hindrance than a help.
While the recommendation may be wise (I return to it in section (C)),
the analysis does not seem to explain why both Britain and Canada (at
opposite ends of the spectrum of authority) have in fact shown
relatively little interest compared with the FASB.

If one considers the dynamics of the role of a conceptual
framework—how it may assist in laying claim to or resisting
challenges to a position of authority—it seems more important to

consider the competitive pressures, how many and how strong are the challengers for the job of standard setting. The FASB has many more active competitors (the Congress; the SEC; the AICPA's Accounting Standards Executive Committee; and now a Governmental Accounting Standards Board) as well as being haunted by the shades of its predecessors (the Committee on Accounting Procedure and the Accounting Principles Board). In Canada their Accounting Research Committee has been given supreme power (and presently has no challengers). It may also take the view that it should let the FASB do the work. In Britain there has been only one ASC[16] and the Government, on the whole, stays in the background.

## *The Wrong Problem?*

Given the unique combination of intellectual and political pressures in the U.S.A., it is understandable how the profession has been forced initially into the search for accounting principles and finally into the conceptual framework. The job has had to be done, and, having been started, has to be completed.

The trouble is that in attacking the variety of accounting practices, critics have, I believe, misunderstood the problem and consequently misunderstood the likely effectiveness of the proposed cure. This seems clear from the circumstances that triggered the start of the standardization programs in the U.S.A. and Britain. Others have reviewed these from a "market" perspective [e.g., Benston, 1976]. Here I offer some case illustrations—British cases as they are the ones I am familiar with. They illustrate that the problem is not so much the use of different accounting principles ("the same economic facts being treated in different ways") but more the difficulty of coping with the uncertainties of business life (disagreement, and often legitimate disagreement, over what the "facts" are).

(1) *GEC/AEI.* The public disquiet over the circumstances surrounding the merger of the General Electric Co. and Associated Electrical Industries in 1967 is commonly adduced as one of the powerful forces that led in 1970 to the establishment of the British ASC [e.g., Leach, 1981; Tweedie, 1981]. Much of the concern centered around the profit forecast (issued by AEI in November in resisting GEC's bid) which forecast pre-tax profits of £10m. After the merger had been completed, GEC in 1968 issued results for 1967 showing that AEI had made a pre-tax loss of £4.5m. AEI's former joint auditors (Deloitte, Plender, Griffiths & Co. and Price Waterhouse &

Co.) issued a letter dated 29th July 1968 to the directors of GEC explaining how the difference had occurred, including a well-known paragraph in which they stated:

> "Broadly speaking, of the total shortfall of £14.5 millions we would attribute roughly £5 millions to adverse differences which are matters substantially of fact rather than of judgment and the balance of some £9.5 millions to adjustments which remain matters substantially of judgment" [Zeff, 1972, p. 33].

There has been a tendency to assume that the "matters of judgment" implied that GEC's directors may have used different accounting principles in preparing the 1967 accounts than would have been used by the former AEI directors (hence the need for standards etc.). This interpretation seems unlikely (as it would probably be unusual in British practice to take the effect of such a change currently rather than retroactively [cf. ASSC, 1974]) and does not appear to be in accordance with the auditors' letter, which, in analyzing differences between forecast and actual included the following items:

|  |  | £m |
|---|---|---|
| (4) | Amounts in excess of forecast, written off stocks for obsolescence and similar reasons | 4.3 |
| (5) | Provisions, in excess of forecast, for estimated losses on contracts in progress and for further expenditure on completed contracts, in the light of subsequent reviews | 4.4 |
| (6) | Additional provisions against debts | 0.5 |

It is not clear if any "matters of fact" are included in these revisions, which total £9.2m and amount to nearly two-thirds of the total shortfall, but they clearly refer to differences in estimates (perhaps as the consequence of a change of business strategy) which no accounting standard on inventories and contract work in progress could have addressed. The former directors' press-statement [Latham, 1969, p. 120] comments that a 5% difference of judgment in the amount at which these items were valued would have amounted to about £15m. (AEI's pre-tax profits in the preceding five years had varied between £6.6m and £13.5m.)

(2) *Leasco/Pergamon.* It was the disputes over Pergamon's 1968 accounts during the takeover negotiations in 1969 that finally triggered the setting up of the ASC. They were the occasion of a famous attack

by Professor Edward Stamp in *The Times* on the flexibility of British accounting principles and the absence of any disclosure of the methods used in arriving at profit [Zeff, 1972, p. 36; Stamp, 1981]. To be sure of the details of the case would require a careful analysis of the massive Board of Trade[17] Inspectors' Report on Pergamon which I have not had the time to do in preparing this paper. But when Price Waterhouse reported in August 1970 on Pergamon's accounts for 1969 they restated the accounts for 1968 (which had originally shown a pre-tax profit of £2.1m when Robert Maxwell was chairman) to £140,000.[18]

*The Times*, in reviewing the report, commented that the affair

> "has aggravated the concern already felt about the comparability of company accounts. It will not be possible to pronounce on these issues until after the Board of Trade inquiry. Meanwhile it needs to be emphasized that it is accounting practice rather than accounting principles which is the main bone of contention in the Pergamon issue" (August 27, 1970, p. 18).

*The Times* pointed out that, in relation to their reductions of stocks and work and progress (which in total reduced 1968 profits by £838,000), Price Waterhouse had mentioned "four instances whereby the normal practice of valuing stocks by the lower of cost and net realizable value was not adhered to" (*ibid.*, p.19). These comments were of course made after the intention to form the ASC had been announced in December 1969. I am reminded of the comment of Grady [1962]:

> "If it is objectively, competently and courageously applied, the scrub brush of good accrual accounting holds the solution to most of the dingy areas of accounting practice."

Nonetheless, however "competently and courageously applied" (a matter for auditing standards), the rule of "lower of cost and net realizable value" can only be as good as the estimates of net realizable value—and where markets for the inventory are highly specialized (as here) such estimates may be no more than guesses about an uncertain future. The accounting problem, once again, is not so much "variety of accounting principles" as how to deal with these uncertainties in preparing useful and informative accounts.

These two cases were of great significance for Britain's adoption of a program of accounting standards. The wisdom of the decision seemed to be confirmed by a series of scandals which followed shortly afterwards, before the new standards had been implemented. Here are two more examples:

(3) *V&G.* The crash in 1971 of the Vehicle and General Insurance Company (with which almost 10% of U.K. private motorists were insured) led to two official inquiries, which are analyzed in Harte and Macve [1982]. Their main criticisms of the position shown by the company's accounts were that provisions for outstanding insurance liabilities at December 31, 1969, had been underestimated by at least £3m (the provision itself being about £3m), and provisions for uncollectible accounts by about £500,000, of which it should have been clear that a provision of at least £250,000 was needed.

The case led, *inter alia*, to the Department of Trade introducing new "valuation regulations" for the purposes of its regulation of the insurance industry (effectively "special purpose" accounting standards)—but to date no valuation regulations have been settled in respect of insurance liabilities. Perhaps in recognition of the difficulties of assessing the uncertainties involved, the Policyholders Protection Act was introduced in 1975 to provide for an indemnity fund to protect policyholders of failed companies, financed by levies on other companies. This may be seen as offering a kind of portfolio diversification not normally available to policyholders insured by any one company, which may reduce their need for reliable information in the way that portfolio diversification for shareholders can reduce their need for information about individual companies [e.g., Beaver, 1981, Ch. 2].

The major criticism made of an "accounting principle" by the Department of Trade inspectors was that the company included in its income its realized gains and losses on investments. This was certainly not the normal practice among British insurers but the severity of criticism it aroused is hard to explain. It was the standard practice in the U.S.A. [Horngren, 1973]! So in this case too, the important issue was how to handle the uncertainties.

(4) *Rolls Royce.* The failure of Rolls Royce in 1971 was accompanied by the realization that development expenditure on the RB.211 engine (designed for Lockheed) carried as an asset on the

balance sheet was worthless. In the period 1961-1970 the company reported profits cumulatively £46.7m higher than it would have if expenditure had been expensed as incurred [Wolnizer and Austin, 1982].

There has been a tendency to believe that the standard on Research and Development in Britain [ASC, 1977] was intended to "prevent another Rolls Royce." However, as the expenditure was separately identifiable development expenditure on a clearly defined project it could probably have been capitalized under the standard that was finally issued—the crucial criterion being "reasonable certainty" of "ultimate commercial viability" and of sufficient future revenues.

As the exposure draft, ED14, had originally proposed expensing of all R&D, many have argued that the development of this standard in Britain is an instance of the ASC bowing to political pressure from the aerospace industry [e.g., Hope and Gray, 1982]. The official view of course is that for that industry an accounting practice which arbitrarily expenses its major form of investment distorts "representational faithfulness," and that a good argument for capitalization can be made even without considering the possible adverse economic consequences of an "expense immediately" standard [e.g., Watts, 1981].

Whatever the reasons for the ASC's change of approach, it is clear that R&D is an extreme case of the conflict between the two aspects of "reliability" ("verifiability" and "representational faithfulness"). There is no conceptual reason why one person should balance these the same as another, or even why one country's standard should be the same as another's.

So, how can uncertainties of the kinds that caused the problems in these four cases be handled? While R&D may be expensed, thus "avoiding" the problem (and particularly the problem of how a standard could require rather than merely permit capitalization [Sprouse, 1979]), a standard proposing that a heavy engineering contractor like GEC or AEI should expense all its contracts in progress seems unlikely to be seriously proposed. How then are such contractors to be made to provide financial reports that are comparable with those of other contractors and of other kinds of businesses? Presumably there are two possibilities (as with choice of accounting principles)— disclosure and "narrowing of differences." To disclosure of accounting policies needs to be added consideration of the disclosure of major assumptions in estimating recoverability of balance sheet assets and the burden of estimated liabilities [Macve, 1980]. Narrowing of differences would be much more difficult. I return to this question in section (B).

To my mind, it is such problems of how to cope with the uncertainties involved that not only led to the difficulties illustrated in these cases (where they became "scandals") but are the major difficulty facing accountants in providing useful financial reports of the kind that modern economies appear to demand—reports on the financial performance and situation of business (and other) enterprises.

### Vision or Chimera?

The FASB's conceptual framework project appears as an impressive attempt finally to sort out and settle troublesome problems that have repeatedly emerged as standard setters have tried to solve questions of "accounting principles." I have argued that, in the U.S.A., the FASB and its predecessors have been compelled to make this attempt largely because of political pressures which have intensified rather than slackened over the last 50, and especially the last 10, years. These political pressures have intertwined with the inheritance of an intellectual tradition that regards the historical cost, "matching" model as a satisfactory basis for resolving problems of relevant and reliable financial reporting.

I have argued that much of the effort has been directed at the wrong problems and the vision of solving them has been a chimera.

However, the acid test of a conceptual framework, like accounting itself, is, "Is it useful?" I now consider the project as a "tool" and ask, "Has it helped in setting accounting standards? How can it be used?"

## (B) TOOL

When Dopuch and Sunder [1980] wrote their critique of the FASB's conceptual framework project, they could not find any evidence to suggest how the objectives and proposed elements would assist policy decisions, e.g., on deferred taxation, on treatment of oil and gas exploration costs, or on reporting of current values. When I finished my report to the ASC in May 1981, four concepts statements had been issued but the rest of the project had not gone beyond discussion memoranda or research reports. Subsequently the exposure draft on "Reporting Income, Cash Flows and Financial Position of Business

Enterprises" was issued on November 16, 1981 [FASB, 1981]. This, in addition to incorporating ideas from several discussion memoranda, also proposed an advance on the statement in SFAC1 [FASB, 1978] (which is to be interpreted as a prescription as well as a description) that "the primary focus of financial reporting is on earnings" (now "comprehensive income"). It proposed that:

> "The measurement of comprehensive income, which measures the overall performance of the enterprise, should be based on the financial concept of capital. Ideally, financial capital should be measured in real terms—that is in reasonably stable financial units" (para. 14).

Although it is only fair to emphasize that the exposure draft stressed the need to focus on the components of income rather than the "bottom line," nevertheless determination of the capital maintenance question would have resolved the issue that was left open when FAS33 [FASB, 1979] and SFAC3 [FASB, 1980b] were issued. It would imply that, if price changes are recognized, then "comprehensive income" is essentially equivalent to "real business income" [Edwards and Bell, 1961], including any real holding gains (whether or not "realized"). It would also have put the U.S.A.'s version of inflation accounting firmly on a basis that has not been adopted in other English speaking countries, where some version of physical capital maintenance is used [e.g., ASC, 1980]. The proposal has now been put back on ice while recognition and measurement criteria are further considered as a unit. The Board will return to reporting issues later (see FASB Status Report, no. 139, January 13, 1983).

So, at present the Board has reached an impasse in considering "historical costs" and "current prices," and the objectives and concepts developed to date do not appear to be helping to clear a way forward. The FASB's Status Report of March 2, 1983, which indicates that the staff are preparing two parallel drafts of accounting recognition concepts that capture the fundamentals of the two general views, states that "each document will show how its conclusions are consistent with the existing concepts Statements."

There have been other developments. In November 1982 the Board issued its Preliminary Views on "Employers' Accounting for Pensions and other Postemployment Benefits" [FASB, 1982]. Appendix B notes that, while the task force on the project was formed in 1975, "by deferring action on the accounting by employers project, the Board also expected to benefit from further progress on its conceptual framework projects." Certainly, the Board makes use in the discussion paper of the definitions of elements from SFAC3, but while it is reasonably confident that the employer's obligation for deferred pension benefits is a liability and argues that it is relevant and sufficiently reliable information to be included in financial statements, it is clearly less happy about the two other proposed elements. The "intangible asset" (for the benefit resulting to the employer from the initiation or enhancement of the pension scheme) is compared with other costs expended in the hope of future benefits (notably research and development) which are not currently recognized as assets. Its recognition is regarded as a "practical" solution (para. 42). The "measurement valuation allowance" (intended to spread out experience gains and losses and the effects of changes in actuarial assumptions over a number of accounting periods) does not seem to qualify as either an asset or a liability under the definitions in SFAC3, but is acknowledged as a "practical" means of reducing unacceptable volatility in pension expense (para. 70). I regard as far-fetched the subsidiary argument that it is intended to be a part of the representation of the pension liability or asset (para. 71). It seems to be in the same category as the "deferred credits" and "deferred charges" which Appendix B to SFAC3 indicated were no longer to be allowed. Naturally, it is these aspects of the proposals that gave most concern to the two dissenting Board members (paras. 118 and following).

It seems to me that the Board could make almost any solution one might reasonably want to consider compatible with its definitions of concepts. Basically this is because they require judgments about "sufficient relevance", "sufficient reliability," "probability of benefits," etc. on which Board members can properly differ. More seriously for the conceptual framework project, the Board in this document seems prepared to argue that "practical" solutions may be chosen even if they seem inconsistent with "concepts" as developed and applied in other areas. I shall suggest in section (C) that, as all good theory must be practical, the conflict here between practical and conceptual indicates that there has been inadequate development of, or understanding of, some of the concepts in the framework.

## Structure for discussion
It is not possible for me to judge whether the FASB would have viewed problems such as "historical cost versus current value," or pension

accounting, in a significantly different way in the absence of the conceptual framework. However, the major intellectual value of the concepts statements may be that they help organize the Board's discussion of problems into a sensible pattern. They focus discussion on the perceived relevance of the proposals to users and how different needs are to be balanced, on the reliability of measurement of the items to be recognized, on whether the information should be included in the financial statements and how it should affect income, on what supplementary disclosures are needed, and so on. In considering these matters, use of the concepts helps to compare proposals in one area of accounting to those in other areas and to consider whether the treatments are consistent or whether practice and standards in other areas need reconsideration too.

The concepts focus on questions of the costs and benefits of change versus continuing the *status quo*—asking about likely economic and other consequences and about what transitional arrangements are needed.

So technical, political and practical issues are tackled in a methodical way which helps identify the areas where judgment is needed, where further research may be helpful, and where compromise to meet the interests of different parties may be required. It also provides a framework for classifying responses from the Board's constituencies. Other standard setting bodies can be "free riders" here and make use of the framework in improving their own discussions.

## Research

The way in which the kind of thinking embodied in SFAC1 and SFAC2 encourages an experimental and research-oriented attitude has often been favorably commented on [e.g., Alexander and Carsberg, 1981; Skinner, 1981; Beaver, 1983], and I suggested to the ASC [Macve, 1981, p. 72] that this was probably the major benefit of the project. It helps identify the questions to be asked. I note however that Solomons (like some who sent comments to the ASC) regards this as a

"somewhat defeatist conclusion. One might suppose that we had already spent enough time asking questions, and that what we needed now was some answers" [1983, p. 111].

I see the definitions in SFAC3 as useful in a similar way. They do not tell us, for example, whether "Deferred Pension Plan Amendment and Initiation Cost" should be treated as an asset in financial statements or how it should be measured, but they do help to focus on some issues of concern. They remind us that, if we treat an item as an asset, we are asserting "probable future economic benefits." To understand what this means we need to be clear about valuation theory [e.g., Bonbright, 1937; Baxter, 1975] and how changes in "value" relate to "income" [e.g., Hicks, 1946]. We need to consider aggregation problems [e.g., Edey, 1974]; the practicalities of the measures proposed [e.g., Dopuch and Sunder, 1980]; and, above all, how to handle the uncertainties that I discussed in the previous section. Can some "accounting principles" be seen as more serviceable "rules of thumb" than others for producing a reasonable answer most of the time [e.g., Edey, 1962; Johnson and Storey, 1982], or are the uncertainties such that disclosure and discussion of assumptions are the most important aspects to be considered [e.g., Macve, 1980]?

I do not know whether the Board, faced with the practical problems of making policy decisions, finds the kind of intellectual discipline the conceptual framework offers valuable—but this is the most valuable feature that I would identify.

## Education

Storey [1981] and Alexander [1982] have expressed the hope that the concepts statements may become important educational texts and Sterling [1982] sees benefits for education. One may wonder why the FASB needs to be involved in such an "academic" endeavor as reviewing and perhaps changing conventional modes of thought. After all there are plenty of accounting academics, themselves no longer very impressed by historical cost and "matching," who are given a captive audience of prospective CPAs in their schools each year and should have a comparative advantage in working on conceptual matters. The process may be slower, but in the long run the effect of new ideas on such *tabulae rasae* may be thought more likely to influence attitudes and practice than an attempt to re-educate the current generations of practising accountants.

There may be relevant differences here between Britain and the U.S.A.. Sterling [1973] bemoans the divorce between much of the classroom teaching of accounting to those students who are going into practice or business (i.e., undergraduate or MBA students) and what the teachers themselves regard as important in their research papers and conference themes. Zeff [1982b] questions how many universities expect such students to study "accounting theory." The major culprit is normally identified as the CPA exam—in particular because many American students take this concurrently with or soon after their degree studies, and are, understandably, motivated to seek forms of learning that will pay off for both. Thus a vicious circle operates (see the discussions in Jensen [1982]).[19]

In Britain there are two significant differences. While university students studying accounting in any depth probably have similar motivations to their U.S. counterparts (the majority are heading towards professional qualification), they cannot, at least for entry into the ICAEW, take the professional exams until a considerable period after graduation and after further courses of professional education [Solomons, 1981]. British university teachers are therefore considerably freer to approach accounting from a variety of different viewpoints, and most undergraduate "majors" and all masters courses will include large helpings of accounting theory—so much so that the professional bodies have increasingly expressed concern about the lack of practical accounting skills to be found among graduates from some programs (accounting graduates are entitled to certain professional examination exemptions) .

The other major difference—which works in the opposite direction—is that, as the British profession does not require an accounting degree for entry, there is not even the opportunity to expose a majority of entrants to accounting theory, and even now only some 20% or so of the new entrants to the ICAEW will have an accounting degree. One may argue therefore that in Britain too, if any significant academic impact is to be had on accounting practice, one cannot leave it to educational institutions. It needs to be channeled through direct influence on the leaders of the profession and on the ASC, and it therefore behooves British academics (if only in their own interests) to urge the ASC to undertake a conceptual framework project.

There is indeed educational value in the FASB's concepts statements, provided they are reviewed from a critical perspective. There are dangers too—if the FASB's lists of objectives, qualities, and definitions are merely tacked on to the existing textbook presentations of "generally accepted accounting principles," they will add little to students' understanding, beyond perhaps providing a specious rationalization for all that follows. They will certainly fail to explain why accounting standards develop and change as they have [Zeff, 1982b].

Rather than leave the job of education to the FASB's conceptual framework project, these difficulties suggest that, both in the U.S.A. and Britain, more attention needs to be given to reform of the institutional relationships between universities and the profession.

## Politics

The intellectual benefits of the project are therefore fairly tentative and difficult to describe. What of its value in "legitimizing" the FASB's activity in standard setting? I have already discussed the forces that have led to the adoption of the project—and perhaps from the political point of view the main benefit is that the FASB has undertaken it—is seen to be "doing something." More than this, the Board has stated the information needs of users to be the primary objective of financial reporting. There is always a tension between the interests of the different parties—users (whether direct or indirect), preparers, and auditors—involved in the financial reporting process [Dopuch and Sunder, 1980, following Cyert and Ijiri, 1974], with a tendency for management and auditors to form a coalition. There is a danger in all professions as they develop of losing touch with the needs of those they are supposed to serve [Burchell *et al.*, 1980]. So re-affirmation of the priority of user needs is important for the public's view of the profession. It helps show that it is trying to respond to the realization that accounting has now become, more than ever before, an area of "public interest" [Olson, 1982]. As George O. May said in 1932:

> "The aim should be to satisfy (so far as is possible and prudent) the investor's need for knowledge, rather than the accountant's sense of form and respect for tradition" [Zeff, 1972, p. 242].

This is even more important today; and if the FASB, in undertaking the project, has helped meet the challenges from the SEC and the Congress in recent years then the profession, and corporate managers too, may judge it a success.

# (C) THREAT

I have reviewed the benefits that may be expected from the development of the FASB's conceptual framework. Finally I consider some dangers. First the "intellectual" dangers.

From an intellectual viewpoint the FASB's and other official conceptual frameworks may be seen as a threat by those who fear that the imposition of an official accounting theory may ultimately destroy any pretense that accounting is a "learned profession" [e.g., Baxter, 1981]. Certainly the preamble to Concepts Statements 2, 3, and 4 [FASB 1980a; 1980b; 1980c] contains a statement that the "conceptual framework . . . prescribes the nature, function and limits of financial accounting and reporting," and the term "prescribes" implies going beyond mere description of current practice to a statement of what "ought" to be (which may of course affirm that current practice is "best").

So when, for example, SFAC1, in discussing the information that financial reporting can provide, says "the information . . . largely reflects the financial effects of transactions and events that have already happened" (para 21), it appears that statements of management plans and projections are thereby excluded from "financial reporting." To many this would be a wholly unjustifiable restriction of the questions that might be addressed, and the possibilities that might be considered in prescribing the best kind of information provision to users, even though they might accept the exclusion as a description of actual current practice, and even as an initial constraint (given moral hazard, problems of litigation, consequences for behavior, etc. that need to be addressed in weighing any proposals to expand forecast information). In fact, however, this particular threat seems empty here—footnote 6 in SFAC1 assures us that the statement "neither requires nor prohibits . . . "management forecast information" . . . Conclusions about . . . [this] . . . are beyond the scope of this Statement." So SFAC1 does not prescribe the "limits of financial accounting and reporting" (even for business enterprises).

Indeed the Board has so far skillfully avoided the danger that it may say too much too early on in the project and has been careful not to foreclose options that may be needed when it gets to grips with more concrete issues. However, the project has now reached the stage of the "nitty-gritty," and the danger that too much may be said is increasing. Given the arguments in section (A) above about the limited scope for the project to produce "answers," the main danger now would seem to be that the Board itself might lose patience with the slow progress it has been making and feel obliged to gloss over conceptual difficulties in the desire to make some decisions about recognition and measurement criteria. I think this would be unwise. If such criteria are adopted in a way that limits sensible options in the future, there will later be a need for making even more distinctions (like those appearing in FASB [1982]) between "conceptual" and "practical" solutions—with a consequent downgrading of the concepts.

In my view, the Board now needs to concentrate on examining and explaining the ambiguities and difficulties associated with the objectives and concepts it has already adopted, and why they do not lead to clear solutions to accounting problems.

There are many such questions that could be explored, and many of them have been discussed at this conference. I will merely mention some that particularly interest me, that seem especially relevant to the focus on "income" in SFAC1, SFAC3, and FASB [1981] and that must be explored if the project is to say anything illuminating about recognition and measurement criteria beyond the suggestions already set out in SFAC2:

(1) How does the objective of providing useful information about a business to help "assess the amounts, timing and uncertainty of prospective net cash inflows" relate to "the primary focus of financial reporting is . . . earnings[20] and its components" [SFAC1, para. 43; cf. Beaver, 1981]? "Unless we can bridge that gap, it doesn't hold together" [Sprouse, 1977, p. 28].

(2) Is the orientation towards "usefulness" of information for investment, credit, and other similar decisions congruent with the need for "fairness" and "objectivity" in the accounting numbers needed for "contractual" purposes and for "accountability" (purposes discussed extensively in the agency theory literature of recent years [e.g., Ronen, 1979]), or are different criteria required [e.g., Gjesdal, 1981; Ijiri, 1982]? The British, to whom the relation of accounting income to the amount legally distributable in dividends has always been a central question, and who are in closer contact with legally oriented European practice [Bromwich and Hopwood, 1983, introduction], think there is an important conflict of purpose here [Edey, 1978; Watts, 1981]. Does the concern among management about what is or is not included in "income" in the financial statements (harder to understand from an "information perspective" [Beaver, 1973]) become more

understandable from a "contractual" perspective where consequences come ready-wrapped in the accounting numbers? Does this suggest, *inter alia*, that proposals to add useful, but often "soft," information should be directed mainly at supplementary disclosures [Burton, 1978]?

(3) More generally, is there congruence or conflict between the objectives for managerial and for financial accounting reports? What are the difficulties in making the latter similar to the former? If the financial reporting environment imposes constraints, how else can the Board minimize the adverse "inductance" effects that may arise if financial reports cannot reflect the benefits and costs of managerial decisions as managers see them [Prakash and Rappaport, 1977; Edey, 1980]?

(4) If "accrual accounting"[21] is superior to past cash flows (whether for informational, contractual, or managerial purposes), how can accounting information be held to be "largely historical" [SFAC1, para 21]? Compare Beaver's [1981, Chapter 4] discussion of accrual accounting as a way of packaging forecasts. If accrual accounting requires use of allocations [Thomas, 1977] or significant subjective estimates of an uncertain future, what is meant by the "representational faithfulness" of accounting measures [cf. SFAC2, paras. 63 and following]?

(5) How does the definition of "comprehensive income" in SFAC3 square with the ambiguities examined, e.g., by Paish [1940], Hicks [1946], and Kaldor [1955] between "income" and "changes in wealth"? For example, when interest rates change, are the resulting changes in wealth usefully treated as income? When estimates are revised in an uncertain world, are the revisions part of income [e.g., Solomons, 1961; Edey, 1963; Bierman and Davidson, 1969]? How much light can analysis of these conceptual difficulties shed on problems such as determining the "capital maintenance concept" [cf. FASB, 1981, para. 14], or deciding whether to recognize a "measurement valuation allowance" in considering pension accounting [FASB, 1982]? Moreover, if income is computed as "change in net assets," how is its significance (e.g., as a performance measure) affected by the limitation that the recorded net assets cannot comprise the "value of the business" [Edey, 1970; FASB, 1981, para. 11]?

(6) In the proper concern in SFAC3 to avoid merely circular definitions (like those in APB Statement 4 [APB, 1970]) that cannot be used to test accounting practice [Storey, 1981], has sufficient attention

been given to developing understanding and explanation of why present practice is as it is [Zeff, 1982b; Burchell *et al.*, 1980; cf. Jaenicke, 1981]?

There are many other such questions one might raise. I believe it is extremely important that they are raised and examined now if the project is to make progress. In other words, I consider the stage to have been reached where what is most needed is development of understanding as to why such plausible arguments as those set forth in the present concepts statements do not either explain present practice, or give clear guidance on how to change it.

The Board has preserved its flexibility so far. It may need to be especially careful not to lose it now and not to override some proper conceptual concerns.

## Politics

There would also be "political" dangers for the FASB in saying too much that is too specific in the conceptual framework, if this were to foreclose options to negotiate and compromise with affected parties in future [Rappaport, 1977; Peasnell, 1982]. The less the power of the standard setters, the greater the danger. I am not arguing for deliberate obfuscation of the issues—rather against the danger of representing the issues to be conceptually clear-cut when generally they are not. It is this very lack of clarity that makes it even harder in accounting to distinguish the "political" and the "technical" than it is in many other fields.[22]

Indeed, I find one of the most fascinating aspects of accounting theory to be how little can be rigorously explained of the "technical" usefulness of a process that is such an important feature of modern economic life (and for which its practitioners are very well remunerated), and how difficult it is to show even what would be a "technical" improvement, apart from the political difficulties that plague all recommendations, scientific or unscientific, in any area of public policy. The danger lies in pretending that such ambiguities about accounting do not exist.

## (D)    CONCLUSION

I have suggested that the conceptual framework should be seen as the crowning effort in the "search for accounting principles." The need for the search is a product of political pressures and intellectual traditions. I have doubted the value of the search in coping with the kinds of problems that accountants face in providing meaningful financial reports about businesses, or users face in relying on those reports. The chief of these problems is the uncertainty inherent in economic activity.

One may speculate whether the "search" could have been avoided if accountants had earlier spelled out the limitations of their art and the nature of the assumptions and conventions they have to adopt in preparing financial reports. However that may be, the search, now begun, must be completed. My own view is that its success will come not from showing how to settle "accounting principles," but from prompting sufficiently deep inquiry into conceptual problems. This kind of inquiry is needed to make clear why there are such difficulties in knowing what is "good accounting," let alone in trying to obtain agreement on this from those variously affected by what the accounts show [Moonitz, 1974; Zeff, 1978]. The inquiry will also show why a government body would be likely to have no more success in establishing good accounting principles, even though it has greater power to coerce.

If I am right, the main danger is that of glossing over conceptual problems. This becomes more critical as the FASB's project now begins to deal directly with recognition and measurement questions. I would have preferred that these conceptual problems had been tackled head-on at the beginning—but I am convinced they will have to be faced in the end. "Truth is the daughter, not of Authority, but of Time" (Bacon, quoted by Baxter [1981]).

If the problems are acknowledged and faced, then I believe the conceptual framework project could considerably enhance respect for the difficult profession of accounting. It may help to reduce the danger of misguided political interference from those who believe that answers to accounting problems should be easy to find, and who attribute all the profession's failures to incompetence or self-serving.

So I will vote with Solomons for the importance of work on the conceptual framework. In doing so I still believe, as I said before [Macve, 1981, p. 72]:

"that the main value of thinking about the conceptual framework of accounting lies in developing understanding of what questions need answering and how they may be approached. In other words, a conceptual framework must be seen as a framework for investigation and research into solutions; not as a package of solutions."

# APPENDIX I. MACVE [1981] CHAPTER 1.

*Not reprinted here as it appears in this volume at pp.35-39*

# APPENDIX II. THE "BARTON" REPORT

This report, prepared by Professor Allan Barton of the Australian National University, Canberra, is entitled "Objectives and Basic Concepts of Accounting" and was published by the Australian Accounting Research Foundation in 1982. It runs to (iv) + 98 pages. I give here an abbreviated summary of its major points.

1)    The author stresses that users of accounting and financial reports need "information about the firm's operations and its resources and obligations for use in economic decision making and control and for accountability purposes" (para. 2.05). The "control" aspect is emphasized as linking published financial and internal (or management) accounting in the same framework.

2)    The users examined and their needs are similar to those in other studies (and include management).

3)    It is deduced that information needs reduce to information on

   a)    cash position and cash flows

   b)    financing of operations and funds flows

   c)    earning power "as this indicates its success in achieving a major goal—the earning of profits . . . the rate of return on investment is crucial information" (para. 3.41).

   d)    the financial position of the firm

   e)    the financial risk incurred in investing funds in the firm.

4) "The functions served by the information are . . . prediction and decision making, control, and accountability for stewardship and evaluation of results" and these are "interrelated" (para. 3.42).

5) The qualitative characteristics are dealt with briefly and are essentially the same as those in other studies ("the differences are largely semantic" (fn. 27)).

6) General concepts underlying accounting are discussed, including the accounting entity, transactions, events, double-entry recording, measurement, monetary measurement, continuing activity and the accounting period, the going concern concept, accrual accounting (defined as in SFAC1), realization, classification.

7) The information required by most users is summarized in four major financial reports—the cash flow statement, funds statement, income statement, and balance sheet. Only the last three of these are needed as published financial statements as the cash flow information is encompassed in the funds statement (para. 7.09). (The funds statement envisaged is a transactions report, "not the conventional statement prepared from comparative balance sheets" (fn. 43).)

8) In discussing the balance sheet it is noted that: "The concept of wealth is fundamental to all financial accounting as all the concepts measured in the income statement and balance sheet are derived from it." Assets and liabilities are defined in similar terms to SFAC3. "More specific definitions of assets depend upon the precise financial measurement system used" (para. 6.12).

9) In discussing the income statement it is noted that income can be defined as the "maximum amount that can be spent without encroaching upon the wealth, net assets or capital held at the beginning of the period; . . . while the business remains as well-off at the end of the period as it was at the beginning." "Again, more precise definitions of income and

capital maintenance depend upon the financial measurement system used" (para. 6.17). "The income statement must articulate with the balance sheet." (para. 6.21). It is noted later that the income statement should disclose, *inter alia*, aggregate sales, variable costs and fixed costs, all major estimates such as depreciation and doubtful debts" (para. 7.12).

10)     Financial measurement systems reviewed include valuation at a) historic cost, b) current market buying price, c) current market selling price, d) present value (potential cash flow, discounted). The dollar has two measurement properties, number of dollars or number of purchasing power units, giving a matrix of eight candidate systems.

The two systems using historic cost valuations are rejected as giving no useful information; and the two using "present value" because they are "*ex ante* and completely subjective" (para. 9.36), and "cannot possibly satisfy any of the history-based functions of control, accountability and measurement of achieved results" (para. 9.43).

The choice must be from the current market value systems. Both of these exclude any asset that does not have a current market value (unlike historic cost). It may be noted that Barton's version of a "current buying price system" values liabilities as in a historic cost system (para 9.21) and regards income as the increase in net assets with both opening and closing components valued at current (i.e. both at period-end) prices—thus income excludes all price changes on the opening stock of assets (so essentially a "physical capital maintenance" concept is applied) (para 9.22). His current selling price system by contrast, admits market prices for marketable liabilities, and computes income as the increase in ending value of net assets over beginning-of-period value (i.e. a "financial capital maintenance" concept) (paras. 9.29-30).

The use of purchasing power units (i.e. "real current value") is preferred as this adds information to the current value systems. Both the real current value systems have their uses (paras. 9.47-48). In the introduction (fn. 2) it was noted that choice of a capital maintenance concept is choice of a socioeconomic objective, about which there is nothing necessarily right or wrong. But once the objective is specified, then the concepts of the indicated measurement system follow. The adoption of a conceptual framework therefore is valuable in analysis and is a necessary but not sufficient condition for the resolution of problems.

# REFERENCES

Accounting Principles Board ("APB"), Statement No. 4, *Basic Concepts and Accounting Principles Underlying Financial Statements of Business Enterprises*, New York: American Institute of Certified Public Accountants ("AICPA"), 1970.

Accounting Standards [Steering] Committee, ("AS[S]C"), Statement of Standard Accounting Practice No. 2 ("SSAP2"), *Disclosure of Accounting Policies*, London: ASSC, November, 1971.

_____, SSAP6, *Extraordinary Items and Prior Year Adjustments*, London: ASSC, April, 1974.

_____, *The Corporate Report: A Discussion Paper*, London: ASSC, 1975.

_____, SSAP13, *Accounting for Research and Development*, London: ASC, December, 1977.

_____, SSAP16, *Current Cost Accounting*, London: ASC, March,1980.

_____, *Setting Accounting Standards: Report and Recommendations of the ASC*, London: ASC, 1981.

Alexander, M.O. (Chairman), *Report of the Ontario Committee on Inflation Accounting*, Toronto: Ontario Government Bookstore, 1977.

_____, "The FASB's Conceptual Framework Project—After Eight Years Is the End in Sight?" *FASB Viewpoints*, Stamford, Conn.: FASB, June 2, 1982.

_____, and Carsberg, B.V., "Glory, Knock-Down Arguments and Impenetrability," in Buckley, 1981, pp.187-204.

American Accounting Association ("AAA"), Committee on Concepts and Standards for External Financial Reports, *Statement on*

*Accounting Theory and Theory Acceptance* ("SOATATA"), Sarasota, Fla.: AAA, 1977.

Barton, A.D., *Objectives and Basic Concepts of Accounting*, Accounting Theory Monograph No.2., Melbourne: Australian Accounting Research Foundation, 1982.

Basu, S. and Milburn, J.A., eds., *Research to Support Standard Setting in Financial Accounting: A Canadian Perspective*, Toronto: The Clarkson Gordon Foundation, 1982.

Baxter, W.T., "A Note on the Allocation of Oncosts between Departments," *The Accountant* (November 5, 1938), pp.633-636 (reprinted in Baxter, 1978).

_____, *Accounting Values and Inflation*, Maidenhead: McGraw-Hill, 1975.

_____, *Collected Papers on Accounting*, New York: Arno, 1978.

_____, "Accounting Standards—Boon or Curse?" *Accounting and Business Research* (Winter, 1981), pp.3-10.

_____, and Davidson, S., eds., *Studies in Accounting*, 3rd edition, London: ICAEW, 1977.

Beaver, W.H., "What Should Be the FASB's Objectives?" *Journal of Accountancy* (August 1973), pp.49-56 (reprinted in Bloom and Elgers, 1981, pp.163-173).

_____, *Financial Reporting: An Accounting Revolution*, Englewood Cliffs, NJ: Prentice-Hall, 1981.

_____, "Research on Monitoring the Accounting Standard Setting Process," in Bromwich and Hopwood, 1983, pp.153-167.

Bell, P.W., *CVA, CCA, and CoCoA: How Fundamental are the Differences?*, Accounting Theory Monograph No.1, Melbourne: Australian Accounting Research Foundation, 1982.

Benston, G.J., *Corporate Financial Disclosure in the UK and the USA*, Lexington, Mass.: D. C. Heath, 1976.

_____, "Are Accounting Standards Necessary?", in Leach and Stamp, 1981, pp.201-214.

Bierman, Jr., H. and Davidson, S., "The Income Concept—Value Increment or Earnings Predictor," *The Accounting Review* (April 1969), pp.239-246.

Bloom, R. and Elgers, P. T., *Accounting Theory and Practice: a Reader*, New York: Harcourt Brace Jovanovich, 1981.

Blough, C.G., "Development of Accounting Principles in the United States," in *Berkeley Symposium on the Foundations of Financial Reporting*, University of California, School of Business Administration, 1967, pp.1-14.

Bonbright, J.C., *The Valuation of Property*, New York: McGraw-Hill, 1937 (reprinted Charlottesville, Va.: Michie, 1965).

Bromwich, M. and Hopwood, A., eds., *Accounting Standards Setting, An International Perspective*, London: Pitman, 1983.

Buchanan, J.M. and Thirlby, G.F., eds., *L.S.E. Essays on Cost*, London: London School of Economics and Political Science/Weidenfeld & Nicolson, 1973.

Buckley, J.W., ed., *The Impact of Accounting Research on Policy and Practice, 1981 Proceedings of the Arthur Young Professors' Roundtable*, Reston, Va.: The Council of Arthur Young Professors, 1981.

Burchell, S., Clubb, C., Hopwood, A., Hughes, J. and Nahapiet, J., "The Roles of Accounting in Organizations and Society," *Accounting, Organizations and Society* (Vol. 5, No. 1, 1980), pp.5-27.

Burton, J.C., "A Symposium on the Conceptual Framework," *The Journal of Accountancy* (January 1978), pp.53-58.

_____, (ed.), *The International World of Accounting, 1980 Proceedings of the Arthur Young Professors' Roundtable*, Reston, Va.: The Council of Arthur Young Professors, 1981.

_____, "Intermediate Accounting from a User Perspective?" in Jensen, 1982, pp.1-11.

Canadian Institute of Chartered Accountants ("CICA"), report prepared by Professor E. Stamp, *Corporate Reporting: Its Future Evolution*, Toronto: CICA, 1980.

Coase, R.H., "Business Organization and the Accountant," *The Accountant* (October 1 - December 17, 1938), (reprinted in Solomons, 1952, pp.105-158 and, with revisions, in Buchanan and Thirlby, 1973, pp.95-132).

*Companies Act 1948*, London: HMSO, 1948.

Cyert, R.M. and Ijiri, Y., "Problems of Implementing the Trueblood Objectives Report," *Studies on Financial Accounting Objectives: 1974*, Supplement to the *Journal of Accounting Research*, 12 (1974), pp.29-45.

Dev, S., *Accounting and the L.S.E. Tradition*, Inaugural Lecture, February 26, 1980, London: London School of Economics and Political Science, 1980.

Dopuch, N. and Sunder, S., "FASB's Statements on Objectives and Elements of Financial Accounting: A Review," *The Accounting Review* (January 1980), pp.1-21 (reprinted in Bloom and Elgers, 1981, pp.107-129).

Edey, H.C., "Income and the Valuation of Stock-in-Trade," *British Tax Review*, (May/June, 1962), pp.164-172 (reprinted in Edey, 1982).

_____, "Accounting Principles and Business Reality," *Accountancy* (November & December, 1963) (reprinted in Edey, 1982).

_____, "The Nature of Profit," *Accounting and Business Research* (Winter, 1970), pp.50-55 (reprinted in Edey, 1982).

_____, "Deprival Value and Financial Accounting," in Edey and Yamey, 1974, pp.75-83 (reprinted in Edey, 1982).

_____, "Why All-Purpose Accounts Will Not Do," *Accountancy* (October 1978), pp.108-109 (reprinted in Edey, 1982).

_____, *The Logic of Financial Accounting*, Deloitte, Haskins and Sells Lecture, February 28, 1980, Cardiff: University College, 1980 (reprinted in Edey, 1982).

_____, *Accounting Queries*, New York and London: Garland, 1982.

_____, and Yamey, B.S., eds., *Debits, Credits, Finance and Profits*, London: Sweet & Maxwell, 1974.

Edwards, E.O. and Bell, P.W., *The Theory and Measurement of Business Income*, Berkeley: University of California Press, 1961.

Edwards, R.S., "The Rationale of Cost Accounting," in Plant, A., ed., *Some Modern Business Problems*, London: Longman, 1937 (reprinted in Buchanan and Thirlby, 1973, pp.71-92).

_____, "The Nature and Measurement of Income," *The Accountant* (July-October, 1938), revised and reprinted in Baxter and Davidson, 1977, pp.96-140.

Financial Accounting Foundation ("FAF"), the Financial Accounting Standards Board and the Financial Accounting Standards Advisory Council, *1982 Tenth Annual Report*, Stamford, Conn.: FAF *et. al.*, January 26, 1983.

Financial Accounting Standards Board ("FASB"), Statement of Financial Accounting Concepts, No.1 ("SFAC1"), *Objectives of Financial Reporting by Business Enterprises*, November, 1978.

\_\_\_\_\_, Statement of Financial Accounting Standards No. 33 ("FAS33"), *Financial Reporting and Changing Prices*, September, 1979.

\_\_\_\_\_, SFAC2, *Qualitative Characteristics of Accounting Information*, May, 1980a.

\_\_\_\_\_, SFAC3, *Elements of Financial Statements of Business Enterprises*, December, 1980b.

\_\_\_\_\_, SFAC4, *Objectives of Financial Reporting by Nonbusiness Organizations*, December, 1980c.

\_\_\_\_\_, Exposure Draft, *Reporting Income, Cash Flows and Financial Position of Business Enterprises*, November 16, 1981.

\_\_\_\_\_, *Preliminary Views . . . Employers' Accounting for Pensions and Other Postemployment Benefits*, November, 1982.

Gjesdal, F., "Accounting for Stewardship," *Journal of Accounting Research* (Spring, 1981), pp.208-231.

Gould, J.R., "Opportunity Cost: The London Tradition," in Edey and Yamey, 1974, pp.91-107.

Grady, P., "Comments" in Sprouse and Moonitz, 1962, pp.67-75 (reprinted in Zeff, 1982a).

Gynther, R.S., "Accounting for Changing Prices: Developments in Australia and Overseas," *The Australian Accountant* (August 1982), pp.468-472.

Harte, G.F. and Macve, R.H., "Lessons of the V&G Crash", paper presented at the annual convention of the Association of University Teachers of Accounting, Lancaster, England, March, 1982.

Hastings, Sir Patrick, "The Case of the Royal Mail", in *Cases in Court*, London: Heinemann, 1949, pp.213-228 (reprinted in Baxter & Davidson, 1977, pp.339-346).

Hicks, J.R., *Value and Capital*, 2nd edition, Oxford: Clarendon Press, 1946 (Ch. 14, pp.171-181, reprinted in Parker and Harcourt, 1969, pp.74-82).

Hope, A. and Gray, R., "Power and Policy Making in the Development of an R&D Standard," *Journal of Business Finance and Accounting* (Winter, 1982), pp.531-558.

Horngren, C., "The Marketing of Accounting Standards," *Journal of Accountancy* (October 1973), pp.61-66.

Ijiri, Y., "On the Accountability-Based Conceptual Framework of Accounting," presented at Conceptual Framework Conference, Harvard Business School, October 1-2, 1982.

Institute of Chartered Accountants in England & Wales ("ICAEW"), "Accountants' Reports on Profit Forecasts" (November 1978), *Members' Handbook*, 3.91.

Jaenicke, H.R., *Survey of Present Practices in Recognizing Revenues, Expenses, Gains and Losses*, Research Report, Stamford, Conn.: FASB, 1981.

Jensen, D.L., ed., *The Impact of Rule-Making on Intermediate Financial Accounting Textbooks*, Columbus, Ohio: Ohio State University, 1982.

Johnson, L.T. and Storey, R.K., *Recognition in Financial Statements: Underlying Concepts and Practical Conventions*, Research Report, Stamford, Conn.: FASB, 1982.

Kaldor, N., "The Concept of Income in Economic Theory," in *An Expenditure Tax*, London: Allen & Unwin, 1965, pp.54-78 (reprinted in Parker and Harcourt, 1969, pp.161-182).

Kirk, D.J., *1980 Annual Report of the FASB*, Stamford, Conn.: FASB, March 4th, 1981.

Latham, Sir Joseph, *Take-over, The Facts and Myths of the GEC-AEI Battle*, London: Iliffe, 1969.

Leach, Sir Ronald, "The Birth of British Accounting Standards," in Leach and Stamp, 1981, pp.3-11.

_____, and Stamp, E., eds., *British Accounting Standards, The First 10 Years*, Cambridge: Woodhead-Faulkner, 1981.

Macve, R.H., *Quaere Verum vel Recte Numerare*, Inaugural Lecture, May 16, 1979, Aberystwyth: The University College of Wales, 1980.

_____, *A Conceptual Framework for Financial Accounting and Reporting; The Possibilities for an Agreed Structure*, London: ICAEW, 1981.

Marple, R.P., *Capital Surplus and Corporate Net Worth*, New York: Ronald Press, 1936.

May, R.G. And Sundem, G.L., "Research for Accounting Policy: An Overview," *The Accounting Review* (October 1976), pp.747-763 (reprinted in Bloom and Elgers, 1981, pp.2-19).

Moonitz, M., *The Basic Postulates of Accounting*, Accounting Research Study No. 1, New York: AICPA, 1961 (reprinted in Zeff, 1982a).

_____, *Obtaining Agreement on Standards in the Accounting Profession*, Studies in Accounting Research No. 8, Sarasota, Fla.: AAA, 1974.

Norris, H., *Accounting Theory*, London: Pitman, 1946 (reprinted, New York: Arno Press, 1980)

Olson, W.E., *The Accounting Profession, Years of Trial: 1969-1980*, New York: AICPA, 1982.

Paish, F.W., "Capital Value and Income", *Economica* (November 1940), pp.416-418 (reprinted in Baxter & Davidson, 1977, pp.179-181).

Parker, R.H. and Harcourt, G.C., *Readings in the Concept and Measurement of Income*, Cambridge: University Press, 1969.

Paton, W.A. and Littleton, A.C., *An Introduction to Corporate Accounting Standards*, American Accounting Association Monograph No. 3, AAA, 1940.

Peasnell, K.V., "Statement on Accounting Theory and Theory Acceptance: A Review Article," *Accounting and Business Research* (Summer, 1978), pp.217-225 (reprinted in Bloom and Elgers, 1981, pp.62-75).

_____, "The Function of a Conceptual Framework for Corporate Financial Reporting," *Accounting and Business Research* (Autumn, 1982), pp.243-256.

Prakash, P. and Rappaport, A., "Information Inductance and its Significance for Accounting," *Accounting, Organizations and Society* (Vol. 2, No. 1, 1977), pp.29-38.

Rappaport, A., "Economic Impact of Accounting Standards – Implications for the FASB," *The Journal of Accountancy* (May 1977), pp.89-98.

Ronen, J., "The Dual Role of Accounting: A Financial Economics Perspective," Ch. 20 in Bicksler, J.L., ed., *Handbook of Financial Economics*, New York: North Holland, 1979.

Sandilands, F.E.P. (chairman), *Inflation Accounting, Report of the Inflation Accounting Committee*, Cmnd 6225, London: HMSO, 1975.

Skerratt, L.C.L. and Tonkin, D.J., *Financial Reporting 1982-83: A Survey of UK Published Accounts*, London: ICAEW, 1982.

Skinner, R.M., "The Impact of Financial Accounting Research on Policy and Practice," in Buckley, 1981, pp.3-36.

Slimmings, Sir William, "The Scottish Contribution," in Leach and Stamp, 1981, pp.12-26.

Solomons, D., ed., *Studies in Costing*, London: Sweet & Maxwell, 1952.

_____, "Economic and Accounting Concepts of Income," *The Accounting Review* (July 1961), pp.374-383 (reprinted in Bloom and Elgers, 1981, pp.201-211).

_____, "Accounting Education: An International Perspective," in Burton, 1981, pp.177-210.

_____, "The Political Implications of Accounting and Accounting Standard Setting," *Accounting and Business Research* (Spring, 1983), pp.107-118.

Sprouse, R.T., in panel discussion in *The Conceptual Framework of Accounting*, proceedings of a conference held at the Wharton School of the University of Pennsylvania, May 4, 1977.

_____, *Prospects for Progress in Financial Reporting*, address at Texas Tech University, April 19, 1979, Stamford, Conn.: FASB, 1979.

_____, and Moonitz, M., *A Tentative Set of Broad Accounting Principles for Business Enterprises*, Accounting Research Study, No.3, New York: AICPA, 1962 (reprinted in Zeff, 1982a).

Stamp, E., "A View from Academe," in Leach and Stamp, 1981, pp.231-247.

_____, "Financial Accounting Standard Setting Criteria: Some Comparisons," in Bromwich and Hopwood, 1983, pp.90-97.

Sterling, R.R., "Accounting Research, Education and Practice," *Journal of Accountancy* (September 1973), pp.44-52 (reprinted in Baxter and Davidson, 1977, pp.368-380, and in Jensen, 1982, pp.121-129).

_____, "The Conceptual Framework; an assessment," *Journal of Accountancy* (November 1982), pp.103-108.

Storey, R.K., *The Search for Accounting Principles*, New York: AICPA, 1964.

_____, "Conditions Necessary for Developing a Conceptual Framework," *FASB Viewpoints*, Stamford, Conn.: FASB, March 3, 1981.

Thirlby, G.F., "The Subjective Theory of Value and Accounting 'Cost'," *Economica* (February 1946), pp.32-49 (reprinted in Buchanan and Thirlby, 1973, pp.135-161).

Thomas, A.L., "Allocation: The Fallacy and the Theorists," in Baxter and Davidson, 1977, pp.182-194.

Tweedie, D.P., "Standards, Objectives and 'The Corporate Report'," in Leach and Stamp, 1981, pp.168-189.

Watts, R.L. and Zimmerman, J.L., "The Demand for and Supply of Accounting Theories: The Market for Excuses," *The Accounting Review* (April 1979), pp.273-301.

Watts, T.R., "Planning the Next Decade," in Leach and Stamp, 1981, pp.27-38.

Wigdor, Alexandra K., and Garner, Wendell R., eds., National Research Council (U.S.), Committee on Ability Testing, *Ability Testing: Uses, Consequences and Controversies*, Washington, DC: National Academy Press, 1982.

Wolnizer, P.W. and Austin, W.T., "Accounting for Research and Development Expenditure: An Analysis of the Rolls Royce

RB.211 Project," *Accounting and Finance* (November 1982), pp.19-32.

Zeff, S.A., *Forging Accounting Principles in Five Countries* (1971 Arthur Andersen lectures at the University of Edinburgh), Champaign, Illinois: Stipes, 1972.

_____, "The Rise of 'Economic Consequences'," *Journal of Accountancy* (December 1978), pp.56-63 or in *Stanford Lectures in Accounting*, Graduate School of Business, Stanford University, 1978, pp.11-19 (reprinted in Bloom and Elgers, 1981, pp.152-162).

_____, "Setting Accounting Standards in the United Kingdom—An American View," in Leach and Stamp, 1981, pp.190-198.

_____, ed., *The Accounting Postulates and Principles Controversy of the 1960s*, New York and London: Garland, 1982a.

_____, "Towards a Fundamental Rethinking of the Role of the 'Intermediate' Course in the Accounting Curriculum," in Jensen, 1982b, pp.33-51.

## NOTES

[1] I am grateful to Pat Armentor, Philip Bell, Harold Edey and Stephen Zeff for their helpful comments on an earlier draft of this paper.

[2] The ASC's representative bodies include the Institute of Chartered Accountants in Ireland. References to "British" here should be understood to include Ireland (Eire and Northern Ireland).

[3] After the Holy Grail was found in Wales, tradition has it that a piece of it came into the ownership of the Powells of Nanteos (whose estate lies about 2 miles southeast of Aberystwyth). Unfortunately it was "mislaid" and a visitor to Nanteos is now shown only a replica.

[4] The summary chapter of my report (Chapter 1) was originally included as Appendix I to this paper but is not reproduced here as it is reprinted in this volume at pp.35-39.

---

[5] *"Essentia non sunt multiplicanda praeter necessitatem."* See, e.g., the entry for "William of Ockham (c. 1284 —c. 1350)", *Collier's Encyclopedia*, New York: Macmillan, 1981.

[6] This is not to say that "paradigm conflicts" or other philosophical explanations are not needed in discussing the problems of knowledge and belief at a deeper level. But "How do we know anything?" is a different kind of question from "Why do we know more about how to put men on the Moon than we do about how to report research and development expenditure in financial statements?".

[7] One may deduce that there has been delay between completion of this study and its publication by AARF as the latest reference date in the bibliography is April 1980, and the Canadian study (published in June 1980) is not referred to.

[8] For further discussion see Basu and Milburn [1982, Session 4].

[9] cf. Skerratt and Tonkin [1982, sections 15(5), 20, and 24] for some examples of companies that have adopted some of its suggestions in their annual reports.

[10] See "Research—Carsberg points the way forward. . . . ," *Accountancy* (April 1983), pp.23-4. In regard to the second of these projects it is noted that "this amounts to what others might describe as the pursuit of a conceptual framework, couched in less emotive language. No ambitions exist to undertake work on a scale similar to that of the United States, though there is much we can learn from the work of the FASB."

[11] Carman Blough has argued that the SEC itself effectively did this part of the job [Blough, 1967].

[12] At this time there was in fact almost no disclosure of method in Britain either and May's proposal would have been very radical. The "Royal Mail" case [Hastings, 1949] had been heard, but it took the Companies Act 1948 to legislate against "secret reserve" accounting for most companies, and "disclosure of accounting policies" did not arrive until SSAP2 in 1971 [ASSC, 1971; Edey, 1970].

[13] Watts and Zimmerman [1979] argue further that it is the influence of the Securities Acts that has directed the orientation and development of the academic accounting literature too. I am concerned here only with how the problems have appeared to professional standard setting bodies.

[14] I am not dealing here with the use of LIFO (normally unacceptable in Britain) or with the undervaluations that arise in a period of inflation. Marple [1936] complained that U.S. companies were writing down fixed assets in the 1930s, so that future income would be enhanced. At least this practice was discoverable by the reader—cf. Hastings [1949].

[15] This criticism is commonly made of the ASC as well.

[16] The committee was originally the "Accounting Standards Steering Committee" but later dropped "Steering" from its title. There has recently been some alteration of its constitution and membership following its own

report on "Setting Accounting Standards" [ASC, 1981] and the installation of a new chairman [Skerratt and Tonkin, 1982, Section 2].

[17] The Board of Trade later became the Department of Trade.

[18] £495,000 if profits on sales to a company owned by Maxwell family trusts, which was now in dispute with Pergamon, are included.

[19] cf. Burton [1982] for a different approach used where only about 5% of the students plan to enter the accounting profession.

[20] Now "comprehensive income."

[21] SFAC1 (para.44) explains that: "Accrual accounting attempts to record the financial effects on an enterprise of transactions and other events and circumstances that have cash consequences for an enterprise in the periods in which those transactions, events and circumstances occur. . . . ." In its most comprehensive form it should therefore presumably include the effects of *everything* that has any consequence for future cash flows—the practical recognition and measurement problems are how much to include and how successfully can the future consequences be reduced to a single number [Edey, 1970].

[22] Solomons [1983] uses the analogy of intelligence testing. However those who administer standardized ability tests are at least able to demonstrate an acceptable degree of "reliability" (in terms of replicability) of the results [Wigdor and Garner, 1981].

# (IV)

# THE CONCEPTUAL FRAMEWORK AND OIL AND GAS ACCOUNTING

[originally published as 'Jock's codicil creates problems at South Fork', *Accountancy Age* (June 30, 1983, p.19); 'Dallas contest needs a few rules' (*ibid.*, July 7, 1983, p.26); 'No accounting for the plot of Dallas' (*ibid.*, July 21, 1983, p.20)].

# The Conceptual Framework and Oil and Gas Accounting

Here in Houston, Texas we are riveted to *Dallas* just as firmly as all y'all are back at home. The difference is that to you it's fantasy; to us, it's what we see all around us.

Presently, J.R. and Bobby Ewing are locked in a battle to the death (of relations, marriages and so on) to decide who is to inherit Ewing Oil. We know that Jock Ewing's will provided in a codicil that, for a year, each brother should take half the company and see who could be the more successful—winner take all.

Of course, Mis' Ellie went to court to try to break the will and stop her two sons tearing the family apart but, luckily for the plot, she lost. The judge ruled that Jock was in his right mind when he added the codicil that provided for the contest. Yet although we see teams of obviously well-paid lawyers, accountants and engineers advising the two brothers each week, the mystery remains—what precisely did Jock intend when he added that codicil? It was not, in fact, read out in court when Mis' Ellie challenged it and, when the will was first read after Jock's death, the wording was vague.

This is not surprising—for if we ask 'what should it have said?' we are plunged straight away into the great oil and gas accounting controversy which has given the Securities and Exchange Commission (SEC) and the Financial Accounting Standards Board (FASB)—to say nothing of the oil and gas industry here—one of their bigger headaches. One can glean from the activity going on at Ewing Oil that the codicil must provide that the winner shall be the brother who produces the bigger profits in the year—but is there any definition of how those profits should be measured? All we know is that each brother was to start with half the company's assets and at the end of the year the brother whose half was the bigger would win.

What is to be the standard for asset and profit measurement? How would one have advised Jock on this problem? The consequences are great but it must be assumed that Jock would have wanted the contest to be quite fair between his two sons—not rigged to favour either J.R. or Bobby—so the method chosen to measure profit must be neutral and concerned only with trying to measure the relevant aspects of the economic reality of the situation in a reliable manner. It must have the qualitative characteristics endorsed by the FASB in its 'conceptual framework' for financial accounting and reporting. In other words, the son who, it is decided, has made the greater profit must be the one who has actually performed better and made his half of the business the better off.

Jock's problem was essentially the same as that faced by the FASB in proposing a standard for the oil industry—to find a measure of assets and profits that would give an unbiased, neutral but reliable representation of the financial position and results achieved by each brother. Or as the ASC in Britain would put it, 'a true and fair view'.

The first problem is to get the contest started. Each brother must start equal with exactly half of the company's assets. Problem one—assets or net assets?

Ewing Oil certainly has extensive borrowings, to judge by all the discussions with bankers and all the computer printouts on cash flow that we have seen J.R. and Bobby wrestling with over the years. But if only the assets are divided between the brothers a possible contest would be to maximize the growth of the assets over the year and treat the liabilities as a fixed burden. Nevertheless this would take away the opportunity to test each brother's relative expertise in a vital area of modern corporate management—the negotiation of favourable financing arrangements. If the net assets were divided then the brothers could, from that base, devise strategies that include altering the amount and structure of borrowings during the year.

This gives us problem two. It is not just the balance-sheet amount of assets or net assets accumulated by each brother that should count. Allowance must be made for the risk characteristics both of different assets and of different levels and forms of gearing. So it is clear that merely using the historical-cost-based figures is likely to leave out a vital dimension—the risk profile—which implies that some form of valuation will be required.

However, talk of risk and values brings us on to problem three—interdependencies between the two halves of Ewing Oil. Thus, borrowing may be available on more favourable terms to a company of the size of Ewing Oil than it is to either of the two halves. Similarly, breach of a loan covenant by one half may bring as bad if not worse consequences for the other half. In planning investment and dividend strategy, the tax consequences (a vital factor in successful business management on behalf of a family as wealthy as the Ewings) will normally result from the joint effect of the activities in the two halves of the business.

So, to make sense of the split, we shall have to assume that the loss of the synergy between the two halves is a necessary cost of running the experiment—noting that this may require the renegotiation of existing contracts, loans and so on in order to allow each half to operate independently. It seems from the plot that this has not been done—the division is internal to Ewing Oil which is still one unit to the outside world. I wonder how they have decided to allocate the rent on the downtown Dallas headquarters.

So let us rule out problem three, and come back to problem two later. For problem one let us simplify the situation by assuming that we only have the assets to deal with. It would be tempting to hope that if we give each brother half of each of the latest balance-sheet categories of assets then we can get the contest started. This is where the FASB enters the game, with its attempt to resolve the 'full cost' *versus* 'successful efforts' controversy.

Ewing Oil is primarily an oil producer and does not even have very many of its own refineries, or else J.R. would not have been spending so much time inveigling Holly of Harwood Oil into a compliant frame of mind for the boardroom as well as the bedroom. We must guess that, some years back, the oil was originally discovered under South Fork's cattle ranges, which turned Jock from cattleman to oilman like most of the other members of the Cattlemen's Club. The wells now operating must have been sunk after some exploratory drillings and the incurring of various amounts of development cost. So now we are faced with the controversy over how these wells should be accounted for—an episode that the FASB would rather forget.

Problem four is 'full cost' *versus* 'successful efforts'. The major oil producers have traditionally favoured successful-efforts accounting— that is to say that if they have spent, say, $10 million, roughly equally, on acquiring and drilling 10 wells and nine of these prove to be dry holes, then $9 million is written off to expense and only $1 million is carried forward to be matched (together with any further development and extraction costs) against the revenues that are received as the extracted oil is sold.

However, since the 1950s smaller oil companies have increasingly adopted the full-cost method. This argues that, given the risks of oil exploration, one needs to take a portfolio approach and treat the full $10 million as the cost of finding the one gusher. This is the amount that should be carried forward to be matched against the sales revenue provided only, of course, that it is not more than is expected to be recovered from future revenue after allowing for future related costs.

The debate over the proper accounting method to be used came forward into the limelight in the US during the 1970s when energy policy, following the OPEC price rises, became a matter of supreme national importance and the government wanted reliable and comparable data on energy costs. And the 1975 Energy Policy and Conservation Act included a requirement for the SEC to see that the appropriate accounting rules were established.

Against this background the FASB, which frequently has to act with the SEC looking over its shoulder, issued its statement No.19 in 1977 requiring 'successful efforts' for all public companies. This action appalled many of the full-costers who feared dire economic consequences if they were compelled to adopt the new standard method, as it would lower their net assets and, if they were still exploring at a rate which added costs faster than old ones were being amortised against sales revenue, would depress their future profits relative to the results under their own full-cost method.

This, they argued, could harm not only their opportunities to raise capital (or at least worsen the terms on which it would be available) but could cause problems in relation to existing borrowing convenants if debt-equity ratios were thereby breached. And in relation to management compensation schemes based on profits (that is, bonuses or commissions). Correspondingly, the (generally larger) companies already using 'successful efforts' might be suspected of favouring the more conservative approach in order to reduce the political risks of 'obscene' high profits (such as further regulation of prices or new penal taxation) or to reinforce barriers to competition.

These various possible consequences to differing vested interests might be regarded merely as unfortunate side-effects if it could be shown that the FASB's proposed method was only the right one—but of course it could not.

More recently the FASB's conceptual framework project has reached the stage of defining an asset for financial statement purposes (essentially as a 'probable future economic benefit'). The definition would not have helped here—as it does not define the boundary between one asset and another. A dry hole cannot be an asset but, if the relevant unit for decision-making is the portfolio of wells explored, then why cannot that be treated as the relevant asset for accounting? More pointedly, as the bankable asset is actually the oil in the ground, why cannot all the costs of finding that oil, including the costs of looking in the dry holes, be capitalized?

Choosing one method over the other is an essentially political decision. Hearings were therefore held at the SEC and the Department of Energy and, in 1978, the SEC overruled the FASB and allowed the continued use of both methods by public companies.

So the ordinary historical cost rules—with their irresolvable disputes over 'full cost' and 'successful efforts' and their inability to cope with inflation, the effects of risk and the benefits of new discoveries of oil—are inadequate to provide a fair and sound basis for judging the contest. We have identified a need to value the oil reserves each brother starts with.

It is possible that we could make the initial division purely by reference to geological and engineering criteria and ensure that each brother started with a similar profile of reserves in terms of their difficulty of extraction. But even if we achieved this in the beginning it will not do when we get to the end of the year as each brother will probably now have a very different mix of extractability of reserve quantities. We can, as it were, give each two apples and two pears to start with but, if one brother ends up with three apples and four pears and the other with four apples and three pears, who shall we say has won? We need to know whether apples are more valuable than pears, or *vice versa*—we need an economic criterion. Similarly, in our case, we cannot get the sort of comparability we need purely by reference to geological and engineering criteria. We want to convert the reserves into some standard unit of recoverable-barrel equivalents in order to allow for the relative difficulty of extraction, risk involved and so on.

This brings us to the second great debate in oil and gas accounting circles. (One can perhaps now see why the problems in this industry are extensive enough for one Texas university to offer a master's degree wholly in the subject of oil and gas accounting—a pointed contrast to the UK.) When the SEC overturned the FASB's standard in

1978 and allowed the continued use of both full-cost and successful-efforts accounting it took the opportunity to add a new requirement—for reserve recognition accounting (RRA).

Estimating a company's oil and gas proved reserves is of course not a new idea—the departure was requiring disclosure of these in supplements to the financial statements in a form which required that they be valued and that the change in the value of reserves over a year be computed in a manner to yield an income figure for the year which would reflect not only the result of extraction and sale but also the results of exploration and development activity.

The valuation procedure required estimating future net cash flows to be obtained from extracting and selling the oil in the reserves and discounting these to a present value. However, certain standardizing rules were built into the SEC's procedures. The cash flows were to be estimated on the basis of current, not estimated future, prices and the discount rate was to be a standard 10% per annum. Initially the disclosures were to be supplementary only but the SEC's intention was that RRA should soon become the primary method of accounting for oil and gas producers (rather as Sandilands[1] envisaged current-cost accounting quickly becoming the means for accounting in the main financial statements, with historical cost figures relegated to a footnote).

These proposals were, to put it mildly, not received enthusiastically by the industry. 'Putting it mildly' is not the custom in Texas—so they kicked and hollered. Why this angry reaction? After all it seems only good sense to say, when looking at an oil company, that the focus of interest is the same as with a mining company—what they have got under the ground. Bankers and other lenders loan money on the strength of these reserves and one would regard them as crucial information in assessing oil-company share values.

One serious objection to basing the accounting for oil companies on reserves and changes in them is the uncertainty involved. While such proved reserves are normally 'audited' by consulting engineers, they are often extremely difficult to estimate and wide margins of error are experienced. Moreover, even if one is fairly sure of the physical quantity of oil, deciding whether it is worth extracting depends also on the price it will command on the market. If the price rises, not only does the value of the oil one is already planning to pump rise but it also becomes worthwhile to extract oil in areas that were previously marginal as the value now exceeds the cost of production. Conversely, when prices fall, both the value of a given quantity and the quantity worth recovering fall as one compares the lower prices with the production costs. Correspondingly, the incentives to further exploration drop—currently Houston's active-drilling-rig count is only about half what it was a year ago.

So there is both engineering and economic uncertainty in estimating the value of a well's proved reserves. More of the change in this value during a year may be due to revisions to previous estimates of quantities and prices than results from new discoveries or extraction. The significance of the figures required by the SEC therefore needed a lot of interpretation in the light of the assumptions being made—and the standardizing procedures may have further garbled the information being provided.

Thus the use of current prices ignores the importance of estimating (guessing) future prices and costs in making decisions about current exploration activity and rate of extraction; the use of a standard discount rate of 10% to convert the estimates of future cash flows to a present value is also questionable. Certainly, 10% is the easiest number to use for those whose arithmetic is weak (and I am told is widely used by bankers—not, I hope, for that reason) but it ignores the different risks of the wells of different companies, changes in the general level of interest rates and the relationship between interest rates and likely price changes.

The economic significance of the RRA figures required by the SEC is far from clear. While the physical estimates of reserves are probably of interest, the packaging of these into standard values in the way described adds no further information and may make it more confusing for those who are seriously trying to estimate the likely prospects of a company. Oil companies in their annual reports have been scathing about the usefulness of the RRA information and strongly opposed to any suggestion that it should form the main basis for accounting. (The paradox is that they seem to think that the historical-cost basis, whether by full-cost or successful efforts, is useful and reliable.)

At the last call, the FASB had issued a consolidating statement (FAS 69) which the SEC supports and which will continue to allow either of the traditional cost methods for the main accounts, but also continues to require supplementary disclosure by public companies of their proved reserves valued on the standardized basis.[2]

So the standard-setters' solutions to the oil and gas accounting problem do not seem likely to tell us what we want to know—which brother has made his half of the company the better off. It would be possible to take a more cynical view and say it does not matter much who has *really* been more successful. We should take the accounting rules as given (like the rules of football) and the one who wins according to the rules is the winner. After all, whoever runs the company in future will continue to be judged by the figures he produces according to the accounting rules in force, so it makes sense to judge who shall run the company the same way.

The three major objections to this line are:

- Other things being equal, different accounting methods only distribute the same total profit to different periods of the life of a business, so that a method which shows one brother more successful this period may show him less successful in a future period.

- One of the major controversies in academic accounting research at present is just how much influence the profits (known to be reported by just one of a choice of methods) have on those who use them, and how far people in fact 'see through' the figures to what is really going on (the 'efficient markets' and 'economic consequences' controversies).

- The activity of the standard-setting bodies makes it likely that the rules will change.

So if we stick to our original and more high-minded objective of choosing an accounting method that will tell us which brother has really been more successful, it is clear that we have got to use a method which incorporates the value of the reserves.

The importance of this can be seen when we look at the dirty tricks J.R. has been getting up to. One of his early moves was to take advantage of the present glut of oil and of the efforts of the producers' cartel, aided by the Energy Commission, to restrict pumping in order to maintain the price. He bribed Walter Driscoll, then on the Commission, to get him a 'variance' so that he could pump more oil and capture the market and Texan consumers' hearts with cheap gasoline prices.

Here the importance of the way in which reserves are calculated for the purposes of this contest becomes clear. If they are not included in the opening and closing position they are effectively free to each brother and the obvious thing to do to win is to pump and sell just as much oil as possible in the year, provided one can get a price that covers any costs of getting it out of the ground and selling it (including the book depletion cost for the well).

Bobby retaliated by trying to expand his own production, against the cartel agreement, and when that failed invoked the clause in the agreement that required the other members of the cartel to buy the relevant fields at a high price—realizing a gain that way.

Both tactics are likely to lead to high profits this year but will unavoidably run down the reserves on which the future profits of Ewing Oil depend. Only if the change in the value of the reserves over the year is included in the accounting can one judge whether J.R.'s 'sell a lot cheap' tactic made economic sense or whether he was squandering his resources. It might have been better to keep the oil in the ground and sell it in the future.

Now we have opened Pandora's box. The crucial economic decision in relation to existing reserves is how fast to extract them, which depends on estimates of how economic conditions will change. In other words, only the brothers can estimate what the reserves are worth and equally well only they can say how well they have done over the year in their stewardship and economic management of the resources they control.

Unless they admit to a mistake (not likely in the circumstances), each will argue that the strategy he has adopted in relation to the amount of oil sold, the price he got, the costs he incurred and the effort he put into discovering new reserves was just the right strategy given the need to balance current and future cash flows and obtain the best pattern over time by which to realize the most wealth for the family to enjoy. Some independent assessment is needed. By whom? The brothers are likely to dispute the competence or fairness of any 'expert' who does not agree with their own assessments.

A more objective assessment could, however, come from the market place. If there is an active and well-developed market in oil wells and exploration sites, then we could use these market values at the beginning and end of the year to judge which half of the business has become the better off—this would deal with all the problems of inflation, risk and valuing reserves—provided we are assured that the market has full information about the characteristics of the assets each brother has accumulated.

Two serious difficulties remain. First, is the market 'efficient' in assessing the value of oil companies' assets? How are they to cope, for example, with those fields where proved reserves are guessed by Bobby or J.R. to be only a fraction of potential reserves? The market price may give a value to these based on some kind of averaging ('you win some, you lose some') of the likely finds to be had from all the fields available on the market. But Bobby or J.R. may, with their intimate knowledge of their own fields, be convinced that this under-estimates the value of particular fields which they are sure will be gushers. Indeed, the more successful an oilman either of them is, the more he is likely to have a nose that smells oil where the rest of the world smells nothing.

The second difficulty lies in all those aspects of the business that cannot be captured in the market prices of its assets, for example the state of management-employee relations, the image of the company in the market place and so on—the intangibles. How are the brothers to be credited with what they achieve? On the other side, how are we to reflect in assessing J.R.'s performance the fact that someone may find out that he illegally exported oil to Cuba? If this became public knowledge could it ruin the company.

We could appeal to the market place again—but now it would have to be the stock-market for the company's shares—and it would only be a fully 'efficient' appraisal if, first, all insider information were made public (which itself might damage the company's prospects) and, second, if the brothers accepted John Q. Public's view of their prospects rather than their own. Moreover, we could only carry out this acid test of their success by selling the two halves of the business. As a result of this neither brother would own Ewing Oil and the purpose of the contest would be defeated.

So Jock's problem has no satisfactory solution. There is no theory which will tell us what accounting standards are the right ones for measuring this year's profit, even for this well-defined purpose. It looks unlikely that either brother will win by showing conclusively that he made more profit than the other. No wonder that *Dallas* and the FASB's search for the conceptual framework often appear to have a lot in common. They both go on and on. There's a lot of money involved and politics and power often seem likely to have more to do with the final outcome than reason and equity.

# NOTES TO THIS REPRINTING

[1] For an analysis of the Sandilands proposals see Appendix IV to Macve, R.H., *A Conceptual Framework for Financial Accounting and Reporting: the possibilities for developing an agreed structure* (London: ICAEW, 1981), reprinted in this volume at pp.137-142.
[2] SFAS69 is still in force in 1997, with the implementation of SFAS19 having been suspended indefinitely by SFAS25 (see e.g. Delaney, P.R., Adler, J.R., Epstein, B.J., and Foran, M.F., *GAAP 97: Interpretation and Application* (New York: Wiley, 1997)).

(V)

# SOLOMONS' GUIDELINES: WHERE DO THEY LEAD?

*Accountancy*, March 1989, pp.20-21

# Solomons' Guidelines: Where Do They Lead?

Last year closed with the Dearing Report[1] calling for more effort to be devoted to developing a 'conceptual framework' for standard setting, so that David Solomons' report, *Guidelines for Financial Reporting Standards*[2], addressed to the Accounting Standards Committee, marks a timely beginning to the New Year. The report (hereafter 'Solomons') is very clearly and well written and sets out in a direct and simple manner its author's well-known views on what he regards as *the* conceptual framework for financial accounting and reporting, and how to 'tell it like it is' (p 8).

There have been a number of such 'conceptual' studies recently, including the International Accounting Standards Committee's exposure draft of a Framework[3], the Scottish Institute's *Making Corporate Reports Valuable*[4], and the ASC's ED 42[5]. There is clearly a strong feeling, at least among the major accounting firms and the standard setters, which is reflected in Dearing, that some such kind of framework of guidelines is necessary in helping standard setters plot their course.

There are a number of reasons why I consider the kind of framework offered by such studies, and now again by Solomons, to be of limited value for these purposes, and I set out some of these reasons here. First, does the 'balance sheet' approach actually make any difference? Solomons sees the primary use of financial reports to be the assessment of entity and managerial performance, and the major concern of these guidelines (as of many accounting standards) is the measurement of profit or 'income'. Relying on the articulation of the balance sheet and the p&l account in conventional 'double entry' accounts, Solomons argues that the way to measure income is to concentrate on faithfully reporting ('recognizing') the entity's assets and liabilities in the balance sheets at the beginning and end of a period, which will provide as residuals the amounts of owners' equity. The change in those amounts (where there are no further contributions or withdrawals by owners and no prior period adjustments) is in turn equal to the income of the period. Echoing Hicks's famous definition[6], 'income is wealth creation' (p 17), Solomons then develops this approach in two ways.

First, he argues that this 'balance sheet' approach, focusing on questions about assets and liabilities, is preferable to focusing first on the elements of income itself (revenues, expenses, gains and losses) as that can lead to creating dubious 'pseudo' assets and liabilities in order to create the desired number. But I see no reasons to believe that the 'balance sheet approach' will make resolving accounting issues (p 28) 'more tractable' than the 'p&l' approach. 'Deferred tax' is discussed as an illustrative example in the appendix, and Solomons argues that the 'timing differences' resulting from depreciation 'give rise to a present obligation to make future payments ... to the Inland Revenue' (p 62), so that full allocation is appropriate (unlike SSAP 15's 'partial allocation'[7]). But the main argument about deferred tax allocation is over whether there is any such 'present obligation'—it is certainly not an obligation that the Inland Revenue can assess. And even if it were a liability there would still remain other 'recognition' issues (uncertainty as to future tax rate changes etc.) which might be persuasive that there is little point in trying to measure it in the accounts.

SSAP 15's own arguments can indeed be criticised (as Solomons criticises them) for being muddled about the nature of a liability—but that disguises the central issue in evaluating the contribution of the Solomons guidelines. While their clarity helps to structure the debate more logically, they do little to move the debate towards a more obvious conclusion.

Solomons' second development of the balance sheet approach is couched in terms that disarm criticism. Although he argues that an important ingredient of the reliability of accounting information is 'comprehensiveness'—'to tell the whole truth' (p 32)—he acknowledges that a balance sheet cannot report the company's 'true net worth' (and so, as income is the change in net worth, nor can 'true income' be reported—p 54) the major omission being that part of net worth which reflects the difference between the total value of recognized net assets and the total net worth of the business as a whole (the present value of its future prospects, reflected, for a listed company, in its market capitalization). This difference is identified, when an acquisition takes place, as 'goodwill'.

Solomons uses this acknowledgment of the limitations of financial statements as a basis for arguing that, while goodwill is an asset, it is only feasible to measure it reliably when there is an acquisition of a business—so that non-purchased goodwill cannot be recognized as an asset in a balance sheet and, in order to be consistent, one should therefore write off purchased goodwill too (as SSAP 22 favours[8]). But logically it is not clear to me why the consequence of the inability to measure non-purchased goodwill should be restricted to not measuring purchased goodwill. Indeed, Solomons himself goes further and states (in Chapter 6) that no intangibles should be included, although no specific examples (like research and development, brands, patents and trademarks) are discussed in the illustrations in the appendix. However, in the appendix on 'financial commitments' the Solomons framework favours extending the class of assets recognized to 'rights' under contracts not yet performed. There is certainly no boundary in economic logic between 'tangibles' and 'intangibles'. The value of some intangible assets can be reasonably ascertained, so why not recognize these? Some 'tangible' assets have very uncertain values and one may doubt whether they should be included as assets (e.g. a highly specialized production complex, or indeed the 'tangible' specialized buildings, equipment etc. employed in a research laboratory). But if some tangible assets should be 'written off' because their values are too uncertain, then for consistency should all assets be written off?

The Solomons line of argument for resolving goodwill seems likely to create more problems than it will cure: what it brings out for me is that standards are often difficult to set, not because standard setters are muddled about the definitions of assets or about the conceptual differences between defining, recognizing and measuring them, but because it is often difficult to know when and how to arrive at a sensible figure at which to include them. Solomons offers his own view of where the boundary should be drawn between what is recognized in the balance sheet and what is excluded—but I see no reason why others should agree on that particular boundary.

My overall evaluation so far of the Solomons exposition of the 'balance sheet approach' is that it adds little to previous attempts by the Financial Accounting Standards Board and others. So there is an important question as to whether we need any more such 'frameworks'. The only merit in an individual country's standard setters adopting distinctive guidelines (apart from misplaced nationalism) is if there are conditions peculiar to that country that render guidelines developed elsewhere inappropriate.

Much of Solomons essentially reiterates the objectives, definitions of assets, liabilities and other elements, the qualitative characteristics and the recognition criteria that are set out in the FASB's *Statements of Financial Accounting Concepts*. Yet the wording differs slightly, and also differs slightly from the IASC's exposure draft, and from ED 42 (see the examples set out below).

---

## DEFINITIONS OF ASSETS

Solomons (1989): 'Assets are resources or rights incontestably controlled by an entity at the accounting date that are expected to yield it future economic benefits' (p 20).

IASC (1988): 'An asset is a resource controlled by the enterprise as a result of past events and from which future economic benefits are expected to flow to the enterprise'. (Exposure draft: *Framework for the Preparation and Presentation of Financial Statements*.)[9]

ED 42 (1988): 'For the purposes of financial statements, assets may be described at a general level as probable future economic benefits controlled by and accruing to a particular enterprise as a result of past transactions or events' (para 14)[10].

FASB SFAC 3 (1980): 'Assets are probable economic benefits obtained or controlled by a particular entity as a result of past transactions or events'.

---

Is the reader to assume that these differences are significant (as a judge would have to look closely at the significance of slight changes in the wording between successive Companies Acts)? Or is it just that Professor Solomons considers his wording more elegant or easier to understand? For the reader (and the ASC) it would have been helpful to have been given a commentary indicating to what extent he regards the FASB's statements and those other attempts as effectively equivalent to his own and where he thinks it important to say something different (and why).

## NOTES TO THIS REPRINTING

[1] CCAB (Consultative Committee of Accountancy Bodies), *The Making of Accounting Standards*, report of the review committee, Chairman, Sir Ron Dearing (London: Institute of Chartered Accountants in England & Wales ('ICAEW'), 1988).

[2] published London: ICAEW, 1989; reprinted London and New York: Garland, 1997. Page references in the text here are to the original 1989 edition.

[3] now published as *Framework for the Preparation and Presentation of Financial Statements* (London: IASC, July 1989).

[4] McMonnies, P. (ed.), *Making Corporate Reports Valuable* (Edinburgh: ICAS & Kogan Page, 1988).

[5] ASC, Exposure Draft 42: *Accounting for Special Purpose Transactions* (March 1988).

[6] Hicks (1946)—see the bibliography to Macve, R.H., 'The FASB's Conceptual Framework—Vision, Tool or Threat?', presented at the Arthur Young Professors' Roundtable, May 7, 1983 (reprinted in this volume at pp.167-217).

[7] ASC, Statement of Standard Accounting Practice No.15 *Accounting for Deferred Tax* (London: ASC, October 1978—last amended December 1992)

[8] ASC, Statement of Standard Accounting Practice No.22 *Accounting for Goodwill* (London: ASC, December 1984—last amended September 1994)

[9] This definition is reiterated in the final version of the IASC's *Framework*—see note 3 above.

[10] see note 5 above. The ASB's November 1995 Exposure Draft: *Statement of Principles for Financial Reporting* now defines assets as follows: 'Assets are rights or other access to future economic benefits controlled by an entity as a result of past transactions or events.'

(VI)

# QUESTIONING THE WISDOM OF SOLOMONS

*Accountancy*, April 1989, pp.26-27

# Questioning the Wisdom of Solomons

In last month's analysis[1] I argued that the framework set out in the Solomons report, *Guidelines for Financial Reporting Standards*, is essentially a reiteration of the approach taken by the FASB in its 'conceptual framework' project; that this 'balance sheet' approach does not resolve fundamental conceptual issues about profit (or income) measurement; and that the conceptual boundary Solomons proposes between the types of assets that should and should not be 'recognized' in the balance sheet is arbitrary and lacking economic logic. This month I examine some individual accounting issues and ask how far the Solomons guidelines will assist decision-making about specific financial reporting problems.

A major element of the Solomons approach (which makes it much more valuable than many of the other frameworks that fudge this issue) is to argue not only for a balance sheet approach but for a balance sheet based on current values, which in turn should be value to the business (VTB) and will often be current cost. The Solomons view is that the income measure derived from changes in these values should be adjusted for inflation to produce 'real financial capital maintenance'.

This is not the place to review all the arguments for and against current values, so I will just address the arguments Solomons uses to dismiss the suggestions in *Making Corporate Reports Valuable* (the Scottish Institute's recent study[2]) that assets should be valued at net realizable value (NRV). These boil down to, first, that NRV is irrelevant in judging the financial position of a going concern, and second, that using NRV would have an unacceptable effect on income by requiring the immediate write-down of many newly acquired fixed assets (particularly the more specialized assets). But as I argued last month, Solomons can live with the requirement to write off goodwill immediately, and anyway, the merit of the balance sheet approach is supposed to be that it 'tells it like it is', and one must accept the income number derived from it. So I consider this second argument to be 'out of court' in the Solomons approach, and the merits of NRV *v* VTB should be argued wholly on which gives a better picture of the financial position. Solomons, though, has provided little basis on which his judgment can be made as he does not systematically develop his idea of what 'financial position' is, independently of its role as a tool for measuring income. True, he refers to an interest of users in assessing present and possible future solvency, but this idea is not developed further, and if anything knowledge of NRV (if practicable) would be at least as relevant as, if not superior to, information about VTB for this purpose.

In the appendix, Solomons deals with more individual accounting issues. Again one of the major merits of this study is that, unlike previous concepts and guidelines which have been drafted with an eye to what will fly politically, Solomons has been able to set out clearly what he sees as the logical implications of the framework he favours. This alone should prompt much further debate of the issues in this country and is to be welcomed. However, my own view is that some of the implications and allusions in the main text indicate that the basic framework is flawed. Four examples spring to mind.

First, Solomons embraces the 'volatility' of income implied by incorporating continuous revaluation of pension assets and liabilities. This is logically consistent with his (and a 'Hicks No 1') view of 'income' as the 'change in the wealth' of the entity, which Solomons measures by the change in the value of net assets. But there are equally respectable theories of the nature of income (e.g. Kaldor's, 'Hicks No 2' and 'Hicks No 3'[3]) which take out not only the inflationary element of changes in net assets but also the effects of 'windfalls' and of changes in interest rates (see Parker, Harcourt and Whittington, *Readings in the Concept and Measurement of Income*[4]).

Solomons ignores these theoretical issues (which go far in illuminating why 'volatility' may be conceptually undesirable as well as being disliked by practical businessmen and certain other users), but I consider they merit examination if one is trying to set out the fundamental principles of accounting.

Second, to illustrate why 'volatility' must be accepted, Solomons mentions self-insurance on several occasions. But the argument that the 'cost' of self-insurance cannot be recognized seems inconsistent with the overall Solomons framework, even if one starts from the balance sheet approach.

Consider two multinational companies, A and B, large and diversified enough to have potential asset losses and potential liabilities that are equivalent to those in an insurance company's portfolio. It is normal to insure, but how should they rationally choose whether to continue to have insurance or not? Ignoring for simplicity transaction and administrative costs, taxes etc., they should presumably compare the premium payable to the insurer with the actuarial expectation of the amount of potential losses. If A decides to continue insurance, then its net assets go down by the cost of the premiums, but the value of its expected future cash flows is protected by insurance. If B now decides not to buy insurance, its net assets are no longer reduced by the cost of the premiums, but the value of its expected future cash flows is lower by the actuarially expected losses. If B has made the wrong decision in not buying insurance, the value of its future cash flows is now lower than those of A by more than the cost of the premiums that A is paying out. Its overall financial position is worse and its management is under-performing A's managers. But the Solomons rule—like FASB's—would require A to charge the premiums and B to do nothing in its financial statements, except as losses actually occur.

In my opinion FASB[5] got this one wrong conceptually, although in practice the uncertainties are of course so great that there may be no practicable way to account for these consequences of 'self-insurance'. More important, this example illustrates the need to relate 'values' to choices and decisions, and makes it surprising that Solomons (p 9) rejects the need to consider how the information in 'external' financial statements should relate to information useful for managerial purposes. At the very least one needs to be aware that the method of financial reporting can influence management behaviour, a phenomenon known as 'information inductance'. For example, under the FASB rules, if B's management wants to show better results this year it could gamble on the timing of losses and not pay the insurance premiums.

The third example is an item that normally increases 'volatility' but which is excluded in the Solomons framework. On p 27 he says that the framework implies that normal corrections and adjustments allowing for new information must be regarded as 'restatements' of previous years' figures—the SSAP 6[6] treatment being regarded as illogical and untruthful. But there are equally respectable theoretical arguments for regarding such 'windfalls' as current period income, and this would be conceptually more consistent with the 'Hicks No 1' model that Solomons appears to espouse in other respects. Indeed his argument here seems inconsistent with his treatment of actuarial gains and losses on pension plans. Moreover, in practical terms, where accounts are used as the basis of sharing out results (e.g. for tax, distributions, bonuses), continuous revisions to prior year figures would be impractical if not inequitable. A Lloyd's syndicate could not operate on that basis. This does not of course mean that it may not be useful to identify such revisions within the analysis of income (as is now done in Lloyd's syndicates in reporting how prior 'closed' years' estimates have 'developed' in the latest 'closed' year) as Solomons recommends.

I do not think this is merely a semantic issue: rather, it illustrates the fundamental problem that Solomons is only addressing one purpose of financial reporting ('telling it like it is' for certain economic decision-making purposes), but not others which are as important (eg providing an equitable basis for sharing out results under trust, contract or statute law). Legally based aspects are dismissed as 'constraints', but legal roles of accounting are as, if not more, important than other roles. This is the major distinction between the US and the UK, which must be addressed in developing implementable UK guidelines, and makes importing FASB's framework 'as it is' inappropriate. Solomons fails to address the British environment, nor does he explicitly consider how far our guidelines should harmonize with European thinking.

Fourth, Solomons argues that 'executory contracts' (i.e. where performance by both parties lies in the future) are both assets and liabilities (p 67), which is indeed logically consistent with the Solomons definitions. (This is no doubt why, in order to be practically acceptable at the present time, ED 42[7] felt obliged to indicate they were not to be separately included in the balance sheet (paras 48, 49, 61) despite the definitions: if one uses asset and liability definitions in the Solomons way to tackle off-balance sheet financing, then the consequences logically do go far beyond the immediate problem of such financing arrangements.) The conclusions and implications may well be right: but the definitions and criteria as presently developed in Solomons cannot bear the weight of establishing, for example, that 'set-off' may be appropriate only where there is (effectively) no counterparty risk (p 68). The balance sheet in the Solomons framework, up to this point, has had as its primary objective the calculation of income (as the difference between net assets) in order to measure performance (p 9). Although users are said at p 9 to be interested in the 'position' of an enterprise too this concept has not been discussed further: but the off balance sheet issues do bring out the need for a 'theory of the balance sheet' independent of its role in assisting calculation of income, and focusing instead on aspects of reporting 'risk profile'. This in turn raises issues such as 'portfolio aggregation' in deciding what may and may not be 'netted off'. There is still much valuable conceptual work that needs to be done here.

I therefore retain a profound scepticism about the value of the FASB type frameworks or guidelines which I find largely reiterated in Solomons, and I consider that guidelines that could really assist standard setters need to devote much greater effort to understanding the variety of roles that financial accounts fulfill and the variety of influences which have shaped the development of present day practices and which need to be taken into account in guiding their future development. It is not enough to seek to 'tell it like it is' (p 8). I believe Solomons goes wrong right at the beginning when he says that 'over the lifetime of an enterprise there is little that accounting can do to increase or decrease aggregate earnings' (p 1). This is only true when the future is certain. Given the uncertainty and limits on our understanding of the business environment, the picture given by accounts can often have a significant effect in shaping what is (whether the business does survive, can raise funds etc.) and that is one reason why there is so much argument over what is 'true and fair', and why standard setting is so difficult. Arguments over the way in which accounting can affect how large a share of enterprise earnings will go to different parties also extend much more widely than just to the tax authorities (p 1). Guidelines that ignore these realities of the accounting process will not lead us very far.

# NOTES TO THIS REPRINTING

[1] Reprinted in this volume at pp.233-9.

[2] McMonnies, P. (ed.), *Making Corporate Reports Valuable* (Edinburgh: ICAS & Kogan Page, 1988).

[3] Hicks (1946); Kaldor (1955)—see the bibliography to Macve, R.H., 'The FASB's Conceptual Framework—Vision, Tool or Threat?', presented at the Arthur Young Professors' Roundtable, May 7, 1983 (reprinted in this volume at pp.167-217).

[4] (2nd Edition: Oxford: Philip Allan, 1986)

[5] See FASB, SFAC3 *Elements of Financial Statements of Business Enterprises* (December 1980), para.101.

[6] Accounting Standards Committee (ASC), Statement of Standard Accounting Practice No.6 (Revised) *Extraordinary items and prior year adjustments* (1986). This standard has now been superseded by FRS3 *Reporting Financial Performance*, issued by ASB in October 1992 (amended June 1993), but FRS3 retains a similar treatment with regard to 'prior period adjustments' (see paras.60-63).

[7] ASC, Exposure Draft 42 *Accounting for Special Purpose Transactions* (March 1988). The relevant standard is now FRS5 *Reporting the Substance of Transactions*, issued by ASB in 1994, which also normally excludes such executory contracts from recognition (para.12).

For Product Safety Concerns and Information please contact our EU
representative GPSR@taylorandfrancis.com
Taylor & Francis Verlag GmbH, Kaufingerstraße 24, 80331 München, Germany

www.ingramcontent.com/pod-product-compliance
Ingram Content Group UK Ltd.
Pitfield, Milton Keynes, MK11 3LW, UK
UKHW021606240425
457818UK00018B/420